Adobe AIR HTML Environment

The HTML environment inside Adobe AIR and depicted in the following figure consists of three main objects:

- The `NativeWindow` object is a container for all objects in a window and provides an interface to the native OS window.
- The `HTMLLoader` object serves a container for HTML content.
- The JavaScript `window` object, which contains the DOM, can access the AIR objects through three properties: `NativeWindow`, `htmlLoader`, and `runtime`.

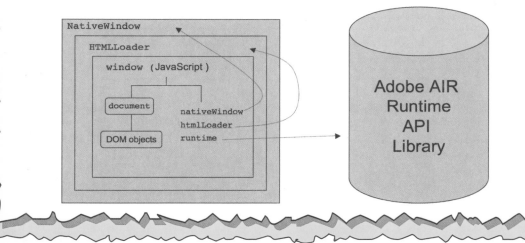

Useful Web Links

You'll find the following Web resources helpful to use as language and API references as you develop your Adobe AIR applications.

Adobe AIR Home
`http://www.adobe.com/products/air`

Developing Adobe AIR Applications with HTML and JavaScript
`http://livedocs.adobe.com/air/1/devappshtml`

Developing AIR Applications with Flex
`http://livedocs.adobe.com/flex/3/html/Part5_AIR_1.html`

Developing AIR Applications with Flash
`http://livedocs.adobe.com/air/1/devappsflash/splash.html`

Adobe AIR Language Reference for HTML Developers
`http://help.adobe.com/en_US/AIR/1.1/jslr/index.html`

File System Directories

The `File` object comes with several properties that give you quick access to a variety of system directories. You'll find these properties shown below.

Directory	File Object Property/Method	Windows Path	Mac OS X Path
Application directory	`[air.]File. application Directory`		
Application storage	`[air.]File. applicationStorage Directory`	`C:\Documents and Settings\userName\ Application Data\ applicationID. publisherID\ Local Store`	`Users/userName/ Library/Preferences/ applicationID. publisherID/Local Store`
User's home directory	`[air.]File.user Directory`	`C:\Documents and Settings\userName`	
User's document directory	`[air.]File. documents Directory`	`C:\Documents and Settings\userName\ My Documents`	`Users/userName/ Documents`
User's desk-top directory	`[air.]File.desktop Directory`	`C:\Documents and Settings\userName\ Desktop`	`Users/userName/ Desktop`
File system root	`[air.]File. getRoot Directories()`	`Returns C: and all other root volumes`	`Returns the / root directory`
Temporary directory	`[air.]File. createTemp Directory();`	`C:\Documents and Settings\rich\Local Settings\Temp\ tempDirName`	`/private/var/tmp/ folders.501/Temporary Items/tempDirName`

AIR Window Types

Adobe AIR enables you to create three major types of native windows that display a variety of OS chrome and UI features.

Type	Description	Chrome	Windows Task Bar	Windows System Menu	Mac OS X Window Menu	Initial window	systemChrome value
`Normal`	Normal window	Full	Yes	Yes	Yes	Yes	`standard`
`Utility`	Palette window	Slim	No	Yes	No	No	`standard`
`Lightweight`	"Lightweight" notification-style windows	None	No	No	No	No	`none`

For Dummies: Bestselling Book Series for Beginners

Adobe® AIR™

FOR

DUMMIES®

by Richard Wagner

WILEY

Wiley Publishing, Inc.

Adobe® AIR™ For Dummies®

Published by
Wiley Publishing, Inc.
111 River Street
Hoboken, NJ 07030-5774
www.wiley.com

Copyright © 2009 by Wiley Publishing, Inc., Indianapolis, Indiana

Published by Wiley Publishing, Inc., Indianapolis, Indiana

Published simultaneously in Canada

For general information on our other products and services, please contact our Customer Care Department within the U.S. at 877-762-2974, outside the U.S. at 317-572-3993, or fax 317-572-4002.

For technical support, please visit www.wiley.com/techsupport.

Wiley also publishes its books in a variety of electronic formats. Some content that appears in print may not be available in electronic books.

Library of Congress Control Number: 2008942265

ISBN: 978-0-470-39044-3

Manufactured in the United States of America

10 9 8 7 6 5 4 3

WILEY

About the Author

Richard Wagner is an experienced Web developer as well as author of several Web-related books. These books include *Building Facebook Applications For Dummies, Professional iPhone and iPod touch Programming, XSLT For Dummies, Creating Web Pages All-in-One Desk Reference For Dummies, XML All-in-One Desk Reference For Dummies, Web Design Before & After Makeovers*, and *JavaScript Unleashed* (1st, 2nd ed.). Richard was previously vice president of product development at NetObjects. He was also inventor and chief architect of the award-winning NetObjects ScriptBuilder. A versatile author with a wide range of interests, he is also author of *The Expeditionary Man* and *The Myth of Happiness*. His tech blog is at subcreatif.richwagnerwords.com.

Dedication

To Kim and the J-boys

Author's Acknowledgments

Thanks so much to all of the great folks on the Dummies team at Wiley. Terrific job, as always. In particular, I would like to thank Susan Christophersen for doing a terrific job managing the book from cover to cover. Hats off also to Russ Mullen for his technical prowess to ensure the accuracy of the code and technical details of the book.

Publisher's Acknowledgments

We're proud of this book; please send us your comments through our online registration form located at http://dummies.custhelp.com. For other comments, please contact our Customer Care Department within the U.S. at 877-762-2974, outside the U.S. at 317-572-3993, or fax 317-572-4002.

Some of the people who helped bring this book to market include the following:

Acquisitions, Editorial, and Media Development

Project and Copy Editor: Susan Christophersen

Acquisitions Editor: Katie Feltman

Technical Editor: Russ Mullen

Editorial Manager: Jodi Jensen

Media Development Project Manager: Laura Moss-Hollister

Media Development Assistant Project Manager: Jenny Swisher

Editorial Assistant: Amanda Foxworth

Sr. Editorial Assistant: Cherie Case

Cartoons: Rich Tennant (www.the5thwave.com)

Composition Services

Project Coordinator: Patrick Redmond

Layout and Graphics: Andrea Hornberger, Christin Swinford, Ronald Terry, Christine Williams, Erin Zeltner

Proofreaders: Melissa Bronnenberg, Caitie Kelly, Penny L. Stuart

Indexer: Broccoli Information Management

Publishing and Editorial for Technology Dummies

    Richard Swadley, Vice President and Executive Group Publisher

    Andy Cummings, Vice President and Publisher

    Mary Bednarek, Executive Acquisitions Director

    Mary C. Corder, Editorial Director

Publishing for Consumer Dummies

    Diane Graves Steele, Vice President and Publisher

Composition Services

    Gerry Fahey, Vice President of Production Services

    Debbie Stailey, Director of Composition Services

Contents at a Glance

Table of Contents

Introduction

Although Adobe AIR is a still new product release, it's already proving to be one of those technologies that is changing the rules of the game. Until AIR was introduced, the runtime environments of the desktop and Web were cleanly divided and clearly distinct from each other. Sure, you had Web-enabled desktop apps and technologies, such as Google Gears, that allowed Web apps some local capabilities. But by and large, the desktop was a stuffy world inhabited by the C++ and Objective-C programmers.

Enter Adobe AIR. It has become a breath of fresh air to Web developers. For the first time, developers can now use Web technologies — such as HTML, JavaScript, Flash, or Flex — to create rich Internet applications (RIAs) that run on desktops and across multiple operating systems. These apps need not be mere "widgets" or "applets" but can be full-fledged, professional, and perhaps even "air-cooled" applications.

About This Book

Adobe AIR For Dummies serves as your friendly, no-nonsense guide to designing and developing Adobe AIR applications. Throughout the book, I focus on covering the essentials you need to successfully deploy your own AIR applications. Using this book, you can

- ✔ Get a solid understanding of the Adobe AIR API
- ✔ Build AIR apps in three different ways: HTML/Ajax, Flex, and Flash
- ✔ Design apps using HTML and CSS
- ✔ Work with local file systems and databases
- ✔ Make sense of application sandboxing and security

You can create Adobe AIR apps using standard Web technologies (HTML, CSS, JavaScript, and Ajax), Flex, or Flash. It would take a book three times as thick as this one to fully cover AIR development equally across these technologies. Consequently, although I give some coverage to Flex and Flash, the book focuses primarily on HTML, CSS, JavaScript, and Ajax. However, because the AIR runtime environment is independent of technologies used to develop the app, Flex and Flash developers can also able to follow along to better their understanding of AIR. You can find source code for many of this book's examples at www.dummies.com/go/adobeairfd.

Foolish Assumptions

In *Adobe AIR For Dummies*, I don't expect you to have any previous experience with Adobe AIR, Flex Builder, or Flash. I do, however, assume that you have at least a working knowledge of HTML, CSS, JavaScript, and Ajax. Oh, yeah, I also assume that you understand the word *arroyo*. (Not that I talk about a deep gully, mind you.)

Conventions Used in This Book

Keep in mind the following conventions, or typographical rules, which I use throughout the book:

- **Text formatting:** I *italicize* new terms that I define. **Bold text** is used to indicate specific commands that you are to perform. Source code and URLs stand out from normal text with a `monospaced` font.

- **Markup terminology:** When working with Adobe AIR, you often work with markup style languages, including Hypertext Markup Language (HTML) and Extensible Markup Language (XML). A markup language consists of many *elements* (also called *tags*), each of which has a *start tag*, *end tag*, and *content* in between. For example:

  ```
  <h1>Are you an AIRhead?</h1>
  ```

  The `<h1>` is the start tag, `</h1>` is the end tag, and `Are you an AIRhead?` is the content. The entire piece of code is called the h1 element or tag.

What You Don't Have to Read

Before you begin the book, let me point out a couple of "optional" modules that you can feel free to avoid without missing the information you absolutely need to know:

- **Text marked with a Technical Stuff icon:** Paragraphs with this icon beside them let you know that this "techie" material provides additional details to round out your understanding. But it is not required reading.

- **Sidebars:** Once or twice, I stick some info in a shaded sidebar, which gives you some "ancillary info" but isn't critical to your understanding of the chapter.

How This Book Is Organized

This book is carved up neatly and cleanly into four distinct parts, like so:

Part I: Airing It Out with Adobe AIR

You begin soaring with AIR after you read Part I. In this part, discover the essentials of the AIR runtime environment and its Web-based framework. Adobe AIR apps can be created using three different Web technologies — standard HTML and Ajax, Flex, and Flash. In this section, I also show you how you can use each of these to build AIR apps. Even if you're familiar with just one of these technologies, you can still find it helpful to work with the other development environments because each has certain advantages and disadvantages over the other.

Part II: AIR Application Design

In Part II, you begin to get deeper into the design of AIR applications using HTML and JavaScript. You will explore how to create HTML/CSS-based user interfaces and add native operating system windows, menus, and icons.

Part III: Programming the Adobe AIR API

Part III is the heart of the book. It is where you discover all aspects of the AIR API. You explore how to interact with the operating system and the file system. If you're developing a database application, this is where you can find out how to work with both local and remote databases. This part also covers deploying your app.

Part IV: The Part of Tens

Part IV is the traditional close to every *For Dummies* book — The Part of Tens. In this action-packed part, you explore ten strategies for security and sandboxing of your application, followed by ten tips to keep in mind for successful AIR debugging. Finally, I close out the book with a survey of ten killer RIAs.

Icons Used in This Book

For Dummies books aren't content with just plain, ordinary pages with ordinary paragraphs. No, we like to make things more interesting and helpful by providing a few icons to point out material of special interest. These are the following

The Remember icon indicates a paragraph that is particularly significant to your understanding of Adobe AIR development.

The Tip icon points out key development tips and techniques that you want to be sure and take note of.

The Warning icon acts as your early warning system, alerting you to potential pitfalls that you may encounter along the way.

As I mention in the "What You Don't Have to Read" section, the Technical Stuff icon points out technical but not required info.

Where to Go from Here

Although you can read this book from cover to cover like a John Grisham novel, it's structured so that you don't have to. Here's a roadmap that will get you going to exactly where you want to go:

- ✔ To explore Adobe AIR and its components, turn the page over and begin reading Chapters 1.
- ✔ To create your first Adobe AIR application using HTML, skip over to Chapter 2.
- ✔ If you're a Flex or Flash developer, you may want to begin with Chapter 3.
- ✔ To dive head first into AIR app design, head over to Part II.
- ✔ To explore the local file and database storage capabilities of AIR, read Chapters 10 and 11.

Part I
Airing It Out with Adobe AIR

The 5th Wave   By Rich Tennant

"We're here to clean the code."

In this part . . .

Perhaps you're a Web developer and the idea of the desktop environment of Adobe AIR seems foreign. Or perhaps you're a desktop programmer but are unfamiliar with Web technologies such as Ajax, Flex, or Flash. If so, then start here. You explore the Adobe AIR environment and the structure of an AIR application. Finally, you roll up your sleeves and develop your first AIR app.

Chapter 1

Getting Started with Adobe AIR

*W*eb developers, unite! For all too long, Web developers have been oppressed by the shackles of the browser window, their creativity stifled by cross-browser compatibility issues, their self-image hurt by the scoffs of desktop app programmers who trivialize browser-based solutions. . .

But that was then; this is now. Or, to mimic the voiceover from an overly dramatic movie trailer, *Everything you know about Web development is about to change. Introducing Adobe AIR. . .*

Adobe AIR promises to liberate developers from the snares, toils, and oppression of their browser-based prisons and enable them to create "rich Internet applications" (RIAs) for the desktop. In true *Braveheart* fashion, maybe you will find yourself shouting from your office or cubicle, "You can take my life, but you can never take my Adobe AIR!"

Okay, perhaps I am guilty of being just a wee bit over-the-top as I introduce Adobe AIR, but I hope the melodrama does serve a purpose. It helps show you that AIR really is not just another flavor of the week. AIR really does provide a greater freedom to do things that HTML/Ajax, Flash, and Flex developers can't do inside the browser.

In this chapter, I introduce you to this "breath of fresh AIR" and get you started working with it. *Viva la RIAs!*

Discovering Adobe AIR

Adobe AIR enables Web developers to create cross-platform desktop applications using and combining familiar Web technologies that they are already skilled in — such as HTML, JavaScript, Ajax, Flash, and Flex.

Even though the technologies used to create it are Web based, an AIR application looks and feels like a normal Windows or Mac OS X program. It runs in its own window, has its own icon, and integrates with the menu system or taskbar. And it generally has the performance you would expect from a native operating system application. In fact, users will interact with an AIR app (see Figure 1-1) just the same as they do with any other application on their desktop.

Creating Internet-savvy apps

An AIR application is technically not standalone. It is actually "powered by" the Adobe AIR runtime that must be installed on any computer in order to run the application. Therefore, when an AIR app is launched, the AIR runtime is automatically loaded behind the scenes prior to the loading of the app.

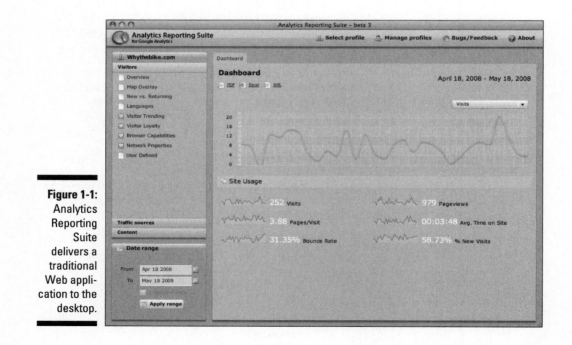

Figure 1-1: Analytics Reporting Suite delivers a traditional Web application to the desktop.

When you create an AIR application, you build the app using Adobe Dreamweaver, Adobe Flex, Adobe Flash, or any text editor. (In Chapter 2, I show you how to create a basic HTML-based app in a text editor and Dreamweaver. Chapter 3 shows you how to create a basic app in Flex and Flash.)

As you can see, many parts of the application use Web techniques and technologies that you're already used to working with. However, core to Adobe AIR is an application programming interface (API) that you can tap into to do real "desktop stuff," such as get access to local files, open native UI windows, create menus, and so on. I walk you through the API in Chapter 4.

As you begin to explore the AIR API, you will see that the key strength of Adobe AIR is not in creating word processors or spreadsheets (although you can), but rather in enabling Web developers to shed the browser and safely deploy Internet-savvy apps onto the desktop.

An AIR application is easily delivered to users with a single downloadable installer (which has an `.air` extension) regardless of the operating system. (See Chapter 14 for more on deployment.)

Developers can create Internet-based desktop apps to some extent through widgets and Java, but both of these technologies have restrictions or limitations that have kept them as niche players. Widgets are intended for limited single screen, display-oriented purposes (such as a stock ticker). Cross-platform applications using Java runtime have traditionally suffered in comparison to native OS apps — in terms of both performance and "look and feel" issues. Also, both widgets and Java apps are much weaker in working with rich media than Flash has been.

In fact, you may want to jump over to Chapter 16 to take a quick look at ten great AIR applications that help demonstrate the power of the platform.

Peeking inside Adobe AIR runtime

The Adobe AIR runtime may be a relatively new platform, but it actually embeds three highly mature and stable cross-platform technologies to power AIR applications. These are the following:

✔ **WebKit:** Used for rendering HTML content inside an AIR app. WebKit is an open source, cross-platform browser and is the underlying rendering engine on which Apple's Safari browser is built.

WebKit is known for its strong support of W3C standards, such as HTML, XHTML, Document Object Model (DOM), Cascading Style Sheets (CSS), and ECMAScript. However, it also provides support for enhanced functionality — enabling the creation of cool stuff such as rounded corners using CSS. Because you're developing solely for WebKit and not for every browser under the sun, you're free to take advantage of these nonstandard extensions.

For more info on WebKit, go to www.webkit.org.

✔ **Adobe Flash Player:** Used for playing Flash media (SWF files). Flash Player is a cross-platform virtual machine used to run media created in the Adobe Flash authoring environment and full SWF-based applications created using Adobe Flex. Flash Player has an embedded JavaScript-like scripting language called ActionScript 3.

Inside your app, you can access existing Flash Player API calls as well as some enhanced functionality for vector-based drawing, multimedia support (see Chapter 13), and a full networking stack (see Chapter 12).

✔ **SQLite:** A database engine for enabling local database access. It's an extremely lightweight, open source, cross-platform SQL database engine that is embedded in many desktop and mobile products. In contrast to most SQL databases, it doesn't require a separate server process, and it uses a standard file to store an entire database (tables, indexes, and so on). If you'd like to explore how to work with SQLite to create database apps, see Chapter 11.

For more info on SQLite, go to www.sqlite.org.

Figure 1-2 shows an overview of the AIR runtime architecture.

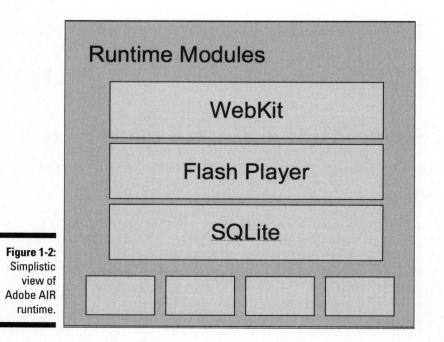

Figure 1-2:
Simplistic
view of
Adobe AIR
runtime.

Blurring the lines between HTML and Flash

Having Flash Player and the WebKit rendering engine integrated inside AIR so tightly opens many possibilities for AIR developers. An AIR app can consist of several different possibilities:

- HTML/JavaScript only
- HTML and Ajax
- Flash only
- Flex only
- Flash/Flex and HTML

In fact, AIR blurs the lines between Flash media, a Flex app, and a traditional HTML-based app. In many cases, an AIR application can be a combination of all these. Consider how these technologies can speak to each other:

- You can access the Flash Player and ActionScript Library APIs from within JavaScript. (See Chapter 5 for more details.)
- ActionScript inside Flash can call JavaScript and access and modify the HTML DOM. (See Chapter 5.)
- You can register JavaScript and ActionScript events anywhere — in Flash, Flex, or JavaScript. (You can thumb over to Chapter 6 to dive fully into events.)

Because an AIR app can use all these technologies interchangeably, you can see that Adobe AIR breaks down the traditional walls that have existed in Web development architecture.

Understanding the AIR Security Model

One of the concepts that is important for you to understand from the get-go is application security. Desktop apps get permission in terms of what they can do and cannot do from the OS and the available permissions of the currently logged-in user. They receive this level of access because the user needs to explicitly install the app — effectively telling the computer that the user trusts the app he or she is about to launch. As a result, native apps have access to read and write to the local file system and perform other typical desktop functions.

Web apps, however, are far more restrictive because of the potentially malicious nature of scripting. Consequently, Web apps limit all local file access, can perform web-based actions only inside the context of a browser, and restrict data access to a single domain.

Playing in sandboxes

The hybrid nature of an AIR application puts it somewhere in between both of these traditional security models. On the one hand, with AIR, you create a desktop application that runs on top of the normal OS security layer. Therefore, it can read and write from the local file system. However, because AIR uses Web technologies that, if unchecked, could be hijacked by a malicious third party and used in harmful ways when accessing the local system, Adobe AIR has a security model to guard against such an occurrence. Specifically, AIR runtime grants permissions to each source or data file in an AIR application based on its origin and places it into one of two kinds of containers it calls sandboxes.

The *application sandbox* contains all content that is installed with the app inside the home directory of an application. These are typically HTML, XML, JS, and SWF files. You can think of files inside the application sandbox as the equivalent of premium frequent flyer members that get full access to the special airport restaurants. Only these files have access to the AIR API and its runtime environment.

Adobe AIR does allow you to link in other local and remote content that is not inside the root directory of the application, but places that content in a *nonapplication sandbox*. Content inside the nonapplication sandbox is essentially handled from a security standpoint just as a traditional Web app is, and is not granted access to the AIR APIs (see Figure 1-3).

Check out Chapter 17 for more on application security and sandboxing.

Additional restrictions within the application sandbox

AIR places strict restrictions over script importing of remote content and the dynamic evaluation of JavaScript code — even inside the application sandbox. Many JavaScript programmers use the `eval()` function as a way to generate executable code on the fly. However, if you're loading data from a remote source, a hacker could potentially inject malicious code into your app without your knowledge. To prevent these security vulnerabilities, `eval()` and other dynamic code methods are prohibited after the `onload` event occurs.

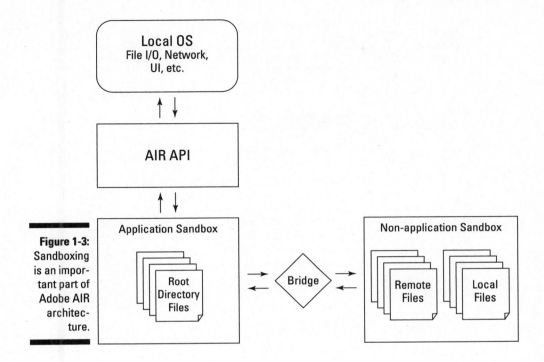

Figure 1-3: Sandboxing is an important part of Adobe AIR architecture.

As it is in Web applications, code being executed inside the application sandbox is free to load data using Ajax (the XMLHttpRequest object). However, any content received using XMLHttpRequest is treated purely as data and cannot be dynamically changed into executable JavaScript code (such as by using eval()).

Table 1-1 lists the specific restrictions of what can be done inside an application sandbox.

Table 1-1   Allowed and Nonallowed JavaScript Activities

Language component	*Before onload*	*After onload*
eval()	Permitted.	Not permitted after an application loads, except when you use with a JSON type parameter to convert JSON strings into objects.
document.write()	Permitted.	Not permitted.
Function constructor	Permitted.	Not permitted.

(continued)

Table 1-1 *(continued)*

Language component	Before onload	After onload
`setTimeout()` and `setInterval()` timing functions	Permitted.	Not permitted when using string parameters.
JavaScript protocol URLs (`javascript:`)	Not permitted.	Not permitted.
`innerHTML`, `outerHTML` properties	Permitted.	Attributes of inserted elements cannot be transformed into executable code.
`XMLHttpRequest`	Synchronous calls outside the application sandbox prohibited.	Asynchronous calls triggered in `onload` always finish after onload.
Remote URL for a `<script> src` attribute	Not permitted.	Not permitted.

Digitally Signing an Application

Because users open their computer to an AIR app, their trust in the software publisher is crucial. They need to know that you won't do bad things to their private data or trash their hard drive. That's why digital signing is a required final step of the AIR application development process before you can deploy it.

To provide a degree of confidence and trust, an AIR application must be signed by a code-signing certificate. There are two types of certificates:

✔ **Self-signed certificates:** "Do-it-yourself" certificates that you can generate with the AIR SDK and then sign your app with. Self-signed certificates provide a minimal degree of trust, but because you have no outside confirmation that you are who you say you are, you are, in effect, telling users, "Hey, you can trust me. Really. Really!" When users install an app with a self-signed certificate, they are warned that the publisher is UNVERIFIED (see Figure 1-4).

Self-signed certificates are intended mainly for internal use when debugging and testing your app.

Figure 1-4:
Self-signed
certificates
give no
assurance
to users.

✔ **Commercial code-sign certificates:** These certificates are purchased
from a certification authority (CA), such as Verisign and Thawte, who
authenticate your identity. A commercial certificate enables you to
be considered a "trusted" publisher and gives users a much higher
degree of confidence in working with your app. A commercial certificate
enables users to verify the corporate or organizational affiliation of the
application and ensures that users can say, "They are who we thought
they were!" (see Figure 1-5).

Commercial certificates, however, are not cheap. Fees are generally around
$300 for one year and $549 for two years for a code-sign certificate.

Figure 1-5:
Commercial
certificates
add trust.

Setting Up Your AIR Development Environment

As you begin to work with Adobe AIR, you should begin by configuring your development environment. First, you should install the runtime and SDK. The SDK comes with two command-line tools that you can use to debug and deploy Adobe AIR apps:

- ✔ ADL is used for testing purposes only, enabling you to run an app without installing it.
- ✔ ADT is used for deploying your app. It packages the app into an installation package.

Adobe also integrates the ability to package AIR apps inside Adobe Flash, Flex, and Dreamweaver (CS3 and later). However, if you use Dreamweaver, you should install the AIR extension to enable you to create AIR apps directly inside the Dreamweaver environment.

The instructions to set up your environment are explained in the sections that follow.

Installing the Adobe AIR runtime

Adobe AIR runtime is the underlying engine that drives any AIR application. As a developer, you need the runtime installed on your machine in order to test and debug your apps. Users also need to download and install it on their computers in order to run an AIR application.

Fortunately, installing the runtime is a quick, "no brainer" process. To install it, follow these four steps:

1. **Go to** `get.adobe.com/air` **in your browser.**

   The Adobe AIR Web page opens.

2. **On the page, click the Download Now button.**

   The installer file is downloaded onto your computer.

3. **Double-click the downloaded Adobe AIR Installer to launch the setup process.**

4. **Follow the on-screen instructions to complete the setup.**

Installing the Adobe AIR SDK

Although the Adobe AIR runtime has a standard installer that you can use for installing on your computer, installing the SDK involves a few more manual steps. Follow these instructions to get it working on your computer:

1. **Go to** `www.adobe.com/products/air/tools/sdk` **in your browser.**

2. **After reading the Adobe AIR SDK license, indicate that you agree with its terms by selecting the check box.**

3. **Click the download link appropriate for your computer (Windows or Mac).**

   The compressed SDK file — `AdobeAIRSDK.zip` (Windows) or `AdobeAIRSDK.dmg` (Mac) is downloaded to your machine.

4. **Create a folder on your machine for the SDK.**

   I recommend something easy such as `c:\airsdk` for Windows or `/Users/[username]/airsdk` for Mac.

5. **Uncompress the SDK file and copy the folders and files into the SDK folder you created in Step 4.**

   The directory structure under your SDK folder (for example, `c:\airsdk`) will look like this:

   ```
   \bin

   \frameworks

   \lib

   \runtime

   \samples

   \src

   \templates
   ```

   You now need to add the `bin` subdirectory to your system path before being able to execute the SDK utilities. Follow the appropriate steps below, depending on your operating system.

Setting the environment path in Windows Vista

1. **Press the Windows key and the Pause/Break key at the same time.**

   The System section of the Control Panel is displayed.

2. **Click the Advanced System Settings link.**

   A User Account Control dialog box is displayed.

3. **If required, enter the password for an Administrator account.**

4. **Click the Continue button.**

5. **Click the Advanced tab in the System Properties dialog box.**

6. **Click the Environment Variables button.**

7. **Edit the system variable named** `Path`.

8. **At the far right end of the existing path value, type a semicolon and then the path for the** `bin` **subdirectory of the Adobe AIR SDK.**

9. **Test the new path by opening a new Console window and typing** adt **at the command prompt.**

   If you see a listing of the various `usage` options available when calling the utility, then you know you have successfully installed the SDK. If not, go back and check to ensure that you correctly added the SDK `bin` path.

Setting the environment path in Windows XP

1. **Press the Windows key and the Pause/Break key at the same time.**

   The System Properties dialog box is displayed.

2. **Click the Advanced tab in the System Properties dialog box.**

3. **Click the Environment Variables button.**

4. **Edit the system variable named** `Path`.

5. **At the far right end of the existing path value, type a semicolon and then the path for the** `bin` **subdirectory of the Adobe AIR SDK.**

6. **Test the new path by opening a new Console window and typing** adt **at the command prompt.**

   If you see a listing of the various `usage` options available when calling the utility, you know you have successfully installed the SDK. If not, go back and check to ensure that you correctly added the SDK `bin` path.

Setting the system path in Mac OS X

Follow these steps to add the path of the AIR SDK to your system path:

1. **Open the Terminal application in your** `/Applications/Utilities` **folder.**

   By default, you will be in your home directory.

2. **Enter** ls –la **at the command prompt.**

   Terminal will display a list of all files in your home directory.

3. **Check to see whether a file called** .profile **exists.**

   If so, go on to Step 5. Otherwise, go to Step 4.

4. **If needed, create the** .profile **file by typing** touch .profile **at the command prompt.**

5. **Type** open -a TextEdit .profile **at the command prompt.**

6. **Add your AIR SDK** bin **subdirectory to the** export PATH=$PATH: **line.**

   Here's how mine looks:

   ```
   export PATH=$PATH:/Users/rich/airsdk/bin
   ```

   If you already have an export PATH line, add the SDK bin folder to the far right, separating it with a semicolon. For example:

   ```
   export PATH=$PATH:/usr/local/bin;/Users/rich/airsdk/
         bin
   ```

7. **Save the file.**

8. **Quit Terminal.**

9. **Restart your computer.**

10. **Open Terminal.**

11. **Type the following in a Terminal window to load the new settings:**

    ```
    . .profile
    ```

12. **Confirm the path by typing** echo $PATH **at the command prompt.**

    You should see the SDK bin path in the output line.

13. **Test the SDK installation by typing** adt **at the command prompt.**

    If you see a listing of the various usage options available when calling the utility, you know you have successfully installed the SDK. If not, go back and check to ensure that you correctly added the SDK bin path.

Prepping Dreamweaver and Flash for AIR

If you use Dreamweaver or Flash CS3 or higher, you can package and preview applications directly inside the authoring environment, eliminating the need to use the command-line SDK tools.

To do so, begin by going to www.adobe.com/products/air/tools and downloading the appropriate software. For Dreamweaver, Adobe provides an MXP extension that you can install using the Adobe Extension Manager. For Flash CS3, you need to install a software update to enable this functionality.

Chapter 2

Building and Deploying Your First AIR Application with HTML and JavaScript

*A*hhhhh, I get it.

I can talk all day about Adobe AIR capabilities and architecture, but in order for you to really understand how to develop apps, nothing works better than walking through each step of the development process. In the experience of many developers, it is only when they build their first Hello World app that those precious words "Ahhhhh, I get it" are uttered.

Developers, quite obviously, do not become instant experts after creating one simple application. But that first app does provide a context and a foundation for understanding the programming and procedural landscape of the platform on which they are working.

In that light, this chapter is intended as the *Ahhhhh, I get it* chapter. I show the steps you need to take to build and deploy a basic Adobe AIR application using HTML and JavaScript.

Overviewing Jot

The application I walk you through in this chapter is one I call Jot. Jot has one limited purpose — to allow a user to enter text in a box and save the text to a file on the desktop. I spice things up a bit by adding my own custom "chrome" user interface. You can follow along with my code to build a duplicate version or download the entire source code at www.dummies.com.

To help you build Jot, I walk you through a series of eight steps, as follows:

1. Prepare the application folder.

2. Create the HTML-based UI.

3. Define CSS styles.

4. Add the JavaScript code.

5. Create the application descriptor file.

6. Create a self-signed certificate.

7. Compile the application.

8. Take a test drive.

The remaining sections of this chapter present the details of each of these steps.

Preparing the Application Folder

Your first step in creating Jot is simply to prepare a folder on your hard drive that will serve as the root for the application files. To prepare that folder, follow these three steps:

1. **On your hard drive, create a new folder named** jot.

   This folder will serve as the root folder containing all the application files.

2. **Inside the new** jot **folder, create two subdirectories:** assets and icons.

   The assets folder will store your .js and .css styles. The icons folder will contain the application icons.

3. **Copy the** AIRAliases.js **file into the** assets **folder.**

   The AIRAliases.js file is located inside the SDK frameworks folder.

With your application folder ready to go, it's time to begin creating the application itself.

Creating the HTML-Based UI

In this section, you create the Jot application using an ordinary HTML page as the user interface (UI). You'll be putting styles and script code elsewhere, so the actual application file contains basic markup only. Here are the steps to create the Jot application:

1. **Use the following code to create a basic XHTML document shell.**

   Yes, an HTML-based AIR application begins its life looking an awful lot like a normal Web page. It's even named `index.html` by default. That's because it *is* a normal HTML file. Here's the code:

   ```
   <!DOCTYPE html PUBLIC "-//W3C//DTD XHTML 1.0
           Transitional//EN" "http://www.w3.org/TR/
           xhtml1/DTD/xhtml1-transitional.dtd">
   <html xmlns="http://www.w3.org/1999/xhtml">
   <head>
   <meta http-equiv="Content-Type" content="text/html;
           charset=utf-8" />
   <title>Jot</title>
   </head>
   <body>

   </body>
   </html>
   ```

2. **Add a** `link` **reference to a stylesheet named** `jot.css` **inside the** `head` **element.**

   You'll create the `jot.css` file in the next section, but for now, add the link:

   ```
   <link type="text/css" href="assets/jot.css"
           rel="stylesheet" />
   ```

3. **Add** `script` **tag references to** `AIRAliases.js` **and** `jot.js` **in the** `head` **element.**

   As with the style sheet above, you'll create the `jot.js` later on. For now, just add the following reference:

   ```
   <script type="text/javascript" language="JavaScript"
           src="assets/AIRAliases.js"></script>
   <script type="text/javascript" language="JavaScript"
           src="assets/jot.js"></script>
   ```

   You use the `AIRAliases.js` file to access the AIR API.

4. **Insert a** `div` **element with an** `id=canvas` **on the line below the opening** `body` **tag.**

   The `canvas` `div` will serve as the container for the UI:

   ```
   <div id="canvas">
   </div>
   ```

5. **Add an** h1 **tag on the first line inside of the** div **element.**

   Because this app has a custom UI, it will not have a normal title bar for the window. So, the h1 tag will serve as the app title:

   ```
   <h1>Jot</h1>
   ```

6. **Add a** textarea **element on the line below the** h1 **element.**

   The textarea box will be used for text entry:

   ```
   <textarea id="jotText">Enter your text here</
       textarea>
   ```

7. **Insert two** input **buttons on the lines below the** textarea.

   These will be used for saving the text file and for closing the application. Here's the code:

   ```
   <input id="btnSave" type="submit" value="Save Jot" />
   <input id="btnClose" type="submit" value="Close" />
   ```

The complete source code to index.html is as follows:

```
<!DOCTYPE html PUBLIC "-//W3C//DTD XHTML 1.0
        Transitional//EN" "http://www.w3.org/TR/xhtml1/
        DTD/xhtml1-transitional.dtd">
<html xmlns="http://www.w3.org/1999/xhtml">
<head>
<meta http-equiv="Content-Type" content="text/html;
        charset=utf-8" />
<title>Jot</title>

<link type="text/css" href="assets/jot.css"
        rel="stylesheet" />
<script type="text/javascript" language="JavaScript"
        src="assets/AIRAliases.js"></script>
<script type="text/javascript" language="JavaScript"
        src="assets/jot.js"></script>
</head>

<body>

<div id="canvas">
  <h1>Jot</h1>
  <textarea id="jotText">Enter your text here</textarea>
  <input id="btnSave" type="submit" value="Save Jot" />
  <input id="btnClose" type="submit" value="Close" />
</div>
</body>
</html>
```

You're now ready to give this basic XHTML file some style.

Adding Styles

Because this is an HTML-based application, I have you add styles and formatting using CSS. You already added the link to `jot.css` in the HTML file, so now you can create this style sheet. To do so, follow these steps:

1. **Create a blank text file and save it as** `jot.css` **in your** `assets` **folder.**

2. **Insert a** `#canvas` **rule to define styles for the** `canvas` `div`.

   The code contains both standard CSS and WebKit extensions:

   ```
   #canvas {
       font-family: 'Lucida Grande', Verdana, Geneva, Sans-
           Serif;
       font-size: 10px;
       text-align:center;
       color: #ffffff;
       padding:5px;
       background:url('background.png') repeat-x 0 0;
       -webkit-background-size: 100%;
       -webkit-border-radius: 5px;
   }
   ```

   The `-webkit-background-size: 100%` rule prevents the background image from tiling and stretches the background image to be the size of the `div`.

   You can use your own background image or else use the one I did by downloading it from the book's Web site at `www.dummies.com/go/adobeair`.

   Notice my use of the `-webkit-border-radius` property. This WebKit extension is used for rounding the corners of the `div`. That's certainly much easier than adding rounded corners using graphics!

   If you're a Web developer, designing for a single browser rather than for all browsers can be a difficult adjustment to make. However, because you're developing your AIR application only for WebKit, be sure to take advantage of WebKit-specific extensions.

3. **Add styles for the** `h1` **and** `textarea` **elements.**

   The `textarea` rule defines the dimensions of the element. It also assigns the `transparent` value to the `background-color` property:

   ```
   h1 { font-size:1.3em; }

   textarea {
       width:210px;
       height: 200px;
       padding:5px;
       margin-bottom: 5px;
   ```

```
      background-color: transparent;
      color: #ffffff;
      border: 0;
      -webkit-border-radius: 5px;

   }
```

Note that I define rounded corners for the textarea, which is displayed when the element receives focus.

4. **Add styles for the submit buttons.**

   To give the submit buttons a rounded look (like everything else in Jot), I turn once again to -webkit-border-radius. However, I also want to give the buttons more of a 3D feel by styling the border-color as follows:

```
input[type=submit] {
   width: 66px;
   color: #ffffff;
   background-color: #222222;
   border: 1px outset #444444;
   border-color: #444444 #000000 #000000 #444444;
   -webkit-border-radius: 8px;
}

input[type=submit]:hover {
   color:#ffffff;
   background-color: #333333;
}
```

   As you can see, I added a :hover pseudo-class definition so that the color changes as the mouse hovers on it.

The full listing for the jot.css file is follows:

```
#canvas {
   font-family: 'Lucida Grande', Verdana, Geneva, Sans-
         Serif;
    font-size: 10px;
   color: #ffffff;
   text-align:center;
   padding:5px;
   background:url('background.png') repeat-x 0 0;
   -webkit-background-size: 100%;
   -webkit-border-radius: 5px;
}

h1 { font-size:1.3em;   }

textarea {
   width:210px;
   height: 200px;
   padding:5px;
   color: #ffffff;
```

```
  background-color:transparent;
  margin-bottom: 5px;
  border: 0;
  -webkit-border-radius: 5px;

}

input[type=submit] {
  width: 66px;
  color:#ffffff;
  background-color:#222222;
  border: 1px outset #444444;
  border-color: #444444 #000000 #000000 #444444;
  -webkit-border-radius: 8px;
}

input[type=submit]:hover {
  color:#ffffff;
  background-color: #333333;
}
```

The user interface of the application is now ready to go. Now you can add the scripting. Read on!

Adding the JavaScript Code

Jot is powered by the JavaScript code that is placed inside of the `jot.js` file that you linked in earlier into the `index.html` file. You need to code Jot to perform four simple functions:

- ✔ Save text to a file when the Save button is pressed.
- ✔ Allow a user to move a window when the mouse button is held down.
- ✔ Automatically resize the application to the size of the HTML content.
- ✔ Close the app when the Close button is clicked.

You begin by adding some basic JavaScript utility routines, and then you can add the custom code for Jot.

Note I've placed in bold type all AIR API-specific calls that I make in the code in some of the following steps.

1. **Add basic JavaScript utility functions for accessing the DOM and binding objects to functions.**

   These core utility functions are both handy and important to have for even the simplest of projects. Here's the code:

```
// Shortcut function to access DOM id
function $(id){
  return document.getElementById(id);
}

// Bind objects to functions
Function.prototype.bind = function(o, args){
  var f = this;
  return function(){
    f.apply(o, args || arguments);
  }
}
```

2. **Define a** `Jot` **object and an** `initialize()` **method.**

   You structure this code by putting all the application logic inside a `Jot` object. At the same time, you define an `initialize()` method that will be called when the application loads. Here's the code:

```
var Jot = {

  initialize:function(){
  }

}
```

   You add the `Jot.initialize()` as a listener to the window load event later on, in Step 10.

3. **Inside** `Jot`, **define the basic shell structure for the** `save()`, `close()`, **and** `refreshSize()` **methods.**

   You can go ahead and leave these empty for the moment, but it's helpful to define them first before you fill in the initialization routine. The code (with empty functions) is as follows:

```
var Jot = {

  initialize:function(){
  },

  save:function(){
  },

  close:function(){
  },

  refreshSize:function(){
  }

}
```

4. **Inside** `initialize()`, **attach the** `onclick` **handlers of the buttons to the newly defined** `save()` **and** `close()` **methods.**

   Here's where the utility functions come in handy:

   ```
   $('btnSave').onclick = Jot.save.bind(Jot);
   $('btnClose').onclick = Jot.close.bind(Jot);
   ```

   You want to place the following code on the first lines inside `initialize()`.

   In this code, the `Jot.save()` and `Jot.close()` methods are assigned as the handlers to the buttons' `onclick` events. The `bind()` methods bind the associated functions to the `Jot` object.

5. **Register an event listener with the window closing event.**

   This is the first interaction you make with the AIR API. You want your app to be able to "listen" to the closing event that is dispatched by the window when it is getting ready to close. This event could be triggered when the Mac OS X `Quit` command or a Windows `Close` command is performed. In this case, I want to call the `Jot.close()` method:

   ```
   window.nativeWindow.addEventListener(air.Event.
       CLOSING, Jot.close.bind(Jot));
   ```

   The `air` object is defined in `AIRAliases.js` that you included previously in the `index.html` file.

6. **Assign a handler to the** `onmousedown` **event of the document body.**

   Because I'm having you use a custom chrome window rather than a normal system window, you need to add the ability for the user to move the window around. You do that by writing your own custom handler for the `onmousedown` event:

   ```
   document.body.onmousedown = function(e){
     if(e.target.tagName != 'input') nativeWindow.
         startMove();
   };
   ```

   This function calls the `startMove()` method of the AIR runtime object `nativeWindow`, which controls the application window. (Note: AIR's `nativeWindow` is technically not the same object as the JavaScript `window` object.)

   The `initialize()` method is now complete.

7. **Define the** `save()` **method.**

   Enter the code as follows (you don't have to use bold, as I do here; the bolded sections just highlight the AIR-specific functionality of the function):

```
save:function(){
  var file = air.File.desktopDirectory.resolvePath(
        'myjot.txt' );
  var jot = $( 'jotText' ).value;
  var stream = new air.FileStream();
  stream.open( file, air.FileMode.WRITE );
  stream.writeMultiByte( jot, air.File.systemCharset
        );
  stream.close();
}
```

The `resolvePath()` method creates a reference (the `file` variable) to a file named `myjot.txt` in the desktop folder of the user. Next, the value of the `jotText textarea` element is assigned to the `jot` variable. You then use the AIR file I/O routines to create a file stream, open it up for writing, write the `jot` variable to the stream, and then close it.

8. **Define the** `close()` **method.**

Before the application quits, the `close()` method checks to see whether the user wants to save the text. If yes, then the `Jot.save()` method is called. Here's the code:

```
close:function(evt){
  var doSave = confirm('Do you wish to save your
        jot? Click OK to save. Click Cancel to close
        without saving.');
  if(doSave) {
    Jot.closeAfterSave = true;
    Jot.save.call(Jot);
  }

  air.NativeApplication.nativeApplication.exit();

}
```

`NativeApplication` is an object created automatically by AIR that contains various application-level properties and methods. However, to actually call any of its members, you access it through its `air.NativeApplication.nativeApplication` property. This property represents the "singleton" instance of the object. The `exit()` method, as you would certainly expect, gives the old curtain call to the application.

9. **Define the** `refreshSize()` **method.**

Although you will be defining a default height and width for the Jot window, you want to be sure to automatically size the height of the window to match the document body. You can accomplish this feat by adding the following code:

```
refreshSize:function(){
  nativeWindow.height = document.body.offsetHeight;
}
```

Given the simplicity of this application, I actually could certainly get by with hard coding the height value for the `nativeWindow`. But this gives you an example of the flexibility you can have in dynamically changing the size of the window during the running of the app.

There's just one more thing you need to do in `jot.css`: trigger `Jot.initialize()` when the document loads, which the next step covers.

10. **Outside the `Jot` definition, add an event listener for the window load event.**

Returning to normal JavaScript stuff, you need to be sure that `Jot.initalize()` is triggered when the app finishes loading:

```
window.addEventListener('load', Jot.initialize,
       false);
```

If you have followed each of the preceding steps, your full source code in `jot.js` should look like the following:

```
// Utility functions (based on Prototype.js)
function $(id){
  return document.getElementById(id);
}

// Bind objects to functions
Function.prototype.bind = function(o, args){
  var f = this;
  return function(){
    f.apply(o, args || arguments);
  }
}

var Jot = {

  initialize:function(){
    $('btnSave').onclick = Jot.save.bind(Jot);
    $('btnClose').onclick = Jot.close.bind(Jot);

    window.nativeWindow.addEventListener(air.Event.
        CLOSING, Jot.close.bind(Jot));

    document.body.onmousedown = function(e){
      if(e.target.tagName != 'input') nativeWindow.
          startMove();

    Jot.refreshSize();

    };
```

```
    },

     save:function(){
      var file = air.File.desktopDirectory.
      resolvePath( 'myjot.txt' );
      var jot = $( 'jotText' ).value;
      var stream = new air.FileStream();
      stream.open( file, air.FileMode.WRITE );
      stream.writeMultiByte( jot, air.File.systemCharset );
      stream.close();
    },

    close:function(evt){

       var doSave = confirm('Do you wish to save your jot?
            Click OK to save. Click Cancel to close without
            saving.');
       if(doSave) {
         Jot.save.call(Jot);
       }

       air.NativeApplication.nativeApplication.exit();

    },

    refreshSize:function(){
      nativeWindow.height = document.body.offsetHeight;
    }

}

window.addEventListener('load', Jot.initialize, false);
```

Creating the Application Descriptor File

Accompanying your main source files is a separate XML file known as the
application descriptor file. This file is required to define metadata for your
application and specify your initial window properties. You can follow these
steps to define the application descriptor file.

1. **In your root application directory, create a blank text file and name it**
   application.xml.

   Technically, you can name the .xml file anything you want, such as
   jot.xml. However, because the name of this file is not related to the
   actual filename of your AIR application, you may find it helpful to keep
   the file generic and use application.xml.

2. **Add the XML header and root** `application` **element at the start of the** `application.xml` **file.**

   The `application` element serves as the root element for the file and goes immediately under the XML header, like so:

   ```
   <?xml version="1.0" encoding="utf-8" ?>
   <application xmlns="http://ns.adobe.com/air/
         application/1.0" minimumPatchLevel="5331">
   </application>
   ```

The `xmlns` namespace specifies that your application targets the 1.0 version of AIR. The `minimumPatchLevel` attribute helps the AIR runtime determine whether a user needs to download and install a required version or patch.

3. **Add basic metadata descriptors inside the** `application` **element.**

   There are several elements that you will want to define for almost any application. These include:

   ```
   <id>com.dummies.jot</id>
   <version>1.0</version>
   <filename>jot</filename>
   <name>Jot</name>
   <description>Jot smart and silly notes</description>
   <copyright>Copyright © 2008, Rich Wagner</copyright>
   ```

   The required `id` element specifies a unique identifier for every AIR application. As you can see, it uses *reverse domain format,* starting with the domain suffix, the domain name, and then the application name. By using every developer's unique domain name, reverse domain formatting ensures that the application can have a unique identifier across the namespace.

   The `version` element is required and indicates the version of your application. The actual notation you use is up to you. AIR doesn't try to determine which version is earlier or later than the next from this value.

   The `filename` element is also required. It defines the filename (without the extension) of your application. The `.air` installer file and actual application executable (Windows `.exe` or Mac OS X `.app`) will use this value.

   The `name`, `description`, and `copyright` elements are optional. If defined, they are displayed in the installer dialog box.

4. **Add descriptive details for the initial window inside the** `application` **element.**

   The `initialWindow` element is used by the AIR runtime to create the opening window based on the settings you specify. Here are the details for Jot:

```
<initialWindow>
  <content>index.html</content>
  <height>350</height>
  <width>250</width>
  <systemChrome>none</systemChrome>
  <visible>true</visible>
</initialWindow>
```

The `content` element indicates the main HTML or SWF (Flash) file of the application. The `height` and `weight` specify the dimensions of the window.

The `systemChrome` element specifies whether to add "chrome" to the window. Possible values are `standard` and `none`. Because this is a custom chrome application, I am specifying `none`.

The `visible` element determines whether the window should be visible as soon as it is created. The default is `false`, meaning that your code would need to show the window.

5. **Specify icon files.**

   You can specify icon files to represent your application on the user's computer. Because different parts of a UI use different sizes of an icon, you can specify 16 x 16, 32 x 32, 48 x 48, and 128 x 128 files.

   I created four `png` icons and copied them to the `icons` directory inside of the application root. Here's the code:

```
<icon>
  <image128x128>icons/128.png</image128x128>
  <image48x48>icons/48.png</image48x48>
  <image32x32>icons/32.png</image32x32>
  <image16x16>icons/16.png</image16x16>
</icon>
```

   If you don't specify any icon files, the AIR compiler will use a default AIR icon.

The `application.xml` file is all set. Here is the full file:

```
<?xml version="1.0" encoding="utf-8" ?>
<application xmlns="http://ns.adobe.com/air/
          application/1.0" minimumPatchLevel="5331">
  <id>com.dummies.jot</id>
  <version>1.0</version>
  <filename>jot</filename>
  <name>Jot</name>
  <description>Jot smart and silly notes</description>
  <copyright>Copyright © 2008, Rich Wagner</copyright>
  <initialWindow>
    <content>index.html</content>
    <height>350</height>
    <width>250</width>
```

```
    <systemChrome>none</systemChrome>
    <visible>true</visible>
  </initialWindow>
  <icon>
    <image128x128>icons/128.png</image128x128>
    <image48x48>icons/48.png</image48x48>
    <image32x32>icons/32.png</image32x32>
    <image16x16>icons/16.png</image16x16>
  </icon>
</application>
```

Testing Your Application Using ADT

If you've followed along through the previous sections of this chapter, you've now assembled all the parts of the core application. It is time to test your application on your computer to make sure it works properly. To do so, you'll use ADT, a command-line utility that is included as part of the AIR SDK.

Before continuing, be sure that you have installed the AIR SDK and that the AIR SDK `bin` directory is in your system path. If either of these need to be done, see Chapter 1 for step-by-step instructions.

1. **To test your application, open a Console (Windows) or Terminal (Mac) window.**

2. **Using the** CD **command, change to your application's root directory.**

   This is the directory in which all your application's source code is located.

3. **Enter** adl application.xml **at the command prompt and press Enter.**

   Figure 2-1 shows the Mac OS X command prompt.

Figure 2-1:
Testing the
AIR app
using ADT.

Jot will launch in debug mode, as shown in Figure 2-2.

4. Perform the following tasks to confirm the functionality that you programmed into the application:

- Type something into the text box and click Save. Open the `myjot.txt` file on your desktop in Notepad or another text editor and check out the contents. If your app is working, you see exactly the same text.

- Click the mouse somewhere on the app (except for the buttons) and drag the window. If your app is functioning correctly, the window moves around the way any other native OS window does.

- Click the Close button and test the save options. If you modified text in the text box, the app should ask you whether you want to save the contents.

  If you modified text and the app just closes, something went awry. In that case, go back through this example and double-check your code.

Figure 2-2:
Jot comes
to life.

Creating a Self-Signed Certificate

As I note in Chapter 1, every AIR application needs to be digitally signed. You can sign the app either through a Certification Authority or through the do-it-yourself econo-mode method of a self-signed certificate. Chapter 1 explains the differences between these two methods and the advantages and disadvantages of each. But for the Jot application you develop in this chapter, you want to keep things simple with a test self-signed certificate. Here's how to create one using the ADT utility.

1. Open a Console (Windows) or Terminal (Mac) window.

2. Enter CD at the command prompt to change to your application root directory.

3. **Enter the following at the command prompt:** adt -certificate -cn cert1 1024-RSA testcert.p12 password **to generate the certificate.**

The basic syntax for creating a self-signed certificate is as follows:

```
adt -certificate -cn commonName keyType
        certificateFile password
```

When you use this syntax in the command line, you instruct ADT to create a certificate with a common name of cert1, a 1024-RSA key type, a filename of testcert.p12, and a password of password.

The testcert.p12 file is created in your application root directory.

Given its weak password, you would not want to use this certificate on an application you intended to distribute. The certificate would work fine for your own internal testing, though.

Also, don't worry: You don't need to create a new certificate for each application. You can use one certificate multiple times.

You're now ready to perform the final step in building and deploying an application: generating a distributable AIR file.

Generating an AIR Installer File to Deploy Your Application

If you've been following along through this chapter, you are nearly finished with your first AIR application. By now, you have all the pieces of the Jot application assembled. Now, you have one final step: produce the .air file that you will use to deploy your app.

To generate the .air file, follow these steps:

1. **Open a Console (Windows) or Terminal (Mac) window.**

2. **Enter CD at the command prompt to change to your application root directory.**

3. **Type in the following command at the prompt:**

```
adt -package -storetype pkcs12 -keystore testcert.p12
        jot.air application.xml index.html assets/jot.
        css assets/jot.js assets/AIRAliases.js assets/
        background.png icons/128.png icons/48.png
        icons/32.png icons/16.png.
```

This long-winded command-line instruction tells ADT to produce `jot.air` using the `application.xml` descriptor file and include all the files of the application. The self-signed certificate `testcert.p12` (created in the previous section) is used as the signing option.

Note that you need to have the proper icons and background image file in the `assets` subfolder in order to make that work. If you don't have your own, go to `www.dummies.com/go/adobeairfd` and download the ones I use.

You will be prompted for the certificate password.

4. **Enter** password **at the command prompt.**

   ADT will do its magic and generate the `jot.air` file in your application directory.

Now, when you double-click the `jot.air` installer file, the Application Install dialog box is displayed, as shown in Figure 2-3.

Figure 2-3:
Installing
Jot with a
self-signed
certificate.

Chapter 3

The Air Feels Different: Building with Flex Builder and Flash

*F*lash and its newer sibling Flex Builder enable developers to create rich media and applications for the Web. However, because Adobe AIR is built on top of underlying Flash technology, they also serve as ideal environments for creating AIR apps for the desktop. In this chapter, I walk you through the steps of creating a basic AIR app in Flex and Flash.

I don't explain how to use Flex or Flash in this chapter or elsewhere in the book; instead, this chapter covers how to access the AIR functionality that you can utilize within these Web development environments.

Developing an AIR Application with Flex Builder 3.0

When you create a new Flex project in Flex Builder, you can choose whether the application you're building is for the Web or for the desktop. Follow these soup-to-nuts instructions to create a sample desktop-based AIR app in Flex Builder that I'm calling JotFlex.

Creating the project

Your first step in creating an AIR-based Flex app is to use the Create Project Wizard to generate the basic files for the project. Follow these steps:

1. **Choose File⇨New⇨Flex Project.**

   The New Flex Project dialog box appears, as shown in Figure 3-1.

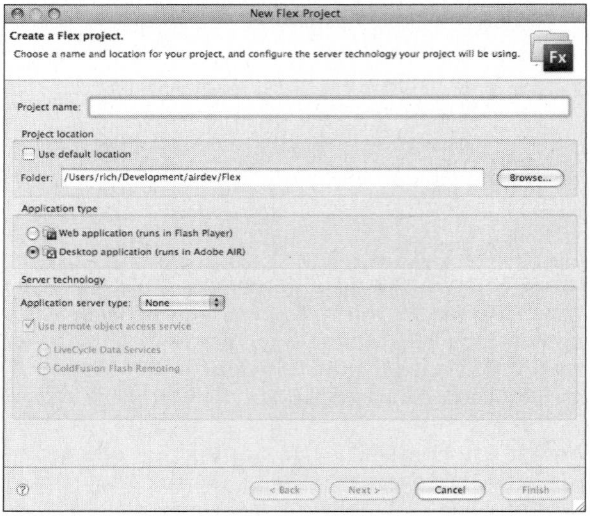

Figure 3-1: The New Flex Project dialog box.

2. **In the Project name box, enter** `JotFlex` **as the name of the AIR project.**

3. **In the Project location box, specify the location of your project.**

   Flex defaults to its own project folder in your Documents folder. Use the default or specify another of your choice.

4. **Select the Desktop Application (Runs in Adobe AIR) option in the Application type box.**

5. **Leave the Server technology box alone.**

6. **Click the Next button to continue.**

   The Configure Output page is displayed.

7. **Specify the desired output location for the compiled application in the Output folder box.**

   Go ahead and leave this at the default folder, `bin-debug`.

8. **Click the Next button to continue.**

   The Create a Flex project is displayed.

You can ignore the top part of the dialog box for this basic example. You use that section to add source code or Flash library files into your app.

9. **If desired, modify the values in the Main source folder and Main application file boxes.**

   You'll probably want to just leave these as is, because these are the typical settings used in Flex apps.

10. **Modify the Application ID to give it a unique, package-like name. To do so, add a** com.*yourdomain.* **prefix to the application name.**

   The application ID I use for this example is com.dummies.JotFlex.

   Be sure to specify a "reverse domain name" — in other words, it's like a Web site address in reverse. The com comes first, followed by a unique domain name, followed by your app name. Flex Builder will not compile your application successfully if you leave the value as is.

   Figure 3-2 shows the dialog box.

11. **Click the Finish button.**

   The new project is created and added to the Flex Navigator, and the main MXML source file is displayed in the editor window, as shown in Figure 3-3.

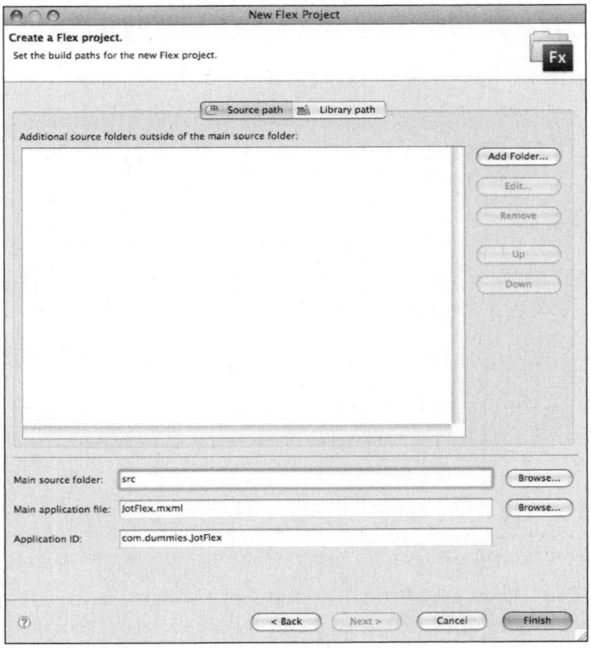

Figure 3-2: Specifying the name of the application.

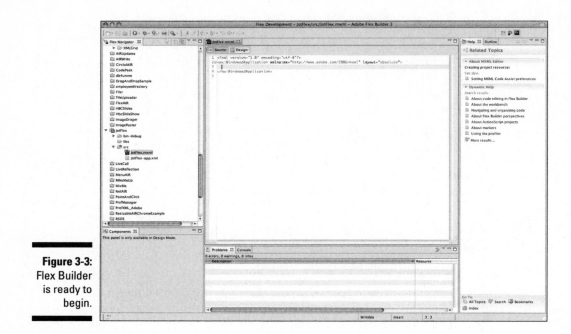

Figure 3-3:
Flex Builder
is ready to
begin.

Notice the root element used in the MXML file. Whereas mx:Application is the root element for Flex Web applications, mx:WindowedApplication is the root for an AIR application.

Adding MXML and ActionScript source code

After you're created your basic files, you're ready to work with MXML and ActionScript to create your app. Follow these steps to continue.

1. **Specify five attributes to the** mx:WindowedApplication **element.**

   In addition to the default settings, specify the title, width, height, verticalScrollPolicy, and horizontalScrollPolicy values, as follows:

   ```
   <mx:WindowedApplication xmlns:mx="http://www.adobe.com/2006/mxml"
       layout="absolute" title="JotFlex" width="321" height="297"
       verticalScrollPolicy="off" horizontalScrollPolicy="off">
   ```

   By setting the verticalScrollPolicy and horizontalScroll Policy properties to "off," you are disabling scroll bars and keeping them from appearing.

2. Inside the `mx:WindowedApplication` **element, add an** `mx:TextArea` **element.**

This element will be used for text entry:

```
<mx:TextArea id="taEditor" x="13.5" y="10" width="292" height="197"/>
```

3. Add two `mx:Button` **elements below the** `mx:TextArea`:

```
<mx:Button id="btnClose" x="100.5" y="215" label="Close"
        click="closeApp()"/>

<mx:Button id="btnSave" x="161.5" y="215" label="Save" click="saveApp()"/>
```

Note the `click` event handlers added in this step. You'll see how to define the `closeApp()` and `saveApp()` functions in Steps 5 and 6.

4. Add an `mx:Script` **element just after the** `mx:WindowedApplication` **start tag:**

```
<mx:Script>
</mx:Script>
```

5. Type the `saveApp()` **function inside the script:**

```
public function saveApp():void {
  var file:File = File.desktopDirectory.resolvePath(
        "myjot.txt" );

  var jot:String = taEditor.text;
  var stream:FileStream = new FileStream();
  stream.open( file, FileMode.WRITE );
  stream.writeMultiByte( jot, File.systemCharset );
  stream.close();
}
```

If you've used Flex before for Web development, the `File` and `FileStream` objects may look foreign to you. That's because you can't use those objects with Web-based apps. (See Chapter 10 for more on `File` and `FileStream`.)

In this function, the `file` variable is assigned as a reference to the `myjot.txt` in the desktop folder of the user. The text contents of `taEditor` are assigned to the `jot` variable. You then use the AIR file I/O routines to create a file stream, open it for writing, write the `jot` variable to the stream, and then close it.

6. Type the `closeApp()` **function inside the script:**

```
public function closeApp():void {
  NativeApplication.nativeApplication.exit();
}
```

NativeApplication contains various application-level properties and methods. However, to actually call any of its members, you access it through its NativeApplication.nativeApplication property. Its exit() method closes the application.

Here's the full source for the JotFlex.mxml file:

```xml
<?xml version="1.0" encoding="utf-8"?>
<mx:WindowedApplication xmlns:mx="http://www.
        adobe.com/2006/mxml" layout="absolute"
        title="JotFlex"
  width="321" height="297" verticalScrollPolicy="off"
        horizontalScrollPolicy="off">


  <mx:Script>
    <![CDATA[

    public function saveApp():void {
      var file:File = File.desktopDirectory.resolvePath(
          "myjot.txt" );
      var jot:String = taEditor.text;
      var stream:FileStream = new FileStream();
      stream.open( file, FileMode.WRITE );
      stream.writeMultiByte( jot, File.systemCharset );
      stream.close();
    }

    public function closeApp():void {
      NativeApplication.nativeApplication.exit();
    }

    ]]>
  </mx:Script>


  <mx:TextArea id="taEditor" x="13.5" y="10" width="292"
        height="197"/>
  <mx:Button id="btnClose" x="100.5" y="215" label="Close"
        click="closeApp()"/>
  <mx:Button id="btnSave" x="161.5" y="215" label="Save"
        click="saveApp()"/>

</mx:WindowedApplication>
```

You're now ready to work with the application descriptor file.

Configuring the application descriptor file

Now you need to configure the application descriptor file, which is an XML file that provides basic application-level details about the application. Follow these steps next.

1. **In the Flex Navigator, double-click the application descriptor file for the AIR project.**

   You'll find it located in the `src` file, with the filename *application-Name-*`app.xml`. For the example project being developed in this section, it's called `JotFlex-app.xml`.

   The file is displayed in the editor, as shown in Figure 3-4.

2. **Locate the** `systemChrome` **element and uncomment it.**

   This property specifies the type of system chrome to use. (See Chapter 7 for more on system chrome.) The `standard` value gives the native OS chrome, whereas `none` removes it.

   By default, the `systemChrome` element is commented out in the XML document. To get a sense of what a Flex chromed AIR app looks like, specify `none` here.

3. **Add** `none` **as the** `systemChrome` **value.**

   The element will look like this:

   ```
   <systemChrome>none</systemChrome>
   ```

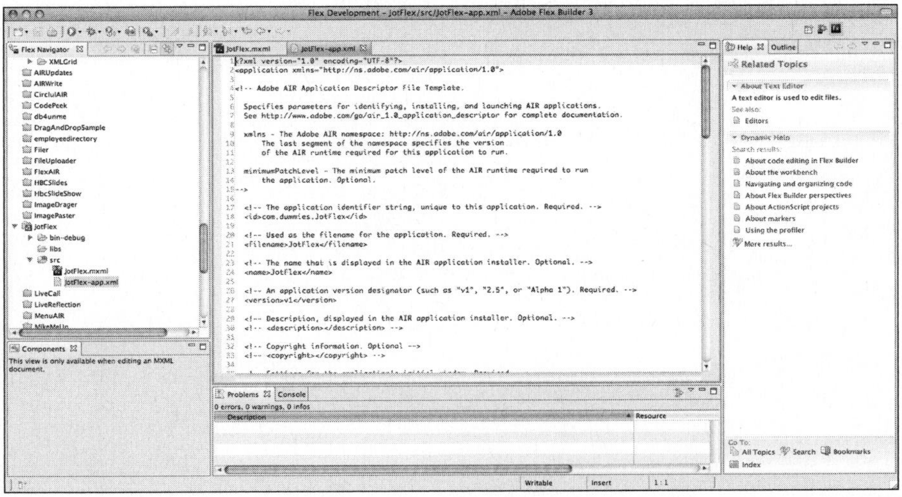

Figure 3-4:
Application
descriptor
file in the
Flex Builder
editor.

4. **Locate the** `transparent` **element and uncomment it.**

   The `transparent` element is commented by default.

5. **Add** `true` **as the** `transparent` **value.**

   The element is as follows:

   ```
   <transparent>true</transparent>
   ```

6. **Choose File⇨Save All from the menu to save all changes.**

   With all the code added to the app, you are ready to test the example application that you've developed in this section.

Testing the app

You now have all the pieces ready for your first AIR app coded and are ready to roll. You can test the app by following these steps:

1. **Choose Run⇨Run JotFlex from the top Flex menu.**

   The JotFlex application is displayed, as shown in Figure 3-5.

2. **Test the functionality of the Save and Close buttons before finishing your testing.**

   When you're satisfied with the state of the application, you're ready to create an installable `.air` file.

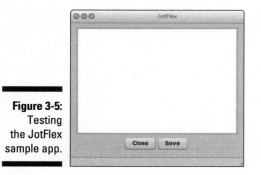

Figure 3-5:
Testing
the JotFlex
sample app.

Preparing the app for deployment

Your AIR app is coded and tested. The final step is to prepare the application for deployment.

1. **Choose Project⇨Export Release Build from the top Flex menu.**

   You can also click the Export Release Build icon on the toolbar.

   The Export Release Build dialog box is displayed, as shown in Figure 3-6.

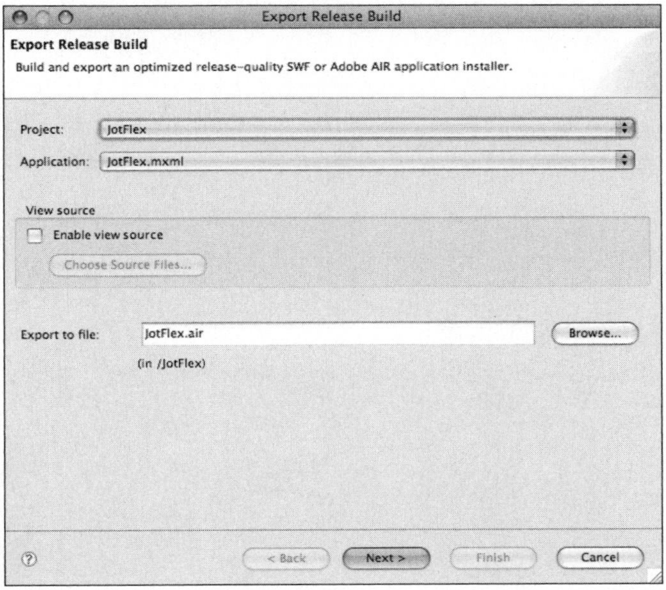

Figure 3-6:
Exporting an AIR project.

You can keep all the default values for this application.

2. **Click the Next button to continue.**

   The Digital Signature page is displayed (see Figure 3-7).

   You now need to create a self-signed digital certificate for this sample application.

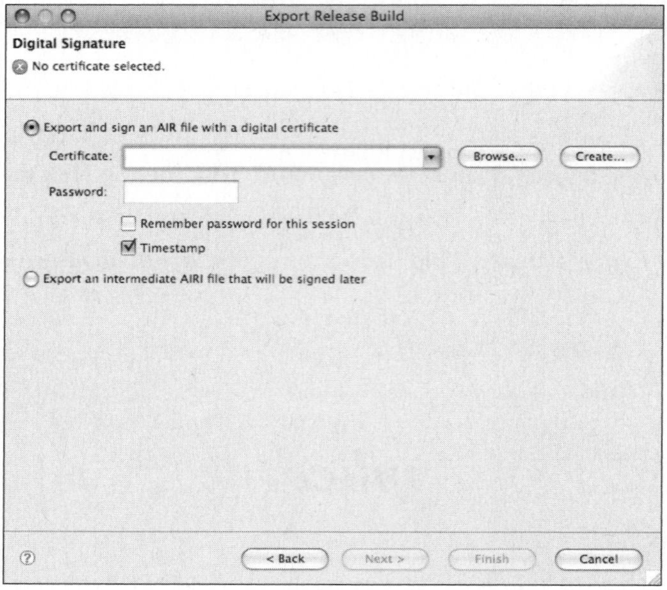

Figure 3-7:
Specifying
a digital
signature
during the
export
process.

3. **Click the Create button.**

   The Create Self-Signed Digital Certificate dialog box is displayed, as shown in Figure 3-8.

Figure 3-8:
Creating a
self-signed
certificate in
Flash.

4. **Enter your name in the Publisher Name box.**

5. **Enter a password in the Password and Confirm Password boxes.**

6. **Click the Browse button.**

   The Save dialog box appears.

7. **Enter the filename of the certificate file and click Save.**

   The Create Self-Signed Certificate dialog box appears again.

8. **Click the OK button.**

   The Digital Certificate page is displayed again.

9. **Click the Finish button.**

   The `JetFlex.air` file is created and now ready for deployment.

   If you would like to deploy the app, jump on over to Chapter 14.

Creating an AIR Application with Flash CS4

Flash has become the clear standard for creating rich media within the browser, so "Flash" and "Web page" are nearly synonymous terms these days. But now, Flash developers are no longer limited to browser-based solutions. Instead, you can take advantage of AIR to create apps for the desktop. This section offers an example of creating a basic AIR application using Flash.

Designing the user interface

Begin creating your application by designing its user interface. I keep the steps short and sweet for this sample app:

1. **Start Flash and, in the first screen that appears, choose the Flash file (Adobe AIR) item.**

   Figure 3-9 shows the opening screen.

2. **From the Properties inspector, resize the document to 300 x 260px.**

   The width and height properties are adjustable here.

3. **Add a `textarea` component onto the stage.**

   I have my `textarea` sized at 250 x 200px. I positioned it at 23 (x) and 13 (y). These sizes and positioning are appropriate for the scope of this app.

4. **From the Properties inspector, change the id of the `textarea` to `taEditor`.**

5. **Add two Button components onto the stage, positioning them side by side under the `textarea`.**

Choose this item to start creating your app.

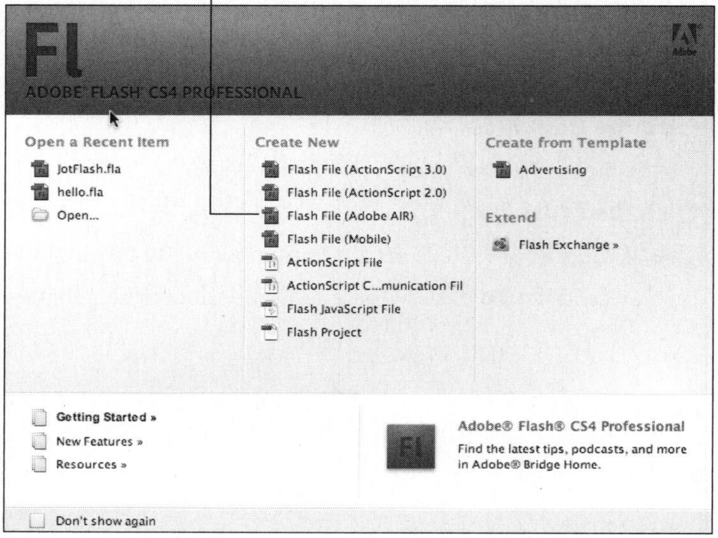

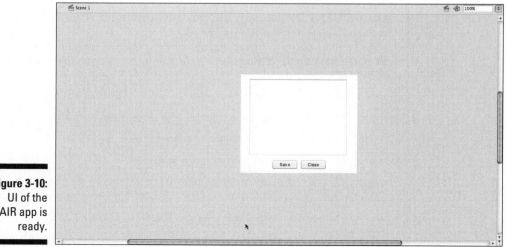

Figure 3-9:
Creating an
Adobe AIR
application
starts here.

6. **Label the first button** `Save` **and give it an id value of** `btnSave`.

7. **Label the second button** `Close` **and give it an id value of** `btnClose`.

Figure 3-10 shows the stage after the components have been added and aligned.

Figure 3-10:
UI of the
AIR app is
ready.

Adding ActionScript code

Now you can attach AIR-based ActionScript code to the user interface by going through these steps:

1. **In the Timeline, select the first frame.**

   The Timeline is at the top section of the Flash window.

2. **Right-click the frame and choose Actions from the pop-up menu.**

   The Actions window is displayed.

3. **Add event listeners for the `click` events of the two buttons.**

   Event listeners are functions you create that respond to events, in this case the clicking of the buttons.

   Type the following code in the Actions window:

   ```
   btnClose.addEventListener(MouseEvent.CLICK,
           closeHandler);
   btnSave.addEventListener(MouseEvent.CLICK,
           saveHandler);
   ```

4. **Add the `closeHandler()` function.**

   Type the following code in the Actions window:

   ```
   function closeHandler(event:Event):void {
       NativeApplication.nativeApplication.exit();
   }
   ```

   This function calls the AIR API to close the app. The `NativeApplication.nativeApplication` object is used to access several application level properties and methods, including `exit()`.

5. **Add the `saveHandler()` function.**

   In the Actions window, enter the following code below the `closeHandler()` function:

   ```
   function saveHandler(event:Event):void {
       var file:File = File.desktopDirectory.resolvePath( "myjot.txt" );
       var jot:String = taEditor.text;
       var stream:FileStream = new FileStream();
       stream.open( file, FileMode.WRITE );
       stream.writeMultiByte( jot, File.systemCharset );
       stream.close();
   }
   ```

The preceding code is some bona fide desktop-related code. This code provides you with the ability to programmatically save files to the user's desktop. The file variable, which is an AIR-based File object, is assigned as a reference to the myjot.txt file in the desktop folder of the user. The text contents of the textarea taEditor is assigned to the jot variable. After that, the code opens a file stream, writes the contents of the jot file to it, and then closes the stream.

Figure 3-11 shows the code added in the Actions window.

Save your changes before continuing. Then you'll be ready to test the code you just added to the Flash project.

6. **Choose Control⇨Test Movie to test your AIR app.**

Your AIR application will run under ADL in its own window. Try typing something in the textarea and then clicking Save. A myjot.txt text file will be saved to your desktop.

Figure 3-11:
The AIR application now coded and ready to go.

Configuring and compiling the AIR application

With the application design and coding now complete, you're ready to establish the AIR settings and compile the application by walking through the following steps:

1. **In the Properties inspector (with the Document selected), click the Edit button beside the AIR Settings label.**

   The AIR – Application & Installer Settings dialog box, shown in Figure 3-12, is displayed. This dialog box is where you specify most of your application-level settings.

2. **If desired, modify the Application ID, Description, and Copyright.**

   The Application ID needs to use a "reverse domain" syntax, which is kind of like a Web site address in reverse. Flash adds the `com.adobe.example.` prefix. Feel free to change to something specific to your context.

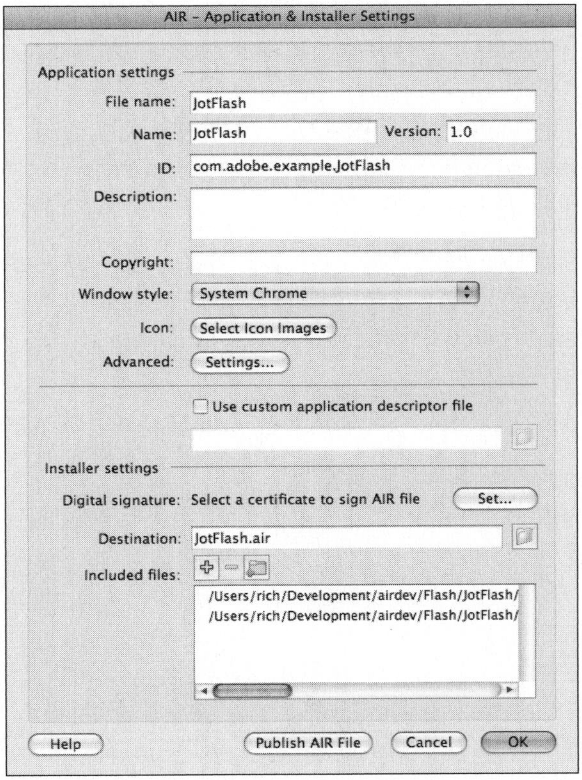

Figure 3-12:
AIR –
Application
& Installer
Settings
dialog box.

You can modify any of the settings that you want, or you can stay with the defaults. But the one task that's mandatory before you publish the application is to create a self-signed digital certificate.

3. **Click the Set button next to the Digital Signature area.**

The Digital Signature dialog box appears (see Figure 3-13).

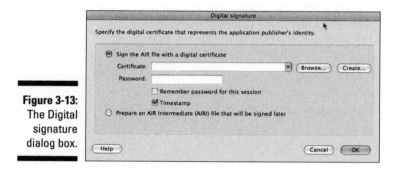

Figure 3-13:
The Digital
signature
dialog box.

4. **Click the Create button.**

The Create Self-Signed Digital Certificate dialog box appears (refer to Figure 3-8).

5. **Enter your name in the Publisher Name box.**

6. **Enter a password in the Password and Confirm Password boxes.**

7. **Click the Browse button.**

The Save dialog box appears.

8. **Enter the filename of the certificate file and click Save.**

The Create Self-Signed Certificate dialog box appears again.

9. **Click the OK button.**

The main AIR – Application & Installer Settings dialog box appears.

10. **Click OK.**

Flash compiles the application and creates the installable `.air` file for you.

Chapter 4

Exploring the Adobe AIR API

· ·

In This Chapter

▶ Showing the relationship between Adobe AIR and JavaScript runtime environments

▶ Accessing the AIR API from within JavaScript and ActionScript

▶ Surveying the Adobe AIR API classes

· ·

Anytime I travel around a new city or country, I'm always sure to throw a reliable map into my suitcase. Before I get out on city streets or country roadways, I want to know what's there, how to get from point A to point B, and what the distances are between major spots of interest. As long as I study my trusty map on the plane trip there, I never feel that I'm going in blind, however foreign the locale may be to me.

In the same way, when it comes to starting to develop applications with Adobe AIR, you can find it helpful to get a lay of the land, by surveying its application programming interface (API). Exploring the Adobe AIR API can give you a solid understanding on what AIR is built for and what you can do to create applications for this new platform.

With that in mind, this chapter walks you through the API. First, however, I show you how you can make API calls from within your code.

Exploring the Relationship between AIR and JavaScript Environments

If you're an HTML/JavaScript developer, it's important for you to have a solid grasp of the impact of AIR on the scripting environment that you're already used to working within. After all, in a traditional Web page, the window is the top-level object that you interact with. The document and other DOM objects (as well as such browser-related objects as history and navigator) are all children of window.

The AIR runtime environment brings in more players:

- ✔ **The** `NativeWindow` **object:** The `NativeWindow` object is a container for all objects in a window and provides an interface to the native OS window. You can perform such functions as creating windows and modifying their look through the `NativeWindow` object.

- ✔ **The** `HTMLLoader` **object:** Inside the `NativeWindow` object, the `HTMLLoader` object serves as a container for HTML content. Each HTML window contains an `HTMLLoader` object. You can use this object to control how HTML content is loaded and displayed.

- ✔ **The JavaScript** `window` **object:** The JavaScript `window` object keeps its traditional role as container for the DOM. However, it also provides three properties that enable you to access the outer world of AIR: the current instance of the `NativeWindow` container (`window.nativeWindow`); the current instance of the `HTMLLoader` container (`window.htmlLoader`); and the rest of the AIR runtime API library (`window.runtime`).

Because of security considerations, only top-level, sandboxed HTML documents have access to the `nativeWindow`, `htmlLoader`, and `runtime` properties. You can't access them from a document inside an `iframe` or `frame`.

Figure 4-1 shows the relationships between the JavaScript and AIR objects.

The `HTMLLoader` object has a `window` property, which is a pointer to the JavaScript `window` object inside of the JavaScript/DOM environment. This property isn't meant to be redundant and is actually not used when you're working inside JavaScript. Instead, ActionScript routines can access the JavaScript/DOM environment using `HTMLLoader.window` as a gateway.

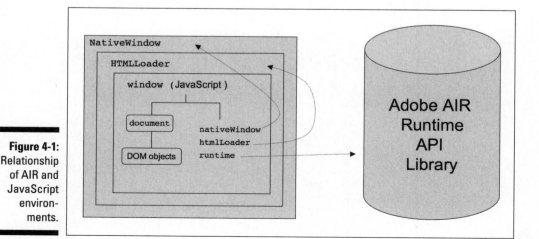

Figure 4-1: Relationship of AIR and JavaScript environments.

Calling the AIR API

The heart of almost any AIR app is the interaction that takes place between the host scripting environment (JavaScript for HTML apps, ActionScript for Flex and Flash apps) and the Adobe AIR runtime. In this section, I provide an overview of how to call the API from inside JavaScript and ActionScript.

Calling from JavaScript

The Adobe AIR API is accessible from JavaScript through a special object called `window.runtime`. The `runtime` object, unique to AIR applications, is used as a gateway to access AIR runtime classes from your code. AIR's classes are logically organized into numerous ActionScript packages. Each package is represented as a property of `runtime`. For example, the `flash` package contains, among other things, the `File` class. So, if you wanted to create an instance of a `File` object, you could use the following declaration:

```
var file = new window.runtime.flash.filesystem.File();
```

That's the long way of doing things, however, and requires you to know the package name for any given object with which you wish to work. Fortunately, there's a better way.

Adobe provides an "aliased" object named `air` that you can use to simplify the access calls and eliminate the requirement of specifying the package name inside the declaration. For example, using the alias definition, you can create a `File` instance using the following, much simpler, syntax:

```
var file = new air.File();
```

To use aliases, include an external script library file called `AIRAliases.js` inside your HTML file, and the world of `air` aliases opens to you:

```
<script src="AIRAliases.js" />
```

A second benefit to using the `AIRAliases.js` file is that the API syntax closely parallels the ActionScript syntax. The only difference is that you need to add the reference to the `air` object in JavaScript, but not in ActionScript. So, here's the JavaScript code to assign the application directory to a variable named `dir`:

```
var dir = air.File.applicationDirectory;
```

The ActionScript code looks remarkably similar:

```
var dir:File = File.applicationDirectory;
```

Calling from ActionScript

You reference Adobe AIR API classes in ActionScript just as you do with other ActionScript packages and classes: Import the package using the `import` statement and then access the class in your code. For example, to use the `File` object, you need to import its package `flash.filesystem.File`. Here's some pseudo code to demonstrate:

```
// first import the package. . .
import flash.filesystem.File;
// . . .and then use the object
var file = new File();
```

Touring the Adobe AIR API

When beginning to work with a new technology, one of the biggest hurdles developers often have is just understanding the lay of the land. In other words, it's hard to develop an application when you don't know exactly the tools you have to work with.

The Adobe AIR API sports a healthy supply of classes that you can use to create desktop-based RIAs. The sections that follow take you on a round-the-world tour of the API to give you a basic understanding of what AIR runtime offers you as a developer and how you can interact with all aspects of the native operating systems. The other chapters of the book give you additional details.

Native OS windows

The Adobe AIR API enables you to create native OS windows, making your application look just like a standard Windows or Mac OS X application. You can also go your own route and create custom window styles and even window shapes.

The following JavaScript function shows you how to create a new, empty window through the API:

```
function createWindow() {
   //Set up the initialization options
   var options = new air.NativeWindowInitOptions();
```

```
    options.systemChrome = air.NativeWindowSystemChrome.
        STANDARD;
    options.type = air.NativeWindowType.NORMAL;
    options.transparent = false;

    //create the native window
    var nativeWindow = new air.NativeWindow(options);
    nativeWindow.title = "The NativeWindows Are Restless";
    nativeWindow.width = 400;
    nativeWindow.height = 300;

    //activate and show the new window
    nativeWindow.activate();
}
```

The `NativeWindowInitOptions()` object enables you to set up certain options related to a window. You then use this `options` object when you create the `NativeWindow` instance. Basic window properties (`title`, `width`, and `height`) are assigned. Finally, the window is activated.

I tell you much more about working with native windows in Chapter 7.

Table 4-1 shows you the window-related classes of the API.

Table 4-1	Window Classes	
Class	*Description*	*ActionScript Package*
[air.]NativeWindow	Creates and controls native desktop windows	flash.display.NativeWindow
[air.]NativeWindow DisplayState	Defines constants for the names of the window display states	flash.display.NativeWindow DisplayState
[air.]NativeWindow InitOptions	Defines the initialization options used to construct a new NativeWindow instance	flash.display.NativeWindow InitOptions
[air.]NativeWindow SystemChrome	Defines constants for the systemChrome property of the Native WindowInitOptions object	flash.display.NativeWindow SystemChrome

(continued)

Table 4-1 (continued)

Class	Description	ActionScript Package
`[air.]NativeWindow Resize`	Defines constants for the possible values of the `edgeOrCor‐ner` parameter of the `NativeWindow.star‐tResize()` method	`flash.display. Native WindowResize`
`[air.]Native WindowType`	Defines constants for the type property of the `NativeWindow InitOptions` object	`flash.display. NativeWindow Type`

Local files

The AIR API lets you work with files and folders with all the usual capabili‐
ties: You can create files and directories, copy and move files around on the
user's hard drive, and display native OS Open and Save dialog boxes. What's
more, you can read and write files from disk or URL (any Internet location).

Following is an example of local file and directory access using JavaScript.
The following function copies a directory to another location and then copies
a text file to the user's desktop:

```
function backup() {

    // Copying user's folder for backup
    var userFolder = air.File.documentsDirectory.
            resolvePath("Giggles");
    var backupFolder = air.File.documentsDirectory.
            resolvePath("Giggles.backup");
    userFolder.copyTo(backupFolder);

    // Copying a file
    var readme = air.File.documentsDirectory.
            resolvePath("Giggles/giggles_readme.txt");
    var readmeDesktop = air.File.desktopDirectory.
            resolvePath("readme_now_or_else.txt");
    readme.copyTo(readmeDesktop, true);
```

In this code, the `userFolder` variable is assigned the `Giggles` folder,
which is a subfolder inside the user's `documentsDirectory` (the user's My
Documents directory in Windows or Documents directory in Mac OS X). Note
the `resolvePath()` method, which allows you to get a path (`Giggles`) that
is relative to another path (`Documents` directory). The `backupFolder`

variable is assigned to a backup directory. The `copyTo()` method then copies the `Giggles` directory to the `backupFolder`.

The second part of the function assigns the `giggles_readme.txt` file to the `readme` variable, and `readmeDesktop` is a variable assigned to a file on the user's desktop folder. The `copyTo()` method copies the `readme` file to the new location.

See Chapter 10 for more about files and folders.

Table 4-2 lists the file-related classes of the AIR API.

Table 4-2	File Classes	
Class	*Description*	*ActionScript Package*
`[air.]File`	Pointer a path to a file or directory	`flash.filesystem.File`
`[air.]FileStream`	Used to read and write files	`flash.filesystem.FileStream`
`[air.]FileMode`	Defines constants used when opening files with `FileStream`	`flash.filesystem.FileMode`
`[air.]FileFilter`	Defines what files on the user's system are displayed in the file browse dialog box	`flash.net.FileFilter`

Menus

Menus — both top level and right-click contextual menus — are one of the fundamental UI building blocks of any Windows or Mac OS X application. The Adobe AIR API provides capabilities to create robust native menus in your application. The following JavaScript code creates a top-level File menu with a single Open item:

```
// Create root menu
var rootMenu = new air.NativeMenu();

// Add a File menu item
var fileMenuItem = rootMenu.addItem("File");

// Create menu and assign it as the submenu
var fileSubmenu = new air.NativeMenu();
fileMenuItem.submenu = fileSubmenu;
```

```
// Add Open item
var fileOpenItem = fileSubmenu.addItem("Open");

// Add event handler
fileOpenItem.addEventListener( air.Event.SELECT,
        fileOpen);

// If running on Windows, add as window menu
if (air.NativeWindow.supportsMenu ) {
        nativeWindow.menu = rootMenu;
}

// If running on Mac OS X, add as application menu
if (air.NativeApplication.supportsMenu) {
    air.NativeApplication.menu = rootMenu;
}

// Handler for the File Open menu item
function fileOpen() {
    alert("An open file can do no harm, so they say.");
}
```

The `rootMenu NativeMenu` instance serves as the container for the submenu and menu items of this example. A File menu item (`fileMenuItem`) is added to the `rootMenu` and then a submenu is created and assigned to it. Next, the Open menu item is added to the `fileSubmenu`.

To have the menu item do anything when a user selects it, you need to add an event handler to it, which I do with the `addEventListener()` method. It tells AIR to execute the `fileOpen()` function (defined at the end of the code) when the `fileOpenItem` is selected.

The final step is to assign the `rootMenu` to the application as a top-level menu. However, Windows and the Mac handle top-level menus differently. A top menu under Windows is contained by the window, whereas under Mac OS X, the top menu becomes the system-wide application menu at the top of the screen. Therefore, before assigning it as a window or application menu, the code checks to see whether that capability is supported at runtime by checking the result of the `supportsMenu` property.

See Chapter 8 for more of the scoop on menus.

Table 4-3 highlights the menu-related classes as well as other UI-related classes in Adobe AIR.

Table 4-3	User Interface Classes	
Class	*Description*	*ActionScript Package*
`[air.]NativeMenu`	Defines a native menu (Application, Window, Dock icon, System tray, Context, Pop-up)	`flash.display. NativeMenu`
`[air.] NativeMenuItem`	Represents a menu item	`flash.display. NativeMenuItem`
`[air.]Screen`	Defines properties to indicate the display screens available	`flash.display. Screen`
`[air.]Icon`	Represents an icon	`flash.desktop. Icon`
`[air.]DockIcon`	Represents a Mac OS X style dock icon	`flash.desktop. DockIcon`
`[air.] InteractiveIcon`	Abstract base class for icons associated with an application	`flash.desktop. InteractiveIcon`
`[air.] NotificationType`	Defines constants for the priority parameter of `DockIcon. bounce()` and the `type` parameter of `NativeWindow. notifyUser()`	`flash.desktop. NotificationType`
`[air.] SystemTrayIcon`	Represents a Windows system tray icon	`flash.desktop. SystemTrayIcon`
`[air.]Loader`	Loads SWF files or image (JPG, PNG, or GIF) files	`flash.display. Loader`
`[air.]Bitmap`	Represents a bitmap image	`flash.display. Bitmap`
`[air.]BitmapData`	Provides a means to work with the pixel data of a bitmap	`flash.display. BitmapData`

Inter-application data exchange

The Adobe AIR API taps into the familiar inter-application exchange mechanism in Windows and Mac OS X, what is ubiquitously known as the Clipboard. You can use the Clipboard's data-exchange capabilities through Copy and Paste routines as well as through drag-and-drop. Tables 4-4 and 4-5 list the Clipboard and drag-and-drop classes of the API.

The following JavaScript example shows you how to copy a piece of text to the Clipboard:

```
function copyMe() {
  var txt = "This little text went to the market.";
  air.Clipboard.generalClipboard.clear();
  air.Clipboard.generalClipboard.setData(air.
        ClipboardFormats.TEXT_FORMAT, txt);
}
```

The `clear()` method of the `Clipboard` object is used to remove existing contents from the Clipboard. Then, the `setData()` method adds the `txt` `String` variable to the Clipboard as plain text.

Chapter 9 dives into more detail on working with the Clipboard and drag-and-drop.

Table 4-4	Clipboard Classes	
Class	*Description*	*ActionScript Package*
`[air.]Clipboard`	Defines a container for transferring data and objects via the Clipboard and drag-and-drop	`flash.desktop. Clipboard`
`[air.]Clipboard Formats`	Defines constants for standard data formats used with the Clipboard	`flash.desktop. Clipboard Formats`
`[air.]Clipboard TransferMode`	Defines constants for the `transferMode` parameter of the `Clipboard.get-Data()` method	`flash.desktop. Clipboard TransferMode`

Table 4-5	Drag-and-Drop Classes	
Class	**Description**	**ActionScript Package**
`[air.]NativeDrag Manager`	Coordinates drag-and-drop operations	`flash.desktop.` `NativeDragManager`
`[air.]NativeDrag Options`	Declares the drag-and-drop actions that are relevant to a drag operation	`flash.desktop.` `Native` `DragOptions`
`[air.]NativeDrag Actions`	Defines constants for the `NativeDragManager.` `dropAction` property	`flash.desktop.` `NativeDragActions`

Multimedia

Adobe AIR provides various media-related classes (see Table 4-6) to work with audio files as well as to interact with such hardware as the system microphone or camera. You can use these multimedia capabilities to add sound effects to your app or develop a full-fledged video, audio, and camera capture app.

The following JavaScript code shows you how to play a sound:

```
var sndFile = new air.URLRequest("ping.mp3");
var snd = new air.Sound(sndFile);
snd.play();
```

The `sndFile` variable references the `ping.mp3` sound file. An instance of a `Sound` object is created using that `sndFile` variable, and then it is played using the `play()` method.

Flip to Chapter 13 for the full scoop on working with audio.

Table 4-6	Media Classes	
Class	**Description**	**ActionScript Package**
`[air.]ID3Info`	Provides properties representing ID3 metadata for an MP3 file	`Flash.media.` `ID3Info`

(continued)

Table 4-6 *(continued)*

Class	Description	ActionScript Package
[air.]Sound	Provides access to sound capabilities, such as playing an audio file	Flash.media. Sound
[air.]SoundChannel	Controls sound in an app (a sound is assigned to a sound channel)	Flash.media. SoundChannel
[air.]SoundLoader Context	Used to perform security checks for files that load sound	Flash.media. SoundLoader Context
[air.]SoundMixer	Provides global sound and mixing control	flash.media. SoundMixer
[air.] SoundTransform	Provides properties for volume and pan control	flash.media. SoundTransform
[air.]Microphone	Captures audio from a microphone attached to the computer	flash.media. Microphone
[air.]Video	Captures video from a video camera attached to the computer	flash.media. Video
[air.]Camera	Captures images from a digital camera attached to the computer	flash.media. Camera

Keyboard and mouse

The AIR API provides access to the keyboard and mouse of the system running your application. You can use it to trap for keyboard or mouse events. Here's an example of how to use JavaScript to listen to keyboard input and then add custom functions when the user clicks the left, right, top, and down arrows. The first thing is to call addEventListener() to listen for the key-Down key in the initialization routine of the app:

```
window.nativeWindow.stage.addEventListener("keyDown",onKe
        y);
```

As a result, when any key is pressed, a function called `onKey()` is triggered, which follows:

```
function onKey(event){

  switch(event.keyCode) {
    case air.Keyboard.LEFT :
      alert("Turn left to surf!");
      break;
    case air.Keyboard.RIGHT :
      alert("Turn right to get chowda!");
      break;
    case air.Keyboard.UP :
      alert("Go up for Hockey!");
      break;
    case air.Keyboard.DOWN :
      alert("Go down for great TexMex!");
      break;
    default
      break;
  }
}
```

In this routine, the `switch` statement evaluates the keycode of the key pressed. If the keycode matches the `air.Keyboard.LEFT`, `air.Keyboard.RIGHT`, `air.Keyboard.UP`, and `air.Keyboard.DOWN`, an `alert()` message box displays. Otherwise, the key passes through without incident.

Table 4-7 shows the classes related to the keyboard and mouse.

Table 4-7	User Interaction Classes	
Class	*Description*	*ActionScript Package*
`[air.]Keyboard`	Defines constants representing keyboard keys and provides an interface to the keyboard	`flash.ui.Keyboard`
`[air.]Key Location`	Defines constants on the location of a key pressed on the keyboard	`flash.ui.Key Location`
`[air.]Mouse`	Allows you to show/hide the mouse pointer	`flash.ui.Mouse`

Database

The SQLite database engine is built inside the Adobe AIR runtime. The AIR API provides a host of database classes (see Table 4-8) for storing and working with local data. You can use the database to store user data or application-specific data.

Consider the following JavaScript example, which uses the API to connect to a database named `chuckles.db` and insert a new record into the `contacts` table:

```
var conn = new air.SQLConnection();
var dbFile = air.File.documentsDirectory.resolvePath
            ("chuckles.db");
// open the database
conn.open(dbFile, air.OpenMode.UPDATE);

// add the customer record to the database
var insertStmt = new air.SQLStatement();
insertStmt.sqlConnection = conn;
insertStmt.text =
    "INSERT INTO contacts (firstName, lastName, phone) " +
    "VALUES ('Rocky', 'Burky', '719-555-1212')";
insertStmt.execute();

conn.close();
```

In this example, a connection is established to the `chuckles.db` database file and opened in update mode. The `conn` variable is used to represent the connection.

The `insertStmt` variable is an instance of `SQLStatement` and is used to send a SQL statement to the database. After that statement is assigned to the text variable, its `execute()` method is called.

Table 4-8	Database Classes	
Classs	*Description*	*ActionScript Package*
`[air.]Encrypted LocalStore`	Manages getting and setting objects in the encrypted local data store	`flash.data. Encrypted LocalStore`

Class	Description	ActionScript Package
`[air.]` `SQLCollationType`	Defines constants for the `defaultCollation Type` parameter of the `SQLColumnSchema` constructor, as well as the `SQLColumnSchema. defaultCollation- Type` property	`flash.data.SQL CollationType`
`[air.]SQLColumn NameStyle`	Defines constants for the `SQLConnection.col- umnNameStyle` property	`flash.data.SQL ColumnName Style`
`[air.]SQLColumn Schema`	Provides info for the speci- fied column within a data- base table	`flash.data.SQL ColumnSchema`
`[air.]SQLConnection`	Manages the creation of and connection to local SQL database files	`flash.data. SQLConnection`
`[air.]SQLError`	Provides details about a failed database operation	`flash.errors. SQLError`
`[air.]SQLError Event`	Triggered by `SQLConnection` or `SQLStatement` when a database error occurs in asynchronous execution mode	`flash.events. SQLErrorEvent`
`[air.]SQLError Operation`	Defines constants for the `SQLError.operation` property	`flash.errors. SQLError Operation`
`[air.]SQLEvent`	Dispatched when a `SQLConnection` or `SQLStatement` instance completes successfully	`flash.events. SQLEvent`
`[air.]SQLIndexSchema`	Provides info for the speci- fied index in a database table	`flash.data. SQLIndexSchema`
`[air.]SQLMode`	Defines the constants for the `openMode` parameter of the `SQLConnection. open()` and `SQL Connection. openAsync()` methods	`flash.data. SQLMode`

(continued)

Table 4-8 *(continued)*

Classs	Description	ActionScript Package
`[air.]SQLResult`	Provides access to data returned by a `SQLStatement` instance	`flash.data.SQLResult`
`[air.]SQLSchema`	Serves as base class for schema for database objects	`flash.data.SQLSchema`
`[air.]SQLSchemaResult`	Provides info from a call to the `SQLConnection.loadSchema()` method	`flash.data.SQLSchemaResult`
`[air.]SQLStatement`	Execute a SQL statement against a local SQL database that is open through a `SQLConnection` instance	`flash.data.SQLStatement`
`[air.]SQLTableSchema`	Defines the specified table in a database	`flash.data.SQLTableSchema`
`[air.]SQLTransactionLockType`	Defines constants for the `option` parameter of the `SQLConnection.begin()` method	`flash.data.SQLTransactionLockType`
`[air.]SQLTriggerSchema`	Defines the specified trigger within a database	`flash.data.SQLTriggerSchema`
`[air.]SQLUpdateEvent`	Dispatched by a `SQLStatement` object when data changes as a result of a SQL statement or trigger	`flash.events.SQLUpdateEvent`
`[air.]SQLViewSchema`	Provides info for the specified view within a database	`flash.data.SQLViewSchema`

Communication

Adobe AIR is all about creating RIAs — rich *internet* applications. Not surprisingly, then, its API sports a healthy supply of internet communication-related classes and functions, as shown in Tables 4-9 and 4-10. You can use this part of the API to do simple tasks, such as calling a URL:

```
var url = "http://www.dummies.com";
var urlRequest = new air.URLRequest(url);
air.navigateToURL(urlRequest);
```

In this JavaScript code, the `url` variable is assigned the value of a Web site. Not just any site, mind you. This variable is then passed as a parameter when a `URLRequest` instance is created. The `navigateToURL()` method is then called using this variable as a parameter.

Chapter 12 tells you more about network connectivity.

Table 4-9	Network Connection Classes	
Class	*Description*	*ActionScript Package*
`[air.]URLLoader`	Downloads data from a URL as text, binary data, or URL-encoded variables	`flash.net.` `URLLoader`

`[air.]URLLoader`
`DataFormat`
	Defines values to specify how downloaded data is received	`flash.net.`
		`URLLoaderData`
		`Format`

`[air.]URLRequest`	Captures data in a single HTTP request	`flash.net.URL` `Request`

`[air.]URLRequest`
`Defaults`
	Defines static properties for defining default values for `URLRequest` class	`flash.net.`
		`URLRequest`
		`Defaults`

`[air.]` `URLRequestHeader`	Encapsulates a single HTTP request header in the form of a name/value pair	`flash.net.` `URLRequestHeader`
`[air.]` `URLRequestMethod`	Determines whether the `URLRequest` object should use POST or GET method when sending data to a server	`flash.net.` `URLRequestMethod`
`[air.]URL` `Stream`	Provides low-level access to downloading URLs (compared to `URLLoader` which is used when a file is completed)	`flash.net.` `URLStream`

(continued)

Table 4-9 *(continued)*

Class	Description	ActionScript Package
`[air.]URL Variables`	Allows you to transfer variables between an app and a server	`flash.net. URLVariables`
`[air.]Socket`	Establish a socket connection and read/write raw binary data	`flash.net.Socket`
`[air.]XML Socket`	Establish a socket connection to communicate with a server computer identified by an IP address or domain name	`flash.net. XMLSocket`
`[air.]Responder`	Used by `NetConnection. call()` to handle return values from the server	`flash.net. Responder`
`[air.]Object Encoding`	Defines serialization settings in classes that serialize objects to work with legacy versions of ActionScript.	`flash.net. ObjectEncoding`
`[air.]NetStream`	Defines a one-way streaming connection between app and Flash Media Server	`flash.net. NetStream`

Table 4-10 **URL-Related Functions**

Function	Description	ActionScript Package
`[air.] navigate- ToURL()`	Opens a URL in the default system browser	`flash.net. navigateToURL`
`[air.] send- ToURL()`	Sends a URL request to server (ignores response)	`flash.net.sendToURL`

In addition to using remote network connections, such as URLs or app servers, you can use the AIR API to connect to other AIR applications, other objects within the same AIR app, and even Flash media running inside the browser (see Table 4-11). For example, if you want to set up your app to converse with another app in the same domain, you write the following:

```
// Create local connection
var clientConn = new air.LocalConnection();
clientConn.connect("rockdude");

// Create object that will be called remotely
var clientCommunicator = new Object();
//
clientCommunicator.talkToMe = function() {
 air.trace("Hey, you rock, dude!");
 }
clientConn.client = clientCommunicator;
```

This code creates a `LocalConnection` object named `lc` and then defines a custom JavaScript object named `clientCommunicator`. The `client` property of `lc` is then assigned to the custom object.

A second application could call the `talkToMe()` method by establishing a local connection with the `rockdude` connection and then specifying the method in the `send()` method:

```
var serverConn  = new air.LocalConnection();
serverConn.connect("rockdude");
serverConn.send("rockdude", "talkToMe");
```

Table 4-11	Application Communication Classes	
Class	**Description**	**ActionScript Package**
`[air.]LocalConnection`	Establish a connection to communicate between two files (SWF<->HTML, SWF<->SWF, etc.)	`flash.net.LocalConnection`
`[air.]NetConnection`	Defines a bidirectional connection	`flash.net.NetConnection`
`[air.]SharedObject`	Enable data sharing between multiple files/objects on local computer or server	`flash.net.SharedObject`
`[air.]SharedObjectFlushStatus`	Defines return values for `SharedObject.flush()` method	`flash.net.SharedObjectFlushStatus`

Part II
AIR Application Design

The 5th Wave   By Rich Tennant

"Okay antidote, antidote, what would an antidote icon look like? You know, I still haven't got this desktop the way I'd like it."

In this part . . .

The introductions are over. It's time to get down to business and focus on application design. You focus in this part on the basics of UI design using HTML and CSS, and on and creating windows and menus from your app. You then explore how to work with menus and icons.

Chapter 5

Using HTML and CSS as Building Blocks

*I*n Chapter 2, I walk you through the basics of creating an HTML-based AIR application. Using that process as a guide helps you realize that working with the content and presentation layer in AIR is nearly identical to designing a traditional Web application. HTML and CSS work the same way. The HTML DOM is still the way in which you access and manipulate the document through scripting. JavaScript works much the same way as it does within a normal Web page.

However, AIR's HTML environment gives you some additional capabilities (such as extended styles or the `canvas` element) that you should understand, regardless of whether you're creating an HTML-based application or even integrating an HTML window inside your Flex or Flash application.

In this chapter, you explore the familiar world of HTML, but do so within this new AIR environment.

Working with HTMLLoader

Whether you're creating an HTML-based AIR application or displaying HTML content in your Flex or Flash app, each HTML document you display is contained in its own `HTMLLoader` object. The `HTMLLoader` manages the behavior and aspects of the appearance of the HTML display. As you work through this section, you explore how to access `HTMLLoader` and display content in it.

Accessing and sizing the HTMLLoader

In an HTML application, an instance of the HTMLLoader object is created automatically for you. You can access this HTMLLoader instance by accessing the htmlLoader property of the JavaScript window object:

```
window.htmlLoader
```

When you're creating an HTML-based app, you can set the initial size of the application through the application descriptor XML file. However, you can also set the size through the width and height of the HTMLLoader, like so:

```
window.htmlLoader.width = 500;
window.htmlLoader.height = 400;
```

In a Flex or Flash application, you need to explicitly create an instance of HTMLLoader by using the following code:

```
var htmlLoader:HTMLLoader = new HTMLLoader();
var urlRequest:URLRequest = new URLRequest("local_help.
        html");
htmlLoader.width = myPanel.stageWidth;
htmlLoader.height = myPanel.stageHeight;
htmlLoader.load(urlRequest);
myPanel.addChild(htmlLoader);
```

The htmlLoader instance uses urlRequest to specify the URL to open using load(). Also, notice that I set the dimensions of htmlLoader. That's because when you're creating an HTMLLoader in ActionScript, the width and height properties are 0, so you need to specify them.

Loading HTML content

HTMLLoader allows you to load HTML content using the load() and loadString() methods. The load(url) method loads the specified URL. For example:

```
window.htmlLoader.load("http://www.dummies.com");
```

You can also use the loadString(htmlContent) method to load HTML content through a string parameter. Here's an ActionScript example:

```
var htmlLoader:HTMLLoader = new HTMLLoader();
var htmlText:String = getHTMLContent();
htmlLoader.loadString(htmlText);
```

Setting the transparency of a window

One of the visual settings that many HTML developers will want to consider when creating an AIR app is the ability to make the background of the window transparent — something that can't be done with a traditional Web app.

However, HTML developers who want to set a transparent background for their applications can become perplexed when they try to do so. It is not so intuitive. When you forget about HTMLLoader, the natural inclination is to set the transparency property of the application descriptor file to false and then set the CSS background to transparent. But, as you'll discover if you try to do both of those things, that's not enough. The reason is that the HTMLLoader container has an opaque background by default.

Therefore, you need to set the paintsDefaultBackground to false:

```
window.htmlLoader.paintsDefaultBackground = false;
```

The HTML document itself does not support alpha blending (other than by using a blended PNG graphic as a background-image). Technically, the HTMLLoader does have an alpha property that you can use for alpha blending, although this property is not used much in HTML applications.

Launching a URL in the default system browser

When you click a link inside of an HTML document or assign a URL to window.location, the requested page will be displayed inside the same HTMLLoader object. However, if you want to launch the URL in the default system browser (typically Internet Explorer, Firefox, or Safari) instead, then you can set the navigateInSystemBrowser property to true:

```
window.htmlLoader.navigateInSystemBrowser = true;
```

History, HTML history that is, can teach you something

By now, you can see how similar the behavior of HTMLLoader is to a browser. It should not be much of a surprise, therefore, that the HTMLLoader is also responsible for maintaining a history list for the URLs that are accessed inside of it.

When a URL is added to the history list, it is stored as a HistoryListItem. You can then use the HTMLLoader history-related properties and methods, as listed in Table 5-1, to work with a HistoryListItem collection to create a virtual browser-like experience inside your application.

Table 5-1	HTMLLoader History-Related Members
Member	**Description**
historyBack()	Goes back in the history list.
historyForward()	Goes forward in the history list.
historyGo(x)	Goes forward or backward x number of spaces.
getHistoryAt(index)	Returns an HTMLListItem element at index position in the list.
HistoryLength	Gives the length of the history list.
HistoryPosition	Shows the current position in the history list.

The following code shows an example of how you can use the history-related functionality in your app:

```
function back()
{
  window.htmlLoader.historyBack();
}

function forward()
{
  window.htmlLoader.historyForward();
}

function getItemInfo(idx)
{
  item = window.htmlLoader.getHistoryAt(idx);
  alert("URL:" + item.url +
        " Title: " + item.title +
        " Original URL: " + item.originalURL);
}
```

Taking Advantage of WebKit Extensions

When you create an HTML-based application in Adobe AIR, you finally have a great excuse to forget about all the cross-browser compatibility issues that continually dog Web developers. Because you're developing for the browser embedded inside the AIR runtime, your only requirement is to ensure that your page looks and performs properly with WebKit. What's more is that although WebKit is standards based, it also features some nonstandard extensions that you can feel free to take advantage of as you develop your interface.

Use this section to help you identify several little secret compartments in that Web developer toolbox of yours.

Table 5-2 lists the major extensions to CSS that you can use in your Adobe AIR applications.

Table 5-2	Major WebKit Extensions to CSS
CSS Property Name	*Description*
`-webkit-background-size`	Specify the size of a background image.
`-webkit-border-horizontal-spacing`	Horizontal component of the border spacing.
`-webkit-border-vertical-spacing`	Vertical component of the border spacing.
`-webkit-border-radius`	Define the rounding radius for the four corners of a box.

`-webkit-border-bottom-left-radius`
`-webkit-border-bottom-right-radius`
`-webkit-border-top-left-radius`
`-webkit-border-top-right-radius`
	Define radius for one of the four corners of a box.

`-webkit-line-break`	Line break rule to use for Chinese, Japanese, and Korean (CJK) text.
`-webkit-margin-bottom-collapse`	Determines how the bottom margin of a table cell collapses.

(continued)

Table 5-2 *(continued)*

CSS Property Name	Description
-webkit-margin-collapse	Determines how the top and bottom margins of a table cell collapses.
-webkit-margin-start	Width of the starting margin (usually left side).
-webkit-margin-top-collapse	Determines how the top margin of a table cell collapses.
-webkit-nbsp-mode	Behavior of nonbreaking spaces within the enclosed content.
-webkit-padding-start	Width of the starting padding (typically left side).
-webkit-rtl-ordering	Overrides the default handling of mixed left-to-right and right-to-left text.
-webkit-text-fill-color	Text fill color.
-webkit-text-security	Replacement shape to use in a password field.
-webkit-user-drag	Use when you need to override the automatic drag behavior.
-webkit-user-modify	Indicates whether the content of an element can be edited.
-webkit-user-select	Indicates whether a user can select the content of an element.

Although some of the extensions are fairly obscure, there are a few jewels to take advantage of, as described next.

Creating rounded rectangles

The -webkit-border-radius and its related properties allow you to define the radius of the border of a block level element. You can use this extension to easily create rounded rectangles rather than resort to image-based corners. The following example creates rounded corners on the top of a div element, but keeps the bottom corners square:

```
-webkit-border-bottom-left-radius: 0px;
-webkit-border-bottom-right-radius: 0px;
-webkit-border-top-left-radius: 15px;
-webkit-border-top-right-radius: 15px;
```

Figure 5-1 shows the result.

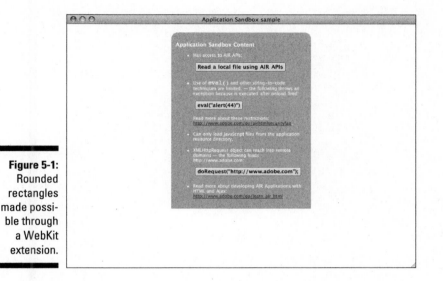

Figure 5-1:
Rounded
rectangles
made possi-
ble through
a WebKit
extension.

See Chapter 2 for another example of using `-webkit-border-radius` in an HTML app.

Making links into push buttons

The `-webkit-appearance` property is a WebKit extension that is designed to change the appearance of an HTML element and transform it into a variety of different UI controls. Adobe AIR supports `-webkit-appearance:push-button`, which can enable you to easily turn a link or other element into a push button. To demonstrate, begin with a link assigned to a class named `special`:

```
<a href="http://www.dummies.com" class="special">Visit Our
         Home Page</a>
```

The `a.special` style can then be defined as follows:

```
a.special
{
  display: block;
```

```
  width: 180px;
  font-size: 14px;
  font-weight: bold;
  line-height: 30px;
  color: #000000;
  text-decoration: none;
  text-align: center;
  margin: 15px auto;
  -webkit-appearance: push-button;
}
```

The `-webkit-appearance: push-button` property transforms the appearance of the a link into a push button. The remaining properties set the formatting and positioning of the element.

Figure 5-2 shows the transformation when the AIR application runs.

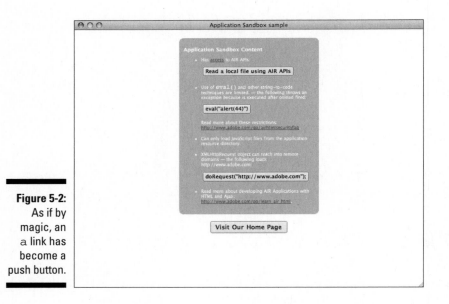

Figure 5-2:
As if by magic, an a link has become a push button.

Setting alpha values

WebKit enables you to set an alpha value when declaring an RGB color with the new `rgba()` declaration. Using `rgba()`, you can add translucent color overlays using CSS and avoid transparent PNGs or GIFs. The syntax for the declaration is as follows:

```
rgba(r, g, b, alpha)
```

The r, g, and b values are integers between 0–255 that represent the red, green, and blue values. The a is the alpha value between 0 and 1 (0.0 is transparent, 1.0 is fully opaque). For example, to set a green background with a 40 percent transparency value, you use the following:

```
background: rgba(0, 255, 0, 0.4);
```

The following example shows five div elements, each with a different alpha value for the background-color. The text-shadow property also uses rgba. Here is the full source code:

```
<!DOCTYPE HTML PUBLIC "-//W3C//DTD HTML 4.01//EN" "http://
          www.w3.org/TR/html4/strict.dtd">
<html>
<head>
<meta http-equiv="Content-Type" content="text/html;
          charset=iso-8859-1" />
<title>WebKit CSS Extensions</title>
<script type="text/javascript" src="AIRAliases.js"></
          script>
<style>
div.blockHead
{
  font-size: 46px;
  text-align: center;
  color: #ffffff;
  text-shadow: rgba(0,0, 0, 0.7) 0 1px 0;
  line-height: 76px;
}
</style>
</head>
<body>
<div class="blockHead" style="background-color: rgba(0, 0,
          0, 0.2);"><span>20%</span></div>
<div class="blockHead" style="background-color: rgba(0, 0,
          0, 0.4);"><span>40%</span></div>
<div class="blockHead" style="background-color: rgba(0, 0,
          0, 0.6);"><span>60%</span></div>
<div class="blockHead" style="background-color: rgba(0, 0,
          0, 0.8);"><span>80%</span></div>
<div class="blockHead" style="background-color: rgba(0, 0,
          0, 1.0)  ;"><span>100%</span></div>
</body>
</html>
```

Figure 5-3 shows the effect of this code when the application runs.

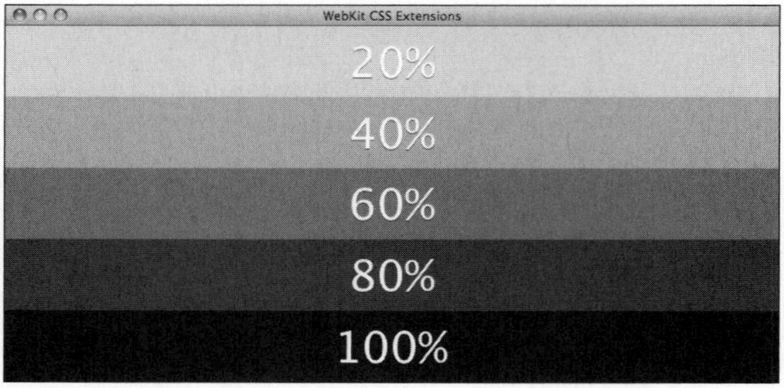

WebKit CSS Extensions

20%

40%

60%

80%

100%

Figure 5-3:
The varying
alpha values
for these
divs form a
gradient.

Drawing Graphics on the HTML Canvas

Although ActionScript developers have the ability to draw graphics on a canvas in their Web or AIR applications, HTML developers have never had this same level of programming power. You can use JavaScript to create or animate DOM elements, but not to create lines or other shapes from scratch. However, WebKit supports the HTML canvas element that defines a drawing region in the document that you then draw on using the WebKit Canvas API.

Canvas drawing can be intimidating because you need to draw on-screen by defining a series of x,y coordinates for lines and rectangles. As you begin, I recommend using a piece of old fashioned graph paper to sketch out the shapes in a grid.

Adding a canvas

You can think of a canvas as a flat, two-dimensional surface that has a default origin (0,0) in the top-left corner. As in an HTML document, all the x,y coordinates that you specify are relative to this position.

To define a canvas in your JavaScript code:

```
<canvas id="whiteboard" style="width:350px;height:350px;"/>
```

You can place as many canvas elements on a page as you want. Each just needs to have its own unique id value.

You can now draw inside the surface region using JavaScript. The following sections show you how.

Getting a context

The `canvas` element serves as the container for your drawing area, but you don't actually work with the `canvas` to do so. Instead, you work with something called a *2d context object*. All the drawing properties and methods that you work with are called from the `context` object.

To get a `context` object to work with, you call the `canvas` element's `getContext()` method:

```
var canvas = document.GetElementById("canvasElement");
var context = canvas.getContext("2d");
```

Drawing a rectangle

In order to draw a rectangle onto a canvas, you can use one of three methods of the `context` object:

- `context.fillRect(x,y,w,h)` draws a filled rectangle.
- `context.strokeRect(x,y,w,h)` draws a rectangular outline.
- `context.clearRect(x,y,w,h)` clears the specified rectangle and makes it transparent.

For example, suppose you'd like to draw a rectangular outline and a solid box inside it. Here's the JavaScript code to draw these two shapes:

```
var canvas = document.getElementById('whiteboard');
var context = canvas.getContext('2d');
context.strokeRect(10,10,100,50);
context.fillRect(15,15,90,40);
```

The `strokeRect()` method creates a rectangular outline starting at the coordinate (10,10) and is 100 x 50 pixels in size. The `fillRect()` method paints a 90 x 40 rectangle starting at coordinate (15,15). Figure 5-4 shows the result of the preceding code.

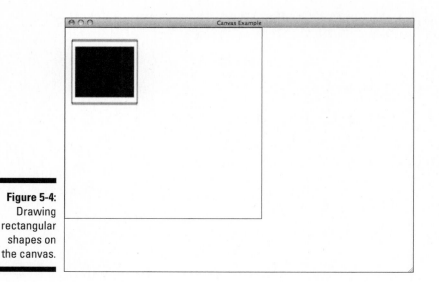

Figure 5-4:
Drawing
rectangular
shapes on
the canvas.

Stroking and filling nonrectangular shapes

To create a shape other than a rectangle, you first need to create a *path,* a sort of connect-the-dots outline of *subpaths.* After you've defined a path, you can then either stroke a line along the path or else fill in the area inside the path.

The following methods of the `context` object are used for drawing nonrectangular shapes:

- ✔ `beginPath()` creates a new path and sets the starting point to the coordinate (0,0).

- ✔ `lineTo(x,y)` adds a line segment from the current point to the specified coordinate.

- ✔ `moveTo(x,y)` moves the starting point to a new coordinate that you define with the x,y values.

- ✔ `closePath()` closes an open path and draws a line from the current point to the original starting point of the path.

- ✔ `stroke()` draws a line along the current path.

- ✔ `fill()` closes the current path and paints the area within it. If you use `fill()`, you don't need to call `closePath()` because `fill()` closes the path automatically.

Here's sample code for a drawing that uses these methods to create two adjacent triangles:

```
var canvas = document.getElementById('whiteboard');
var context = canvas.getContext('2d');
// Triangle outline
context.beginPath();
context.moveTo(10,10);
context.lineTo(10,75);
context.lineTo(100,40);
context.lineTo(10,10);
context.stroke();
context.closePath();
// Filled triangle
context.beginPath();
context.moveTo(110,10);
context.lineTo(110,75);
context.lineTo(200,40);
context.lineTo(110,10);
context.fill();
```

Figure 5-5 shows the incredible work of art that was just created.

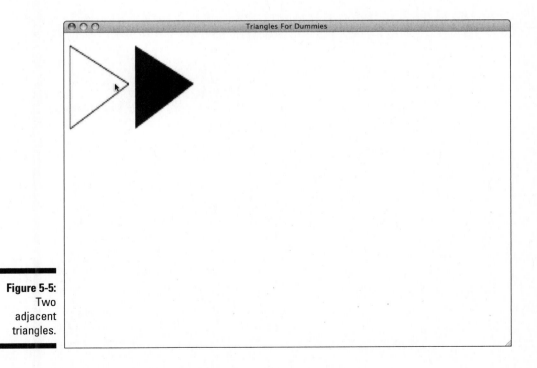

Figure 5-5:
Two
adjacent
triangles.

Working with color and transparency

The context object has fillStyle and strokeStyle properties that enable you to define the color, style, and alpha value of your drawing. Table 5-3 lists all the properties of the context object.)

Table 5-3   Available Properties of the context Object

Property	Description
FillStyle	Provides CSS color or style (gradient, pattern) of the fill of a path.
GlobalAlpha	Specifies the level of transparency of content drawn on the canvas. Floating value between 0.0 (fully transparent) and 1.0 (fully opaque).
GlobalCompositeOperation	Specifies the compositing mode to determine how the canvas is displayed relative to background content. Values include: copy, darker, destination-atop, destination-in, destination-out, destination-over, lighten, source-atop, source-in, source-out, source-over, xor.
LineCap	Defines the end style of a line. String values include: "butt" for flat edge, "round" for rounded edge, "square" for square ends. (Defaults to "butt".)
LineJoin	Specifies the way lines are joined together. String values include: "round", "bevel", "miter". (Defaults to "miter".)
lineWidth	Specifies the line width. Floating point value greater than 0.
miterLimit	Specifies the miter limit for drawing a juncture between line segments.
shadowBlur	Defines the width that a shadow covers.
shadowColor	Provides CSS color for the shadow.
shadowOffsetX	Specifies the horizontal distance of the shadow from the source.
shadowOffsetY	Specifies the vertical distance of the shadow from the source.
StrokeStyle	Defines the CSS color or style (gradient, pattern) when stroking paths.

You can set color values by using either hex or rgb values:

```
context.fillStyle="#111202";
context.strokeStyle=rgb(255,120,125);
```

The alpha value can be assigned to the shape you're filling in using the rgba(). For example:

```
context.fillStyle = "rgba(13,44,50, 0.9)";
```

For example, the following code draws two circles in the canvas. The large circle has a 60 percent transparency value, whereas the smaller circle has a 50 percent transparency value:

```
var canvas = document.getElementById('myCanvas');
var context = canvas.getContext('2d');
context.fillStyle = "rgba(23,44,70, 0.6)";
context.beginPath();
context.arc(50,90,50,0, 360, false);
context.fill();
context.fillStyle = "rgba(0,100,0,0.5)";
context.beginPath();
context.arc(80,70,70,0, 360, false);
context.fill();
```

Figure 5-6 shows the two colored, semitransparent circles.

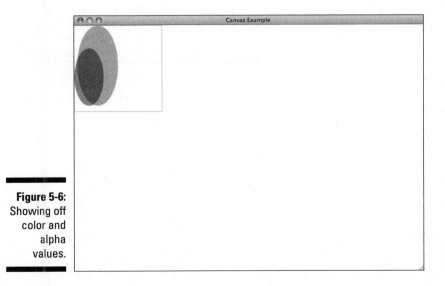

Figure 5-6:
Showing off
color and
alpha
values.

Chapter 6

Anyone Listening? Working with Events

*W*hen you create an AIR application, one of your major objectives is to be able to respond to events that occur from the time your application loads to the time it finishes. When the app loads, you will probably have an initialization routine. When the user clicks the Save button, perhaps you have a `saveToFile()` function that is called. Or, suppose a user wants to retrieve a list of customer records she needs to contact. Your application sends off a database query and then waits for the database engine to deliver results before processing them. Each of these is an example of an event-driven application.

In this chapter, I show you to how to work with and respond to user and system events in Adobe AIR.

Responding to Events

The heart of Adobe AIR event system is a matching pair of events consisting of an event and an event listener. To illustrate the nature of this pair, I'll draw some parallels with the real world. Suppose you're charged to go to a press conference introducing a new soft drink and are responsible for writing an article on that beverage for *Soda Monthly* magazine. You don't think much about it, but actually much of what you do to cover that conference is listen and wait for something to happen and then respond to those events when they transpire. For example:

✔ At the start of the press conference, you get your notepad out.

✔ When the maker of the soda makes an outrageous claim, you laugh and write it down.

✔ When two reporters behind you are bickering, you choose not to listen to their conversation.

✔ When samples of the new carbonated soda called *Gel-ola* are passed out, you eagerly jump in line to get your free drink.

✔ When you taste the new beverage, you nearly gag as you drink the sickeningly sweet, cola-tasting liquid with a semi-solid, gel-like substance.

✔ When the conference ends, you travel back to the office to finish the story, armed with a case of *Gel-ola* to hand out to your coworkers.

Bringing this back to the world of AIR development, much of the normal operation of an AIR app operates in the same event-driven manner. AIR has a vast cornucopia of events that you can choose whether to react (or, in programming terms, *listen*) to. For those events that you want to listen to, you define functions that are called when the event occurs during the execution of the application. A function that responds to an event is called an *event listener* or *event handler*.

Event handling in the HTML DOM

Since the early days of JavaScript, Web pages have had the idea of event handlers. In fact, if you've ever worked with client-side JavaScript, you are very familiar with event handlers. HTML elements have certain "on" events associated with them that you can assign JavaScript functions to. For example, the following code uses several "on" events to respond to both browser and user events:

```
<body onload="init()"></body>
<input type="submit" onclick="submitForm()"></input>
<img src="button_on.png" onkeydown="showInfo()"/>
```

Or, in a normal Web page, you could also use a callback function, such as:

```
document.getElementById("btnSubmit").onclick = submitNow;
```

Using this, you tell the submitNow() function to execute when the btnSubmit object is clicked.

Perhaps most significant, however, the W3C DOM Level 2 event model introduced the concept of "event listeners" with the `addEventListener()` method. Event listeners are arguably the best way to attach an event with its handler. Not only can you define a listener all inside of your script, but you can also attach multiple event handlers to the same event.

Here's an example of adding the `init()` function as a listener to the `load` event of the window object:

```
window.addEventListener("load", init);
```

Notice that the function does not have parentheses included when you assign it as a handler.

You can continue to associate events to handlers in any of these three fashions for standard DOM object events in HTML applications.

Registering events in the AIR event model

The Adobe AIR event model is based on the W3C DOM Level 3 events specification. As a result, to "register" an event listener to the event of an AIR object, you need to call the associated object's `addEventListener()` method. This method says, in effect: "Hey, Mr. Object, when event X occurs, you need to execute function Y." The basic structure looks like this:

```
eventTarget.addEventListener([air.]EventClass.EVENT_NAME,
        eventHandler);
```

For example, suppose you want to execute a function after an AIR `File` object (with the instance name `fs`) has opened a local file for reading and writing. The associated AIR event is `[air.]Event.COMPLETE`. Here is the code:

```
fs.addEventListener(air.Event.COMPLETE, onFileRead);
```

Working with Event Objects

When the event occurs and triggers the event handler, it dispatches an event object to the handler. This object is an instance of the `Event` class or one of its many subclasses, such as `HTTPStatusEvent` or `IOErrorEvent`. You will often use this object instance to help you process the event successfully.

For example, an `HTTPService` object dispatches a `FaultEvent` in case something goes awry during an HTTP request. The `FaultEvent` instance is passed to its handler as a parameter. The handler can then use the event object as needed. In the case of an error handler like this, you can display the `message` property of the event object (see the bolded call that follows) to let the user know what went wrong. Here's the JavaScript code:

```
httpService.addEventListener(air.FaultEvent.FAULT,
        onFetchError);
function onFetchError(event)
{
  alert("The following error occurred when fetching the
        RSS feed: " + event.message);
}
```

Here's a second example of using the event object (see bolded code) to display details of an error that occurs during a SQL database operation. In ActionScript:

```
private function onDatabaseError(event:SQLErrorEvent) :
        void
{
  Alert.show(event.error.message + " Details: " + event.
        error.details);
}
```

But event objects are far more useful than just providing error details. Consider the handler of a drag drop event. In the following code, the handler uses the `event.clipboard.hasFormat()` and `event.clipboard.get-Data()` methods of the `NativeDragEvent` object (see bolded code) to capture the data being dropped onto the application:

```
public function onDragDrop(event:NativeDragEvent) : void
  {
    if (event.clipboard.hasFormat(ClipboardFormats.TEXT_FORMAT)) {
      var s:String = (event.clipboard.getData(ClipboardFormats.TEXT_FORMAT,
            ClipboardTransferMode.ORIGINAL_PREFERRED) as String);
      processDroppedText(s);
    }
  }
```

When you register an event to be captured, you identify it by its event class and its `type` property (which is expressed as a constant value). For example, the `NativeDragEvent` class has several specific events that you can capture:

```
NativeDragEvent.NATIVE_DRAG_COMPLETE
NativeDragEvent.NATIVE_DRAG_DROP
NativeDragEvent.NATIVE_DRAG_ENTER
```

```
NativeDragEvent.NATIVE_DRAG_EXIT
NativeDragEvent.NATIVE_DRAG_OVER
NativeDragEvent.NATIVE_DRAG_START
NativeDragEvent.NATIVE_DRAG_UPDATE
```

Therefore, if you wanted to assign a listener to the `NativeDragEvent.NATIVE_DRAG_ENTER` and `NativeDragEvent.NATIVE_DRAG_DROP` events, your code would look like this:

```
addEventListener(NativeDragEvent.NATIVE_DRAG_ENTER,
        onDragIn);
addEventListener(NativeDragEvent.NATIVE_DRAG_DROP,
        onDragDrop);
```

For the `onDragIn()` and `onDragDrop()` functions, the `NativeDragEvent` is passed as a parameter. So, in ActionScript, the empty functions are shown as follows:

```
private function onDragIn(event:NativeDragEvent): void
{
}

private function onDragOut(event:NativeDragEvent): void
{
}
```

`Event` is the base class of all AIR event objects. However, most AIR objects that you work with will have events that are subclasses of the base `Event`. There are far too many to simply list here, so you'll want to check the event type for each event you want to listen to in your application.

Overriding Default Behaviors

In addition to the handlers that you explicitly define in your source code, you should also be aware of *default behaviors,* or behaviors that automatically are performed when an event is triggered. You can prevent most default behaviors from occurring by adding `preventDefault()` in an error handler. For example, the cut, copy, and paste commands automatically send data to or receive it from the Clipboard in edit boxes of an AIR application (such as a `textarea`). To prevent this default behavior, you need to define a handler and then add `preventDefault()`. The handler code might look something like this in JavaScript:

```
function onCopy(event)
{
  var sel = window.getSelection();
  event.clipbardData.setData( selection + " (Text portions
          copyright © 2009, WackyTacky, Inc. So there.)"
          );
  event.preventDefault();
}
```

In this sample code, the default onCopy event is intercepted so that a copyright notice can be appended to the end of the text selection.

If you want to test to see whether you can cancel an event using prevent Default(), you can check its cancelable property. For example:

```
if (event.cancelable)
{
  event.preventDefault();
}
else
{
  cry();
}
```

Understanding the Flow of Events

When a nonvisual AIR object, such as HTTPRequest or File, is the target of an event, AIR dispatches the event object directly to it. If there is a default behavior, that behavior executes. Or, if an event listener is attached, that routine is called.

However, when there is a visual object that is in the Flash/Flex display list (the list of visible UI objects) or in the HTML DOM, the flow of events is trickier. The reason is that some events can be associated with more than one element on-screen. For example, if a user clicks a textarea, the click event could potentially be associated with the textarea, its div container, or maybe even the document itself. Suppose you have click event handlers defined for each of these DOM objects. Which handler is triggered first? Given this reality, you should have an understanding of the event flow of an AIR app to help you anticipate how your AIR application will respond. The following sections show you the event flow in the Flex/Flash display list as well as the HTML DOM.

In a Flex/Flash application, for example, the `stage` object is at the top of the display list. The rest of the display objects are then structured in a hierarchy node list beneath the `stage` object. When AIR dispatches an event object for a display list event, the event object travels through the display list in three distinct phases, as follows:

- ✔ **Capture phase:** During the capture phase, the event object travels from the `stage` object down the node list to the target object.
- ✔ **Target phase:** During the target phase, the event object is at the target object.
- ✔ **Bubbling phase:** In the bubbling phase, the event object travels back up through the hierarchy all the way back to the stage.

The practical implication of this event flow is that you can add event listeners to any object within the display list hierarchy rather than just to a single target.

By default, events are ignored during the capture phase and captured first at the target phase followed by the bubbling phase. That's the normal event flow and will work for you under most situations.

However, if you'd prefer to capture during the capture phase, you need to add a new parameter to `addEventListener()` that I have not mentioned yet. Specifically, you need to include the optional `useCapture` parameter to `addEventListener()` and set it to `true`:

```
var useCapture = true;
eventTarget.addEventListener([air.]EventClass.EVENT_NAME,
          eventHandler, useCapture);
```

When `useCapture` is true, the listener processes the events during the capture phase and the events in the target and bubbling phase are ignored.

If you wanted to listen for an event in all three phases, you would actually need to call `addEventListener()` two times, toggling the value of the `useCapture` parameter.

Figure 6-1 shows the display list of a Flex application.

Now suppose the following handlers are defined:

```
stage.addEventListener( MouseEvent.CLICK,
          stageClickHandler);
text1.addEventListener( MouseEvent.CLICK,
          textClickHandler;
```

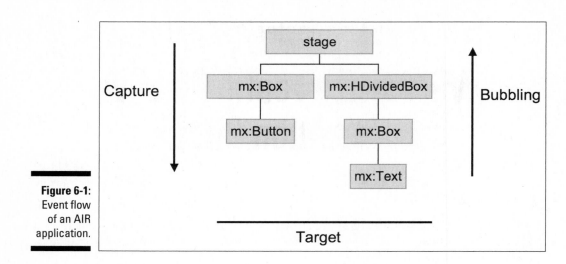

Figure 6-1:
Event flow
of an AIR
application.

When the user clicks the mx:Text element, AIR runtime sends the event object to the stage. However, since useCapture=false, its listener is not dispatched during the capture phase. Instead, the event object continues down the hierarchy to the mx:HDividedBox, to the mx:Box, and finally to the target mx:Text. Once here, its event listener is triggered, calling textClickHandler(). The event object then bubbles back up through the display list hierarchy. When it reaches the stage this time around, the stageClickHandler() is called.

Chapter 7

Windows: Creating Native Application Shells

*O*ne of the ways in which college students or young adults know that they're on their own and away from the apron strings of their parents is when they get their own digs — their own place to live in and call home. Likewise, the primary way in which an AIR-based rich Internet application is distinct from a browser-based app is that it has its own on-screen home — a window independent from the browser in which it can do its own thing.

In this chapter, I show you how to create and work with windows as you develop your Adobe AIR applications. You discover how to "style" them like other native windows. Heck, I even show you how to create nonrectangular windows.

Although it may be more work to deal with native windows than with a normal Web application, you'll find your efforts paying off in terms of the power and control doing so brings you.

Exploring AIR Windows

There are three different categories of native windows that can be part of an AIR application. In most cases, the type that you use will often depend on the development tool you're working with to create your app. The three categories of windows are as follows:

✔ **HTML window:** An HTML window contains a normal HTML document, which displays content using a mixture of HTML, CSS, and JavaScript. It is created from the `air.HTMLLoader` object.

HTML windows are a special type of `NativeWindow` window (see the next bullet). You can access the `NativeWindow` instance of an HTML window through its `nativeWindow` property.

HTML developers will primarily work with HTML windows, although Flex and Flash developers can create HTML windows as well.

✔ **ActionScript NativeWindow:** A NativeWindow window contains Flash or Flex content and is created programmatically using the `NativeWindow` class.

Flash developers will typically work with ActionScript windows using the Flash stage and display list, although they can be created programmatically by Flash, Flex, and HTML developers.

✔ **Flex mx:Window:** When working with Flex Builder, you create windows typically composed of MXML components that you add inside Flex Builder or through ActionScript code. These windows are contained by `mx:WindowedApplication` or `mx:Window` elements.

As you would expect, the Flex windows are available only for Flex developers.

Creating the Initial Window

The main window of an application is created by AIR runtime based on the property settings inside of the `initialWindow` element of the application descriptor file (typically `application.xml`).

Because you can specify the visibility of the initial window, the main window can serve as your main application window, or it can remain hidden and be used to open other windows.

There are several required and optional properties that are defined as child elements inside of `initialWindow`. These are listed in Table 7-1.

Table 7-1		Initial Window Properties	
Property	*Values*	*Description*	*Required*
content	*Filename*	HTML or SWF filename containing the main content of the app. URL is relative to the root application folder.	Yes

Property	Values	Description	Required
title	*Apptitle*	Title of the main application window. (Note: A `title` defined in the content file will override this setting.)	No
systemChrome	standard, none	Indicates whether to use the chrome of the native OS. (See the "Setting the Window Style" section below.)	No
transparent	true, false (default)	Indicates whether the main window supports alpha blending. When set to true, then `system Chrome` must be `none`. (See the "Setting the Window Style" section.)	No
visible	true, false (default)	Specifies whether to make the main window visible when it loads. However, in Flex-based apps, this property is ignored. Instead, Flex apps use the `visible` property in `mx:Win dowedApplication` instead.	No
minimizable	true (default), false	Determines whether the window can be minimized.	No
maximizable	true (default), false	Determines whether the window can be maximized. (On Mac OS X, both `maximizable` and `resizable` must be set to `false` to prevent resizing.)	No
resizable	true (default), false	Determines whether the window can be resized. (On Mac OS X, both `maximizable` and `resizable` must be set to `false` to prevent resizing.)	No

(continued)

Table 7-1 *(continued)*

Property	Values	Description	Required
width	Integer	Specifies initial width (in pixels) of the main window.	No. If not specified, then size and positioning are determined by the OS (for HTML files) or the root file (SWF files).
height	Integer	Specifies initial height (in pixels) of the main window.	
x	Integer	Specifies initial *x* position of the main window.	
y	Integer	Specifies initial *y* position of the main window.	
minSize	*width height* (in pixels)	Indicates the minimum size of the window.	No
maxSize	*width height* (in pixels)	Indicates the maximum size of the window.	No

Here's an example of the `initialWindow` section of the application descriptor file, using all the available properties:

```
<initialWindow>
    <content>index.html</content>
    <title>My Application</title>
    <systemChrome>standard</systemChrome>
    <transparent>false</transparent>
    <visible>true</visible>
    <minimizable>true</minimizable>
    <maximizable>true</maximizable>
    <resizable>true</resizable>
    <width>600</width>
    <height>400</height>
    <x>10</x>
    <y>10</y>
    <minSize>200 200</minSize>
    <maxSize>900 900</maxSize>
</initialWindow>
```

You can also set some of the properties of the initial window in your code when the application loads. If your changes would be noticeable on-screen, you want to set the `visible` property to `false` (`<visible>false</visible>`). Setting this property to `false` enables the processing to occur without noticeable redraws on-screen when the window's position, size, or layout is changing. Then, after your changes are made, you can activate the window to make it visible.

However, if you're using Flex Builder to create your app, forget the `visible` property in the application descriptor file. It is ignored. Instead, set the visibility through the `visible` property of the `mx:WindowedApplication` element.

In HTML, you add the code in the window's `load` handler:

```
<!DOCTYPE html PUBLIC "-//W3C//DTD XHTML 1.0
        Transitional//EN" "http://www.w3.org/TR/xhtml1/
        DTD/xhtml1-transitional.dtd">
<html xmlns="http://www.w3.org/1999/xhtml">
<head>
<meta http-equiv="Content-Type" content="text/html;
        charset=utf-8" />
<title>Test</title>
<script type="text/javascript" language="JavaScript"
        src="assets/AIRAliases.js"></script>
<script type="text/javascript" language="JavaScript"
        src="assets/util.js"></script>
<script type=»text/javascript» language=»JavaScript»>

  window.addEventListener('load', initialize, false);

  function initialize() {
    window.nativeWindow.y = 10;
    window.nativeWindow.x = 10;
    window.nativeWindow.activate();
  }

</script>
</head>

<body>
<div id="canvas">
<h1>Welcome to Adobe AIR.</h1>
<p>Don't go messin' with my Adobe AIR.</p>
<input id="btnLaunch" type="submit" value="Launch" />
</div>
</body>
</html>
For a Flex mx:WindowedApplication, assign a handler to its
        windowComplete event:
<?xml version="1.0" encoding="utf-8"?>
<mx:WindowedApplication xmlns:mx="http://www.
        adobe.com/2006/mxml" layout="absolute"
        title="AIRBaby!" width="429" height="209"
        windowComplete="initWindow()" visible="false">
<mx:Style source="default.css"/>

<mx:Script>
  <![CDATA[
```

```
    private function initWindow():void {
      stage.nativeWindow.maximize();
      stage.nativeWindow.visible = true;
    }

    ]]>
</mx:Script>

  <mx:Label text="Super!" x="17" y="19"/>

</mx:WindowedApplication>
```

In this example, the `window` instance is referenced using `stage.nativeWindow`. The `maximize()` method is then called to maximize the window. Finally, the `stage.nativeWindow.visible` property is set to `true`.

Setting the Window Style

The initial window and additional windows you create on your own have several style options that you can specify at the time you create the window. After the window is created, you can't change its properties. You can define a window style by its system chrome, transparency, and type.

System chrome

Normal windows that you work with have chrome around them. *Chrome* is a techie term that refers to the UI controls of the operating system that are outside the content area of a window. So, just as a car might have shiny chrome trimming, a bumper, and a grill that cover the vehicle, so the chrome of an OS window surrounds and complements the window itself. Examples of chrome include the title bar, the Minimize/Maximize/Restore buttons, menu bars, and toolbars.

AIR does not support the following chrome UI elements: Windows title bar icon, Mac OS X proxy icon (icon on the toolbar), Mac OS X toolbars, and alternate or nonstandard system chrome.

You can set the chrome of an application by setting the `systemChrome` property of the `NativeWindowInitOptions` object and, for initial windows, the `systemChrome` element of the application descriptor file. I discuss the `NativeWindowInitOptions` object more in the "Creating a Window Programmatically" section, later in this chapter, but for now, I show you how to assign the `systemChrome` value from code. In HTML, you write:

```
var options = new air.NativeWindowInitOptions();
options.systemChrome = "standard";
```

Or, using Flex/Flash:

```
var options:NativeWindowInitOptions = new
        NativeWindowInitOptions();
options.systemChrome = NativeWindowSystemChrome.STANDARD;
```

There are three types of chrome:

✔ **Standard OS chrome:** When you assign `standard` (HTML) or
  `NativeWindowSystemChrome.STANDARD` (Flex/Flash) to the `system`
  `Chrome` property, the window uses the system chrome of the native OS.
  Figures 7-1 and 7-2 show the standard chrome surrounding the same
  AIR window running under Windows and Mac. Notice that the chrome
  changes based on OS, but the content inside the window remains the
  same.

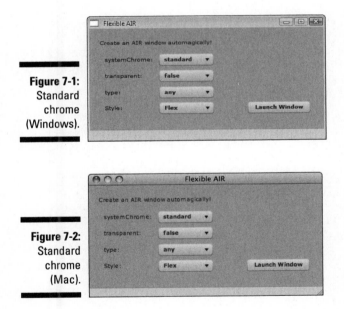

Figure 7-1:
Standard
chrome
(Windows).

Figure 7-2:
Standard
chrome
(Mac).

✔ **Custom chrome:** By assigning `none` (HTML) and `NativeWindow`
  `SystemChrome.NONE` (Flex/Flash) to the `systemChrome` property, you
  disable the standard chrome of the OS. When you use `none` with HTML
  or NativeWindow windows, you need to handle user interactions with
  the window, such as window movement.

When you're working with transparent or nonrectangular windows, you need to use `none`.

✔ **Flex chrome:** When you assign `systemChrome = NativeWindow SystemChrome.NONE` for a Flex `mx:Window` or `mx:Windowed Application` window, Flex adds its own custom titlebar, Minimize/Maximize/Restore buttons, status bar, and resize gripper. Figure 7-3 shows the customized Flex chrome running on Windows.

Figure 7-3:
Flex style
chrome
(Windows).

You can get rid of the Flex chrome by setting the window's `showFlex Chrome` property to `false`. (You can see an example of this in the "Creating a Window Programmatically" section, later in the chapter.) Or if you want to hide a single chrome element, you can do that by setting the `showTitleBar`, `showGripper`, or `showStatusBar` property to `false`.

Although the Flex chrome appears to surround the window content replacing the native OS chrome, the custom chrome is actually drawn by Flex inside the window boundaries and is automatically programmed to handle user interactions. However, when sizing your window, you'll need to account for the extra height that the custom chrome takes up.

Flex chrome is available only for AIR applications written in Flex Builder that use `mx:Window` or `mx:WindowedApplication` windows. If you create a Flash or HTML-based app and want your own custom chrome, you need to create it yourself.

Transparency

Adobe AIR supports *alpha blending,* which is the process of combining a window with the desktop or other windows to create partial or full transparency.

The AIR window and each UI object contained by the window has an assignable alpha value from 0 to 1.0 that determines the level of transparency: 1.0 means fully opaque, and 0 means fully transparent (elements default to 1.0). Therefore, when a window is set to transparent, its background is partially or fully hidden (depending on its alpha value), and any window area that does not contain a UI element is not visible.

To enable this functionality, you need to do the following:

- ✔ Set the `transparent` property to `true` at the time the window is created.
- ✔ Because a transparent window can't have system chrome, set the `systemChrome` property to `false`.
- ✔ Because HTML apps display windows with an opaque background even when you set `transparent` property to `true`, you also need to set the `air.HTMLLoader.paintDefaultBackground` property to `false`.
- ✔ Optionally assign an alpha value to the window.

You can do this in HTML through the `alpha` property for a window you create with `air.HTMLLoader.createRootWindow()`. Flex also enables you to specify an alpha value through the Property Inspector when you're designing an `mx:WindowedApplication` or `mx:Window`.

The following HTML code shows you how to create a transparent window:

```
var options = new air.NativeWindowInitOptions();

options.systemChrome = "none";

options.transparent = "true";

var windowBounds = new air.Rectangle(200,250,300,400);

htmlLoader = air.HTMLLoader.createRootWindow(true,
          options, true, windowBounds);

htmlLoader.paintsDefaultBackground = false;

htmlLoader.load(new air.URLRequest("win2.html"));
```

I cover the `createRootWindow` method in the upcoming section "Creating a Window Programatically," so don't concern yourself with the particulars of window creation for now. Instead, notice how the three bolded property assignments in the preceding code are used to create a transparent HTML window.

For Flex/Flash, use the following code to set up the initialization options for a window you will be creating:

```
var options:NativeWindowInitOptions = new
          NativeWindowInitOptions();

options.systemChrome = NativeWindowSystemChrome.NONE;
options.transparent = true;
```

Figure 7-4 displays a transparent window with Flex chrome. As you can see, the desktop wallpaper partially shows through the semitransparent window (set at 0.5). Figure 7-5 shows a fully transparent window, with just its controls showing up.

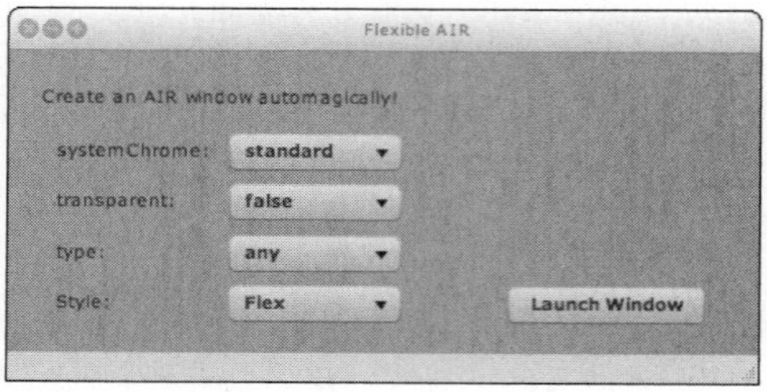

Figure 7-4:
Transparent
window
with Flex
style
chrome
(Mac).

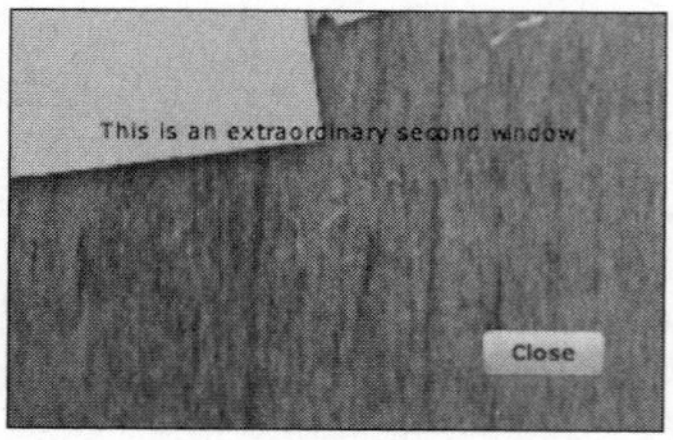

Figure 7-5:
Chromeless,
transparent
window
with desk-
top showing
through
(Mac).

Window type

You can use the `type` property of an AIR window as a shortcut to define both the chrome and visibility attributes of a window you create programmatically. There are three types of AIR windows that you can define using the `type` property:

- **Normal** is a standard OS window. The initial window of an AIR application is always defined as a normal window. See Figures 7-1 and 7-2.

- **Utility** is a palette style window. See Figures 7-6 and 7-7.

- **Lightweight** is designed for notification type windows.

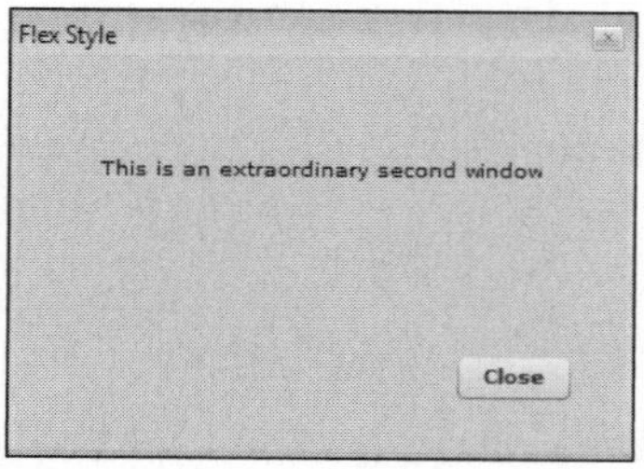

Figure 7-6:
Utility
window
(Windows).

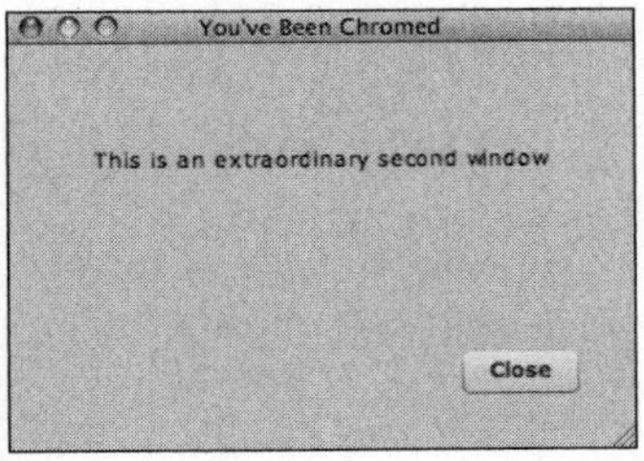

Figure 7-7:
Utility
window
(Mac).

The `type` property is not available for the initial window of an application.

Table 7-2 shows the support of OS chrome and other UI features based on the window type.

Table 7-2			AIR Window Types				
Type	**Description**	**Chrome**	**Windows Task Bar**	**Windows System Menu**	**Mac OS X Window Menu**	**Initial window**	**system Chrome value**
`Normal`	Normal window	Full	Yes	Yes	Yes	Yes	`standard`
`Utility`	Palette window	Slim	No	Yes	No	No	`standard`
`light weight`	"Lightweight" notificationstyle widows	None	No	No	No	No	`none`

To create a utility window in HTML, you use the following windows initialization options:

```
var options = new air.NativeWindowInitOptions();

options.systemChrome = "standard";

options.transparent = false;

options.type = "utility";
```

Or, to set the initialization settings for a lightweight window in Flex/Flash:

```
var options:NativeWindowInitOptions = new
       NativeWindowInitOptions();
options.systemChrome = NativeWindowSystemChrome.NONE;
options.transparent = false;
options.type = NativeWindowType.LIGHTWEIGHT;
```

Table 7-3 shows all the window initialization properties that you can work with.

Table 7-3	Window Initialization Properties		
Property	**Values**	**Default value**	**Valid for initial window**
systemChrome	standard, none	standard	Yes
Type	normal, utility, lightweight	normal	No (initial window is always normal)
Transparent	true, false	false	Yes
Maximizable	true, false	true	
Minimizable	true, false	true	
Resizable	true, false	true	

Creating a Window Programmatically

Although the initial window is created automatically by AIR on app launch, additional windows must be explicitly created programmatically. The following sections show you how to create HTML windows, mx:Windows (Flex), and NativeWindows (Flash, Flex, or HTML).

Creating an HTML window

In a typical HTML-based AIR application, when you're working with additional windows, you want to display sandboxed HTML content inside the new window. To do so, you want to do four tasks:

✔ Set the basic window style properties through air.
  NativeWindowInitOptions().

✔ Set the dimensions and position of the window using an air.
  Rectangle() instance.

✔ Create the window using the `air.HTMLLoader.createRootWindow()` method, passing along the info specified by the first two tasks.

✔ Load the HTML page using the window's `load()` method.

Using this four-step process, here's how you can create a utility window to display an HTML named `win2.html`:

```
function launch(){

  var options = new air.NativeWindowInitOptions();
  options.systemChrome = "standard";
  options.transparent = false;
  options.type = "utility";

  var windowBounds = new air.Rectangle(100,100,300,200);

  newWindow = air.HTMLLoader.createRootWindow(true,
          options, true, windowBounds);
  newWindow.load(new air.URLRequest("../win2.html"));
}
```

Figure 7-8 shows the window that is created.

Figure 7-8:
Utility win-
dow shown
on a Mac.

The following code is used to create a chrome-less, transparent window with an alpha value of 0.7. Note the property assignments in bold:

```
function launch(){

  var options = new air.NativeWindowInitOptions();
  options.systemChrome = "none";
  options.transparent = true;

  var windowBounds = new air.Rectangle(100,100,300,200);

  newWindow = air.HTMLLoader.createRootWindow(true,
          options, true, windowBounds);
  newWindow.alpha = 0.7;
  newWindow.paintsDefaultBackground = false;

  newWindow.load(new air.URLRequest("../win2.html"));
}
```

The windows that you create with `createRootWindow()` are independent of the opening window.

Figure 7-9 displays the same `win2.html` content, but in a different style of window container.

Figure 7-9:
Transparent
window
with
desktop
windows
showing
through.

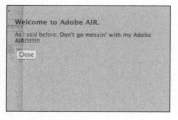

If you're trying to display nonsandboxed content in a window you're creating, use the JavaScript `window.open()` method. For example, the following code creates a new window:

```
newWindow = window.open( 'http://www.dummies.com/air/
           getsupport.php', 'Get Application Support',
           'width=400,height=303' );
```

Note that this nonsandboxed window would not have access to the AIR API.

Creating a Flex mx:Window

When working with Flex Builder, you typically create your application windows as separate MXML files, each of which uses `mx:Window` as the root tag of the document.

Listing 7-1 lists the contents of the MXML file for this example.

Listing 7-1: SecondWindow.mxml

```
<?xml version="1.0" encoding="utf-8"?>

<mx:Window xmlns:mx="http://www.adobe.com/2006/mxml"
           layout="absolute" width="300" height="200"
           styleName="sanschrome">
<mx:Style>
.sanschrome { showFlexChrome: false; background-color:"";}
```

```
</mx:Style>

<mx:Script>
  <![CDATA[
    private function closeWindow():void {
      this.close();
    }

  ]]>
</mx:Script>


  <mx:Button x="217" y="151" label="Close"
         click="closeWindow()"/>
  <mx:Text x="39" y="49" text="This is an extraordinary
         second window&#xd;&#xd;" color="#000000"/>
</mx:Window>
```

Note that the `mx:Window` element is assigned the `sanschrome` CSS style. This style hides the default Flex chrome and any background color.

When you want to open a chrome-less, transparent instance of this window in your app, you simply call the following routine:

```
public function openWindow():void {
   secWindow = new SecondWindow();
   secWindow.systemChrome = NativeWindowSystemChrome.NONE;
   secWindow.transparent = true;
   secWindow.open();
}
```

In this example, I create an instance of the `mx:Window` contained in `SecondWindow.mxml` called `secWindow`. `SecondWindow()` is the name of the subclass of the Window class. Its name is taken from the MXML filename. After you set the basic property settings of the window, you use `open()` to display it.

Creating an ActionScript NativeWindow

The third kind of window you can create is a `NativeWindow` through ActionScript. When creating an HTML or `mx:Window` window, you typically already have content defined by the HTML or MXML file that you reference. However, a `NativeWindow` does not have an associated content file, meaning that you need to programmatically add the content yourself at the time the window is created.

The following example creates a NativeWindow window:

```
public function createWindow():void {

    // Set init options
    var options:NativeWindowInitOptions = new
        NativeWindowInitOptions();
    options.systemChrome = NativeWindowSystemChrome.
        STANDARD;
    options.transparent = false;
    options.type = NativeWindowType.NORMAL;

    // Create new NativeWindow
    var newWindow:NativeWindow = new
        NativeWindow(options);
    newWindow.title = "You've Gone Native";
    newWindow.width = 500;
    newWindow.height = 400;

    // Create HTML container
    var htmlViewer:HTMLLoader = new HTMLLoader();
    htmlViewer.width = 490;
    htmlViewer.height = 390;

    // Add to stage
    newWindow.stage.align = StageAlign.TOP_LEFT;
    newWindow.stage.scaleMode = StageScaleMode.NO_SCALE;
    newWindow.stage.addChild( htmlViewer );

    // Load URL
    htmlViewer.load( new URLRequest("http://www.dummies.
        com") );

    // Make visible
    newWindow.activate();
}
```

The ActionScript routine begins by setting the initialization options. It then creates a NativeWindow instance called newWindow and assigns basic size properties. An HTML viewer is created to be displayed as content inside the window, which is added to the newWindow stage through the addChild() method. The window is activated and made visible through the activate() method.

Listing 7-2 lists the source code for FlexAir.mxml. (See Figure 7-1 for a view of the window during runtime.) It's an example of creating a window based on the input of the user.

Listing 7-2:   FlexAir.mxml

```
<?xml version="1.0" encoding="utf-8"?>
<mx:WindowedApplication xmlns:mx="http://www.
         adobe.com/2006/mxml" layout="absolute"
         title="Flexible AIR" width="429" height="209">
<mx:Style source="default.css"/>

<mx:Script>
<![CDATA[
  import mx.controls.Label;
  import mx.controls.Text;
  import mx.collections.ArrayCollection;
  import mx.controls.HTML;

  private var secWindow:SecondWindow;

  [Bindable]
   public var chromeOptions:ArrayCollection = new
          ArrayCollection(
     [ {label:»standard», data:NativeWindowSystemChrome.
        STANDARD},
       {label:»none», data:NativeWindowSystemChrome.NONE}
       ]);

  [Bindable]
  public var transparentOptions:ArrayCollection = new
          ArrayCollection(
     [ {label:»false», data:false},
       {label:»true», data:true}
       ]);

  [Bindable]
  public var typeOptions:ArrayCollection = new
          ArrayCollection(
     [ {label:»any», data:null},
       {label:»normal», data:NativeWindowType.NORMAL},
       {label:»utility», data:NativeWindowType.UTILITY},
       {label:»lightweight», data:NativeWindowType.
        LIGHTWEIGHT}
       ]);

  [Bindable]
  public var flexOptions:ArrayCollection = new
          ArrayCollection(
     [ {label:»Flex», data:true},
       {label:»NativeWindow», data:false}
       ]);
```

(continued)

Listing 7-2 *(continued)*

```
public function createWindow():void {

    // Set init options
    var options:NativeWindowInitOptions = new
            NativeWindowInitOptions();
    options.systemChrome = cbSystemChrome.selectedItem.
        data;
    options.transparent = cbTransparent.selectedItem.data;
    if ( cbType.selectedItem.data != null )
      options.type = cbType.selectedItem.data;

    // Create new NativeWindow
    var newWindow:NativeWindow = new
            NativeWindow(options);
    newWindow.title = «You've Gone Native»;
    newWindow.width = 500;
    newWindow.height = 400;

    // Create HTML container
    var htmlViewer:HTMLLoader = new HTMLLoader();
    htmlViewer.width = 490;
    htmlViewer.height = 390;

    // Add to stage
    newWindow.stage.align = StageAlign.TOP_LEFT;
    newWindow.stage.scaleMode = StageScaleMode.NO_SCALE;
    newWindow.stage.addChild( htmlViewer );

    // Load URL
    htmlViewer.load( new URLRequest(«http://www.dummies.
        com») );

    // Make visible
    newWindow.activate();
}


  public function launchWindow():void {

    // Flex style window or native?
    if ( !cbFlexStyle.selectedItem.data ) {
      createWindow();
    }
    else {
      // Create window and assign title
      secWindow = new SecondWindow();
      // Assign chrome value
      secWindow.systemChrome = cbSystemChrome.
          selectedItem.data;
      // Assign transparent
```

```
        secWindow.transparent = cbTransparent.selectedItem.
            data;
        // Assign window type
        if ( cbType.selectedItem.data != null )
         secWindow.type = cbType.selectedItem.data;
        // Open window

        if ( ( secWindow.systemChrome ==
            NativeWindowSystemChrome.NONE ) &&
            ( secWindow.transparent == true ) ) {
          secWindow.title = «You're Flexible»;
         }
        else {
          secWindow.title = «You've Been Chromed»;
        }

        secWindow.open();
      }
   }

  ]]>
</mx:Script>


<mx:Label text=»Create an AIR window automagically!»
        x=»17» y=»19»/>
<mx:Button x=»289.75» y=»140» label=»Launch Window»
        click=»launchWindow()»/>
<mx:ComboBox x=»127.75» y=»49» id=»cbSystemChrome»
        dataProvider=»{chromeOptions}»  width=»100»/>
<mx:ComboBox x=»127.75» y=»79» id=»cbTransparent» dataProv
        ider=»{transparentOptions}»  width=»100»/>
<mx:ComboBox x=»127.75» y=»110» id=»cbType»
        dataProvider=»{typeOptions}»  width=»100»/>
<mx:ComboBox x=»127.75» y=»140» id=»cbFlexStyle»
        dataProvider=»{flexOptions}»  width=»100»/>

<mx:Label x=»25.75» y=»51» text=»systemChrome:»/>
<mx:Label x="25.75" y="81" text="transparent:"/>
<mx:Label x=»25.75» y=»112» text=»type:»/>
<mx:Text x=»25.75» y=»142» text=»Style:&#xd;» width=»74»/>

</mx:WindowedApplication>
```

In this example, the user specifies the window properties through the
mx:ComboBox controls and then clicks the Launch Window button. The
Launch Window button calls the launchWindow() function, which first
determines whether the type of window should be NativeWindow or Flex.
If NativeWindow, then the createWindow() function is called. Otherwise,
the launchWindow() creates an instance of the SecondWindow window
(SecondWindow.mxml).

Creating Nonrectangular Windows

Taking advantage of windows transparency, you can create nonrectangular windows for your AIR apps. Although you can use ActionScript advanced drawing techniques to draw nonrectangular shapes, the most straightforward way to achieve a common nonrectangular window is to combine transparency with an image background.

Because nonrectangular windows have no chrome, you need to code basic window functionality, such as Move, Close, and Minimize.

Nonrectangular windows in HTML

To create a nonrectangular window in an HTML application, begin by defining a basic HTML file that includes a `div` element to contain any content. Also included here is the reference to include the `AIRAliases.js` file:

```
<html>
<head>
<title>CirculAIR</title>
<script type="text/javascript" src="AIRAliases.js"></
        script>
</head>
<body>
<div id="canvas">
</div>
</body>
</html>
```

Next, assign a background image to the body. The following example uses a circular image named `badge.png`. The example also adds a basic style for the `canvas div`:

```
<style media="all">
  body { background:url('badge.png') no-repeat 0 0; }
  #canvas { text-align: center; }
</style>
```

You can add any content to the HTML file. In this example, some basic text and two images are added, which are being used for Minimize and Close buttons inside the `div` container:

```
<img id="btnMinimize" src="minimize.png"
        onclick="minimizeWindow()"/>
<img id="btnClose" src="close.png"
        onclick="closeWindow()"/>
<p class="circleCaption">This may be a lame app, but what
        do you expect? <br/><br/>It's a circle!</p>
```

As you can see, this code assigns `onclick` event handlers to the two image buttons. The `minimizeWindow()` and `closeWindow()` functions are defined shortly.

Add styles as needed for the page elements. Here's the code:

```
#btnMinimize {
  position: absolute;
  top: 55px;
  left: 220px;
}

#btnClose {
  position: absolute;
  top: 55px;
  left: 235px;
}

.circleCaption {
  margin: 150px 50px 30px 50px;
  color: #ffffff;
  font-family: 'Lucida Grande', Verdana, Geneva, Sans-
        Serif;
    font-size: 17px;
}
```

To give basic functionality to the app, you define handlers for the two image buttons:

```
function closeWindow() {
  air.NativeApplication.nativeApplication.exit();
}

function minimizeWindow() {
  window.nativeWindow.minimize();
}
```

Because the window has no chrome, you need to add window move functionality. (If you don't, the user won't be able to move the AIR app around the screen.) The handiest way is to trap for the `onmousedown` event, which you can do when the page is loaded, like so:

```
function initialize() {
  document.body.onmousedown = function(e){
    window.nativeWindow.startMove();
  };
}

window.addEventListener('load', initialize, false);
```

Before building the app, you need to make sure that the application descriptor file contains the appropriate settings for the `initialWindow` tag:

```
<initialWindow>
    <content>index.html</content>
    <systemChrome>none</systemChrome>
    <transparent>true</transparent>
</initialWindow>
```

Figure 7-10 displays the AIR app when it is run.

Figure 7-10:
Non-
rectangular
AIR app.

Listing 7-3 shows the HTML source file.

Listing 7-3: index.html

```
<html>
<head>
<title>CirculAIR</title>
<style media="all">

  body {
    background:url('badge.png') no-repeat 0 0;

  }

  #canvas {
    text-align: center;
  }

  #btnMinimize {
    position: absolute;
    top: 55px;
    left: 220px;
  }
```

```
  #btnClose {
    position: absolute;
    left: 235px;
  }

  .circleCaption {
    margin: 150px 50px 30px 50px;
    color: #ffffff;
    font-family: 'Lucida Grande', Verdana, Geneva, Sans-
          Serif;
     font-size: 17px;
  }


</style>
<script type="text/javascript" src="AIRAliases.js"></
          script>
<script type="text/javascript">

  function initialize() {
    //window.nativeWindow.addEventListener(air.Event.
          CLOSING, closeWindow);

    document.body.onmousedown = function(e){
      window.nativeWindow.startMove();
    };
  }

  function closeWindow() {
    air.NativeApplication.nativeApplication.exit();
  }

  function minimizeWindow() {
    window.nativeWindow.minimize();
  }


  window.addEventListener('load', initialize, false);

</script>

</head>
<body>
<div id="canvas">
<img id="btnMinimize" src="minimize.png"
          onclick="minimizeWindow()"/>
```

(continued)

Listing 7-3 *(continued)*

```
<img id="btnClose" src="close.png"
        onclick="closeWindow()"/>
<p class="circleCaption">This may be a lame app, but what
        do you expect? <br/><br/>It's a circle!</p>
</div>
</body>
</html>
```

Nonrectangular windows in Flex

A background image can also be used with mx:WindowedApplication and mx:Window elements in Flex Builder to create nonrectangular windows. The first step is to create an mx:WindowedApplication and set its showFlex Chrome property to false and be sure that no background is set:

```
<?xml version="1.0" encoding="utf-8"?>
<mx:WindowedApplication xmlns:mx="http://www.adobe.
        com/2006/mxml" layout="absolute" height="378"
        width="356"
 styleName="sansChrome">
  <mx:Style>
  .sansChrome { showFlexChrome: false; background-
        color:"";}
  </mx:Style>

</mx:WindowedApplication>
```

Next, you can use an mx:Image element to display the background image:

```
<mx:Image id="imgCircle" x="0" y="0" source="badge.png"
        width="354" height="376"/>
```

Now you add desired content to the mx:WindowedApplication. In this example, I add basic text and two mx:Image elements for the Minimize and Close buttons. (You can use mx:Button elements instead.) Here's the code:

```
<mx:Text id="txtLabel" x="81" y="126" text="This
        may be a lame app, but what do you expect?
        &#xd;&#xd;It's a circle!" width="192"
        height="131" color="#FFFFFF" fontSize="17"
        textAlign="center" enabled="true"
        selectable="false" useHandCursor="true"/>
  <mx:Image x="211" y="54" source="minimize.png"
        click="minimizeWindow()" id="ibtnMinimize"/>
  <mx:Image x="226" y="54" source="close.png"
        click="closeWindow()" id="ibtnClose"/>
```

As you can see, I add `click` event handlers to the images. You can define these in an `mx:Script`, as follows:

```
<mx:Script>
<![CDATA[

  public function closeWindow():void {
     this.close();
   }

  private function minimizeWindow():void {

      stage.nativeWindow.minimize();
   }

]]>
</mx:Script>
```

To add window movement functionality, mouse down events need to be captured for the image and text elements. These are defined in an initialization routine to be triggered when the application is loaded adding `application Complete="initWindow()"` in the `mx:WindowedApplication`. Here's the attached function:

```
  private function initWindow():void {
     this.imgCircle.addEventListener(MouseEvent.
        MOUSE_DOWN, onMouseDown);
     this.txtLabel.addEventListener(MouseEvent.
        MOUSE_DOWN, onMouseDown);
   }
```

One final effect that you can add using ActionScript is a drop shadow for the image (named `imgCircle`) using a `DropShadowFilter`. To do so, declare a `shadowFilter` variable:

```
  public var shadowFilter:DropShadowFilter;
```

Then add the following to `initWindow()`:

```
     shadowFilter = new DropShadowFilter();
     shadowFilter.color = 0x000000;
     shadowFilter.alpha = 0.5;
     shadowFilter.blurX = 5;
     shadowFilter.blurY = 5;
     shadowFilter.distance = 3;
     addShadow(this.imgCircle);
```

Finally, add the `addShadow()` function, which is referenced in the preceding code. This adds the `shadowFilter` to the image:

```
public function addShadow(comp:DisplayObject):void {
    comp.filters = [this.shadowFilter];
}
```

Before building the app, you need to make sure the application descriptor file contains the appropriate settings for the `initialWindow` tag:

```
<initialWindow>
    <content>index.html</content>
    <systemChrome>none</systemChrome>
    <transparent>true</transparent>
</initialWindow>
```

Figure 7-11 displays the running nonrectangular AIR app.

Figure 7-11: Non-rectangular AIR app written in Flex Builder.

Listing 7-4 shows the main MXML source file for the application.

Listing 7-4: CirculAIR.mxml

```
<?xml version="1.0" encoding="utf-8"?>
<mx:WindowedApplication xmlns:mx="http://www.adobe.
        com/2006/mxml" layout="absolute" height="378"
        width="356"
 styleName="sansChrome" applicationComplete="initWindow()
        ">
  <mx:Style>
  .sansChrome { showFlexChrome: false; background-
        color:"";}
  </mx:Style>
```

```
<mx:Script>
<![CDATA[

  public var shadowFilter:DropShadowFilter;

  private function initWindow():void {
    this.imgCircle.addEventListener(MouseEvent.
      MOUSE_DOWN, onMouseDown);
    this.txtLabel.addEventListener(MouseEvent.
      MOUSE_DOWN, onMouseDown);

    shadowFilter = new DropShadowFilter();
    shadowFilter.color = 0x000000;
    shadowFilter.alpha = 0.5;
    shadowFilter.blurX = 5;
    shadowFilter.blurY = 5;
    shadowFilter.distance = 3;
    addShadow(this.imgCircle);

  }

  public function closeWindow():void {
    this.close();
  }

  private function onMouseDown(evt:MouseEvent):void {
    stage.nativeWindow.startMove();
  }

  private function minimizeWindow():void {
    stage.nativeWindow.minimize();
  }

  public function addShadow(comp:DisplayObject):void {
    comp.filters = [this.shadowFilter];
  }


]]>
</mx:Script>

<mx:Image id="imgCircle" x="0" y="0" source="badge.
        png" width="354" height="376"
        doubleClick="closeWindow()"/>
```

(continued)

Listing 7-4 *(continued)*

```
<mx:Text id="txtLabel" x="81" y="126" text="This
        may be a lame app, but what do you expect?
        &#xd;&#xd;It's a circle!" width="192"
        height="131" color="#FFFFFF" fontSize="17"
        textAlign="center" enabled="true"
        selectable="false" useHandCursor="true"/>
<mx:Image x="211" y="54" source="minimize.png"
        click="minimizeWindow()" id="ibtnMinimize"/>
<mx:Image x="226" y="54" source="close.png"
        click="closeWindow()" id="ibtnClose"/>

</mx:WindowedApplication>
```

Chapter 8

Working with Menus and Tray and Dock Icons

......

......

Mindlessly going along with the crowd may be a bad thing in the real world, but I strongly recommend that you go along with the "in" crowd when it comes to creating applications. The cool kids, in this case, are apps that conform to the basic UI standards and core functionality of the native OS. UI conventions help ensure that users instantly know how to interact with your app, where to go to find it, and how to get it to perform an action.

With that in mind, Adobe AIR enables developers to build apps that conform to the user interface conventions and functionality of the native OS. In addition to windows (discussed in Chapter 7), an AIR application also interacts with other key parts of a native OS user interface, including the menu system, taskbar (Windows), and Dock (Mac OS X). In this chapter, you discover how to add these capabilities to your AIR app.

Exploring the Types of Native Menus

For Web applications, menus are typically used as a way to navigate to different pages of the application. However, these menus are implemented inside a page as an on-screen control — not that much different from a button or text field. Native OS menus, however, are foreign territory for Web apps; these menus are stuff the browser deals with. But Adobe AIR empowers you to use menus as a primary way in which a user interacts with your native application.

There are several types of menus that you can implement, depending on the needs of your app. Table 8-1 lists each of the menu types and indicates the native OS for which they are applicable. Also note the Default column in the table. Adobe AIR automatically adds a default application menu, as well as some context (right-click) menus, to your app when running under Mac OS X.

Table 8-1		Menu Types			
Menu Type	*Description*	*Accessed By*	*Windows*	*Mac OS X*	*Default*
Application menu	Top menu of app displayed in Mac OS X Menubar	`Native Application. native Application. menu`	No	Yes	Default is provided under Mac OS X
Window menu	Top menu of a window displayed below its title bar	`NativeWindow. menu`	Yes	No	
Pop-up menu (also called a context menu)	Generic right-click pop-up menu that can be displayed anywhere in an AIR window	`Interactive Object. context Menu`	Yes	Yes	Default is pro-vided for selected text in a TextField object
HTML/SWF context menu	Right-click menu dis-played when an HTML doc or SWF file is right-clicked	`Interactive Object. context Menu`	Yes	Yes	Default is pro-vided for selected text/ images in HTML
System tray icon menu	Menu displayed when the app's Windows system tray icon is clicked	`Native Application. native Application. icon.menu`	Yes	No	

Menu Type	Description	Accessed By	Windows	Mac OS X	Default
Dock icon menu	Menu displayed when the app's Mac OS X Dock icon is clicked	`Native Application. native Application. icon.menu`	No	Yes	Default is provided under Mac OS X
`mx:Flex Native Menu`	Flex-based non-visual component that acts as a wrapper for the `NativeMenu` class Enables you to work with native menus through a Flex component	Instance of `Flex Native Menu`	Yes	Yes	

Creating a Menu

Adobe AIR menus are created using the `NativeMenu` and `NativeMenuItem` classes. These menus and menu items that you create in code are distinct and independent from the various application, window, and context menus that appear on-screen. You can therefore designate a `NativeMenu` object to serve as any of these types of menus.

Keep in mind the following basic rules of thumb to consider when you create AIR menus:

- ✔ **You have a hierarchy of menu objects.** When you create a menu, you are creating a hierarchy. A `NativeMenu` object, which is always at the top level of the hierarchy, contains one or more `NativeMenuItem` objects.

- ✔ **`NativeMenuItem` objects are flexible.** A `NativeMenuItem` can represent one of three things: a command item, a separator, or a submenu.

✔ **The root menu is boss.** The `NativeMenu` instance you designate to serve as the application and/or window menu is often called the *root menu* or *top-level menu*. Its `NativeMenuItem` children are displayed horizontally to form a Menu bar.

✔ **Submenus are implemented through two objects.** A submenu is just another `NativeMenu` instance. However, it is always contained by a `NativeMenuItem` and is never directly added to a `NativeMenu`. Given those facts, you can think of a submenu as consisting of two components:

  • A `NativeMenuItem` instance that serves as the container of the submenu and displays a menu label for the submenu.

  • The actual menu, a `NativeMenu` instance that is assigned to the `submenu` property of a `NativeMenuItem` instance.

Because a submenu is a `NativeMenu` instance contained by a `NativeMenuItem`, be wise in your variable naming, or your code can become confusing to read and work with. For example, if you assign `fileMenu` as the `NativeMenuItem` instance that contains the File submenu, you can be confused as to whether you're working with the container item or the actual submenu.

✔ **Two names for right-click menus.** Adobe AIR features both *context menus* and *pop-up menus*. However, these two menus are essentially the same thing — namely, a menu displayed in place when the mouse is right-clicked. The only difference is in usage; context menus have menu items specific to a particular on-screen object, whereas a pop-up menu is more general purpose in nature.

✔ **Root menus and context menus have structural differences.** The menu item children of a root menu should be submenus, not commands or separators. However, context and pop-up menus often have commands and separators in the highest level of their menu structure.

✔ **Menus trigger two events.** `NativeMenu` and `NativeMenuItem` objects dispatch displaying and select events:

  • The `displaying` event is triggered just before the menu or menu item is displayed.

  • The `select` event is triggered when a `NativeMenuItem` command item is selected by the user. (Separators and submenus don't trigger a `select` event.)

Creating a root menu

To create an application (Mac OS X) and window (Windows) menu for your application, you create a `NativeMenu` instance that will serve as your root menu. You can assign this same `NativeMenu` object to serve as both the application and window menu.

In JavaScript, you create the top-level `NativeMenu` instance using `air.NativeMenu()`:

```
var rootMenu = new air.NativeMenu();
```

In ActionScript, use the following:

```
var rootMenu:NativeMenu = new NativeMenu();
```

Creating submenus

A root `NativeMenu` isn't much good on its own, however. Instead, it needs a set of `NativeMenuItem` objects to serve as submenus. To do so, create the `NativeMenuItem` and then assign a new `NativeMenu` instance to its `submenu` property. You then add new items to the submenu.

Here's the code in JavaScript:

```
var fileMenuItem = rootMenu.addItem("File");

var fileSubmenu = new air.NativeMenu();
fileMenuItem.submenu = fileSubmenu;
var newFileItem = fileSubmenu.addItem("New");
```

A `NativeMenuItem` is added to the `rootMenu` instance using `air.NativeMenuItem()`. As you can see from the preceding code, the `addItem()` creates a new menu item with the menu label specified in the parameter.

Using ActionScript, you write the following:

```
var fileMenuItem:NativeMenuItem = rootMenu.
        addItem("File");

var fileSubmenu:NativeMenu = new NativeMenu();
fileMenuItem.submenu = fileSubmenu;
var newFileItem:NativeMenuItem = fileSubmenu.
        addItem("New");
```

You could also use the `addSubmenu()` method as a shortcut to eliminate one line of code. It enables you to assign a `NativeMenu` instance as a submenu at the same time that you create the menu item. In JavaScript:

```
var fileSubmenu = new air.NativeMenu();
var fileMenuItem = rootMenu.addSubmenu(fileSubmenu,
        "File");
```

Using this shortcut, you can go one step further and create separate routines for creating each submenu. The following example creates a root menu and then adds four submenus to it, each of which is created in a helper function:

```
var rootMenu = new air.NativeMenu();
var fileMenuItem = rootMenu.addSubmenu(createFileMenu(),"File");
var editMenuItem = rootMenu.addSubmenu(createEditMenu(),"Edit");
var viewMenuItem = rootMenu.addSubmenu(createViewMenu(),"View");
var helpMenuItem = rootMenu.addSubmenu(createHelpMenu(),"Help");
```

The following syntax is also valid, although you would not be able to reference by name the `NativeMenuItem` children of `rootMenu`:

```
var rootMenu = new air.NativeMenu();
rootMenu.addSubmenu(createFileMenu(),"File");
rootMenu.addSubmenu(createEditMenu(),"Edit");
rootMenu.addSubmenu(createViewMenu(),"View");
rootMenu.addSubmenu(createHelpMenu(),"Help");
```

Creating menu commands

A menu command is created using the `NativeMenu addItem()` method and then adding an event listener that triggers a function when the item is selected. Consider the following JavaScript:

```
var fileSubmenu = new air.NativeMenu();

var newFileItem = fileSubmenu.addItem(new air.
        NativeMenuItem("New"));

newFileItem.addEventListener( air.Event.SELECT, fileNew);


function fileNew() {
  alert("You created a new document. You must be proud!");
}
```

`newFileItem` is added as a new `NativeMenuItem` under `fileSubmenu` and given the label of New. A `select` event listener is added to execute the `fileNew()` function.

Consider a slightly more complete ActionScript example. Pay special attention to the bolded lines, which create a menu item and attach a `SELECT` event handler to it:

```
private function initWindow():void {
  var rootMenu:NativeMenu = new NativeMenu();
  var fileSubmenu:NativeMenu = new NativeMenu();

  var fileMenuItem:NativeMenuItem = rootMenu.addItem(new
          NativeMenuItem("File"));
  fileMenuItem.submenu = fileSubmenu;

  var newFileItem:NativeMenuItem = fileSubmenu.addItem(new
          NativeMenuItem("New"));
  newFileItem.addEventListener( Event.SELECT, fileNew);
}

public function fileNew(evt: Event):void {
  mx.controls.Alert.show( "You created a new document. You
          must be proud!");
}
```

Notice that the event handler function needs to pass the Event instance as a parameter even if you don't plan on using it.

Creating menu separators

A menu separator is a horizontal line that does what its name implies — separates items in your menu into logical groupings. To create a menu separator, you set to true an optional isSeparator parameter in the NativeMenuItem constructor.

The following JavaScript code adds separators between the New, Save, and Exit menu items:

```
var fileSubmenu = new air.NativeMenu();
var newFileItem = fileSubmenu.addItem(new air.
        NativeMenuItem("New"));
newFileItem.addEventListener( air.Event.SELECT, fileNew);
var sep1 = fileSubmenu.addItem(new air.NativeMenuItem("",
        true));
var saveFileItem = fileSubmenu.addItem(new air.
        NativeMenuItem("Save"));
saveFileItem.addEventListener( air.Event.SELECT,
        fileSave);
var sep2 = fileSubmenu.addItem(new air.NativeMenuItem("",
        true));
var exitFileItem = fileSubmenu.addItem(new air.
        NativeMenuItem("Exit"));
exitFileItem.addEventListener( air.Event.SELECT,
        fileExit);
```

The equivalent ActionScript looks like this:

```
var fileSubmenu:NativeMenu = new NativeMenu();
var newCommand:NativeMenuItem = fileSubmenu.addItem(new
        NativeMenuItem(«New»));
newCommand.addEventListener(Event.SELECT, fileNew);
var sep1:NativeMenuItem = fileSubmenu.addItem( new
        NativeMenuItem(«B», true));
var saveCommand:NativeMenuItem = fileSubmenu.addItem(new
        NativeMenuItem(«Save»));
saveCommand.addEventListener(Event.SELECT, fileSave);
var sep2:NativeMenuItem = fileSubmenu.addItem( new
        NativeMenuItem(«B», true));
var exitCommand:NativeMenuItem = fileSubmenu.addItem(new
        NativeMenuItem(«Exit»));
exitCommand.addEventListener(Event.SELECT, fileExit);
return fileSubmenu;
```

Adding keyboard shortcuts to menu items

You can add keyboard shortcuts (or accelerators) to your menu items to enable users to select a menu command directly through the keyboard rather than navigate the menu.

A keyboard shortcut normally consists of two parts: a primary (or normal) key plus one or more modifier keys (such as Shift, Alt, Ctrl, and, for Mac users, Command [⌘]). Take the familiar `Paste` command as an example. Under Windows, the keyboard shortcut is Ctrl+P. Under Mac OS X, the shortcut is ⌘+P.

Adobe AIR has a default modifier key when running under Windows and Mac — the Ctrl key for Windows and ⌘ key for Mac. Each of these is automatically added as a modifier key unless you specify otherwise.

Keyboard shortcuts are applicable only to application and window menus.

Setting the primary key

To set the key for a `NativeMenuItem`, assign a single character string to its `keyEquivalent` property. For example:

```
fileNewItem.keyEquivalent = "n";
```

The lowercase n in this code assigns Ctrl+N as a shortcut key for the `fileNewItem` menu item for Windows; it assigns ⌘+N under Mac.

If you use an uppercase letter, the Shift key is added as one of the modifiers. Therefore, the following:

```
fileNewItem.keyEquivalent = "N";
```

assigns the shortcut keys of Shift+Ctrl+N (Windows) and Shift+⌘+N (Mac).

Setting the modifier keys

To change the set of modifiers, assign the `keyEquivalentModifiers` array property one or more of the following values:

- `air.Keyboard.CONTROL`
- `air.Keyboard.COMMAND`
- `air.Keyboard.SHIFT`
- `air.Keyboard.ALTERNATE`

In ActionScript, you want to lose the initial `air.` reference.

Because the property is an array type, you can add multiple modifiers inside the brackets. For example, to set Ctrl+Alt+N, you use

```
fileNewItem.keyEquivalent = "N";
fileNewItem.keyEquivalentModifiers = [air.Keyboard.
        CONTROL+air.Keyboard.ALTERNATE];
```

When you change the `keyEquivalentModifiers` property, the default modifier values are overwritten, so you need to include the Ctrl or ⌘ key as part of the new modifier array.

Adding mnemonic key assignments

Both Windows and Mac allow users to access and navigate menus through the keyboard through what is known as *mnemonics*.

On Windows, a menu command is assigned a mnemonic, which is usually the first character of the label. If that character is already used by another item, then the next significant character is used. A user is then able to select the menu command by pressing and holding the Alt key (to access the window menu) while then pressing the mnemonic key. The mnemonic key is often underlined (for example, File).

On Mac, the mnemonic is slightly different. After one of the top-level application menus is selected, a user types the first letter or two of the command. The closest match is highlighted. If that's the desired item, press Return to select the item.

To assign a Windows mnemonic key, you specify the zero-based index of the desired character inside the string. The first character is 0, the second 1, and so on. Therefore, to assign the F as the mnemonic key for the File command, for example, you use the following:

```
fileMenuItem.mnemonicIndex = 0;
```

Selecting and deselecting menu items

You may wish to use a menu command to show the state of your application, such as whether a toolbar or status bar is visible. A check mark appearing next to the label means that the item is selected and is the standard way to indicate an "on" or "true" state. To display a check mark:

```
viewStatusBarItem.checked = true;
```

To remove the check mark:

```
viewStatusBarItem.checked = false;
```

Disabling and enabling menu items

Menu items can be disabled, causing the item to be grayed out. To disable a menu item, use the `enabled` property of a `NativeMenuItem`. Here's an example:

```
editCutItem.enabled = false;
```

When selected, disabled menu items do not trigger a `select` event.

See the section "Updating menus before they display," later in this chapter, for more on working with the `enabled` property.

Attaching an object to a menu item

You can take advantage of the `data` property of a `NativeMenuItem` instance to attach data or an object to it. A common example in which this storage mechanism can come in handy is for a Recent Documents submenu. You can assign a `File` object to the associated menu item and then open the `File` instance when the menu item is selected. For example, here's a JavaScript snippet that assigns an image to the `data` property of a recent item:

```
var imgFile = air.File.applicationStorageDirectory.
        resolvePath("wallpaper-1.jpg");
recentItem1.data = imgFile;
```

Setting the Application, Window, Pop-Up, and Context Menus

You can set `NativeMenu` objects to the application, window, pop-up, and context menus. (You can also assign them to the taskbar icon and Dock icon menus as well, but I cover that later in the chapter.)

Before assigning application and window menus, you first want to check to see whether the OS that the app is running on supports the associated menu. Therefore, evaluate the OS before making these menu assignments.

Setting a window menu (Windows)

A window menu is supported on the Windows OS, but only for windows that have system chrome. Therefore, you want to perform two checks before assigning the window menu. In JavaScript, the code to perform these checks is as follows:

```
if (air.NativeWindow.supportsMenu &&
    nativeWindow.systemChrome != air.
        NativeWindowSystemChrome.NONE) {
    nativeWindow.menu = rootMenu;
}
```

Here's how you check for proper OS support in ActionScript:

```
if (NativeWindow.supportsMenu &&
    nativeWindow.systemChrome !=
        NativeWindowSystemChrome.NONE) {
    nativeWindow.menu = rootMenu;
}
```

Setting an application menu (Mac)

To set the application menu for Mac OS in JavaScript, use this code:

```
if (air.NativeApplication.supportsMenu) {
  air.NativeApplication.menu = rootMenu;
}
```

In ActionScript, use this code to set the application menu:

```
if (NativeApplication.supportsMenu) {

    NativeApplication.nativeApplication.menu = rootMenu;
}
```

Setting a context menu

A context menu is a menu that you can add to your app that is context aware — in other words, the menu choices that are displayed are applicable to that particular UI control or part of the app in which the user is working. It is accessible in your app by right-clicking an on-screen object.

Setting a context menu in an HTML app

For HTML apps, you can set a NativeMenu instance as the context menu for an HTML element. To do so, you begin by adding an event handler to the element's oncontextmenu event, as follows:

```
<div id="canvas" oncontextmenu=»displayContextMenu
        (event)»>
<p>Content is good. </p>
</div>
```

Next, define the event handler:

```
function displayContextMenu(event) {
  event.preventDefault();
```

```
rootMenu.display(window.nativeWindow.stage, event.
        clientX, event.clientY);
}
```

Because text selections and images have their own default menus, you can disable any built-in menus by calling `preventDefault()`. The `display()` method of the `NativeMenu` instance `rootMenu` is called, using the `stage` object and the mouse x,y coordinates received from the `event` parameter.

You can prevent text selection (and the text selection context menu from being displayed) by adding the style rule `-khtml-user-select:none`. This WebKit extension selector disallows text selections.

Setting a context menu in Flex

In Flex Builder, every `mx:` UI element contains a `contextMenu` property. You can assign a `NativeMenu` menu instance to this property either in your code or in the designer.

Using ContextMenu and ContextMenuItem

When creating AIR apps in Flex and Flash, you can also use `ContextMenu` and `ContextMenuItem` to create context menus. However, `ContextMenu` and `ContextMenuItem` are used primarily when you need to output to a SWF for in-browser use, because Flash Player doesn't support `NativeMenu` and `NativeMenuItem`. Therefore, if you're focused on developing AIR apps and not Flash media, I recommend sticking with `NativeMenu` and `NativeMenuItem`.

Setting a pop-up menu

As are context menus, pop-up menus are accessible anywhere inside sandboxed content of your app by right-clicking an on-screen object. You can display a `NativeMenu` instance as a pop-up simply by calling its `display()` method.

In an HTML application, you can trap for the `onmouseup` handler:

```
<div id="canvas" onmouseup="displayPopupMenu(event)">
<p>Content is good. </p>
</div>
```

The handler then calls the `display()` method of the `NativeMenu` instance named `popupMenu`:

```
function displayPopupMenu( event ) {

  popupMenu.display(window.nativeWindow.stage, event.
        clientX, event.client
}
```

In Flex, you can usually get the functionality you're looking for by assigning a `NativeMenu` instance to the `contextMenu` property of the `mx:WindowedApplication` element. But you can also show a pop-up menu anywhere in your code simply by calling the `display()` method:

```
private function onMouseClick(event:MouseEvent):void {
  popupMenu.display(event.target.stage, event.stageX,
        event.stageY);
}
```

Handling Menu Events

As I mention earlier in the chapter, `NativeMenu` and `NativeMenuItem` objects dispatch `select` and `displaying` events. To make menu items functional, you need to respond to these events. In this section, I walk you through how to add support in your apps.

Responding to menu selections

`NativeMenuItem` commands are the only part of a menu that can respond to a user selection. This makes sense because the root menu, submenus, and separators exist only to allow the user to easily navigate a logical grouping of selectable menu commands.

You can respond to select events directly from each menu command by adding an event listener (also called an event handler). (See Chapter 6 for more on event listeners.) The following JavaScript example assigns the `fileNew()` function to serve as the `select` event handler for the `newFileItem` menu command:

```
newFileItem.addEventListener(air.Event.SELECT, fileNew);
```

However, because `select` events of menu items bubble up to the menu, you can also listen for all `select` events in the menu. When you do so, you can use the `target` property of the event object to determine the specific menu command that was selected.

The following code assigns the `selectTrapper()` function as the official event listener for `rootMenu`, which is a top-level menu used throughout the project. Here's the JavaScript version:

```
function selectTrapper(event) {
  var menuItem = NativeMenuItem(event.target);
  alert( menuItem.label + " has been selected, so don't
         try to stop it!");
}

rootMenu.addEventListener(air.Event.SELECT,
         selectTrapper);
```

Here's the ActionScript version:

```
public function selectTrapper(evt: Event):void {
  var menuItem:NativeMenuItem = evt.target as
         NativeMenuItem;
  mx.controls.Alert.show( menuItem.label + " has been
         selected, so don't try to stop it!");
}

rootMenu.addEventListener(Event.SELECT, selectTrapper);
```

When the application runs, the `selectTrapper()` function will serve as the handler for all menu commands.

If you add listeners to both the `NativeMenuItem` and its `NativeMenu` container, *both* event handlers will be triggered. The `NativeMenuItem`'s select event is dispatched first and then the event bubbles up to its parent. If you have a listener at the container level, it will be called as well.

Updating menus before they display

Menus and menu items also dispatch a `displaying` event just before the menu is displayed on-screen. By attaching a listener to this event, you can update the contents of a menu or the state of a menu item before the user sees it. For example, the following code sample updates the `enabled` state of a menu item depending on settings stored in an object called `appProperties`. In JavaScript, you write:

```
rootMenu.addEventListener(air.Event.DISPLAYING,
         updateMenuState);

function updateMenuState(event):void {
  var menuItem = NativeMenuItem(event.target);0
  if (menuItem.label = 'Allow Updates') {
    menuItem.enabled = appProperties.allowUpdates;
  }
  if (menuItem.label = 'Offline Mode') {
    menuItem.enabled = appProperties.offlineMode;
  }
}
```

```
In ActionScript, you write it this way:
rootMenu.addEventListener(Event.DISPLAYING,
        updateMenuState);

public function updateMenuState(evt: Event):void {
  var menuItem:NativeMenuItem = evt.target as
          NativeMenuItem;
  if (menuItem.label = 'Allow Updates') {
    menuItem.enabled = appProperties.allowUpdates;
  }
  if (menuItem.label = 'Offline Mode') {
    menuItem.enabled = appProperties.offlineMode;
  }
}
```

The FlexNativeMenu Alternative

Flex developers can use the `mx:FlexNativeMenu` component as an alternative to working directly with `NativeMenu`. `mx:FlexNativeMenu` serves as a nonvisual wrapper for `NativeMenu`, allowing you to interact with native menus in your MXML file much the same as you would with Flex's other visual menu components. For example, the following code defines a root menu:

```
<mx:FlexNativeMenu id="rootMenu"
        dataProvider="{rootMenuData}"
labelField="@label" keyEquivalentField="@
        key" showRoot="false"/>
```

The `dataProvider` property points to an XML hierarchy of menu items that I define as follows:

```
<mx:XML format="e4x" id="rootMenuData">
    <root>
      <menuitem label="_File">
        <menuitem label="_New" key="n"
        ctrlKey="true" cmdKey="true"/>
        <menuitem type="separator"/>
        <menuitem label="_Save" key="s"
        ctrlKey="true cmdKey="true"/>
        <menuitem type="separator"/>
        <menuitem label="Exit"/>
      </menuitem>
```

```
      <menuitem label="_Edit">
        <menuitem label="_Undo" key="z"
        ctrlKey="true" cmdKey="true"/>
        <menuitem label="_Redo" key="y"
        ctrlKey="true" cmdKey="true"/>
        <menuitem type="separator"/>
        <menuitem label="Cut" key="x"
        ctrlKey="true" cmdKey="true"/>
        <menuitem label="_Copy" key="c"
        ctrlKey="true" cmdKey="true"/>
        <menuitem label="_Paste" key="v"
        ctrlKey="true" cmdKey="true"/>
      </menuitem>
      <menuitem label="_Help">
        <menuitem label="_About MyApp"/>
      </menuitem>
    </root>
  </mx:XML>
```

You can attach an event listener to the `FlexNativeMenu` instance much the same as you would with `NativeMenu`:

```
rootMenu.addEventListener(FlexNat
        iveMenuEvent.ITEM_CLICK,
        rootMenuHandler);
```

See http://livedocs.adobe.com/flex/3/html/help.html?content=FlexApolloComponents_10.html for more complete details on working with the `mx:FlexNativeMenu` component.

Enabling Your App for the Windows System Tray and Mac OS X Dock

Windows and Mac OS X each have dock areas that display icons of opened applications.

Windows has two areas:

- **Taskbar:** Displays currently running apps as buttons across the bar.
- **System tray:** The notification section of the taskbar, usually located at the bottom right of the desktop. It contains icons for access to system functions or minimized apps.

By default, your AIR app displays in the taskbar, not the system tray. However, if you add a bitmap array to your app for display as the system tray icon, the app moves to the system tray. Although you can't modify the taskbar icon or menu, you can customize the system tray icon, icon Tool Tip, and icon menu.

The Mac OS X Dock displays application icons. It's used both to launch apps and indicate opened apps by displaying a triangle or dot below the icon. The right side of the Dock is used for showing application windows that are open.

You can customize the Dock icon and icon menu, but app window Dock icons always use your application's default icon.

You can work with the icon and its menu on both Windows and Mac through the NativeApplication.nativeApplication.icon property. The object type is SystemTrayIcon under Windows and DockIcon under Mac.

Before accessing the icon property, you want to check OS support by checking the NativeApplication.supportsSystemTrayIcon or NativeApplication.supportsDockIcon property. If you attempt to access a property specific to SystemTrayIcon or DockIcon on an OS that doesn't support it, you'll trigger a runtime exception. And that's not good for anyone!

Enabling your app for the Windows system tray

You can transform your application to work in the system tray by assigning one or more bitmaps to the NativeApplication.nativeApplication.icon.bitmaps array property. If that property is assigned, Adobe AIR assumes that you'd like your app displayed in the system tray using the designated bitmap. You can provide one or more image sizes in the array. When more than one image is included, AIR displays the image that is most appropriate to the size of system tray icons, typically 16 x 16 pixels.

The following code shows how to add system tray support. First, assign an array of images to the `bitmaps` property (see the upcoming "Putting it All Together with MenuAIR" section for more details on how `trayDockIcons` is loaded):

```
air.NativeApplication.nativeApplication.icon.bitmaps = [trayDockIcons];
```

Next, add the icon menu and Tool Tip:

```
if (air.NativeApplication.supportsSystemTrayIcon) {
  SystemTrayIcon(air.NativeApplication.nativeApplication.icon).menu =
            createDockMenu();

  SystemTrayIcon(air.NativeApplication.nativeApplication.icon).tooltip =
            "MenuAIR Command & Control";
}
```

Remove the `air.` for ActionScript.

Enabling your app for the Mac OS X dock

By default, the icons you assign in the application descriptor file are used as the Dock icon for your application. However, you can also assign a separate icon through the `air.NativeApplication.nativeApplication.icon.bitmaps` property.

AIR automatically defines a Dock icon menu for your app. However, you can append additional menu commands above the default menu items. To assign a menu for your app's icon on the Mac OS X Dock, use the following:

```
if (air.NativeApplication.supportsDockIcon) }
  DockIcon(air.NativeApplication.nativeApplication.icon).menu = iconMenu;
}
```

Once again, remove the `air.` for ActionScript.

Putting It All Together with MenuAIR

Previous sections of this chapter walk you through the process of creating and enabling menus. Here, it's time to get practical. The following sample app makes use of the menu-building techniques discussed in this chapter.

MenuAIR: The HTML Edition

Listing 8-1 shows the HTML version of my simple menu demo, MenuAIR.

Listing 8-1: MenuAIR.html

```
<!DOCTYPE HTML PUBLIC "-//W3C//DTD HTML 4.01//EN" "http://www.w3.org/TR/html4/
           strict.dtd">
<html>
<head>
<meta http-equiv="Content-Type" content="text/html; charset=iso-8859-1" />
<title>MenuAIR</title>
<script type="text/javascript" src="AIRAliases.js"></script>
<script type="text/javascript">

          window.addEventListener('load', initialize, false);
          var contextMenu;

  /**
  * Initializes the app after loading
  *
  */
  function initialize() {

    // Create root menu
    var rootMenu = new air.NativeMenu();

    // Create root submenus
    rootMenu.addSubmenu(createFileMenu(),"File");
    rootMenu.addSubmenu(createEditMenu(),"Edit");
    rootMenu.addSubmenu(createViewMenu(),"View");
    rootMenu.addSubmenu(createHelpMenu(),"Help");

    // Attach event listener routine to root menu
    rootMenu.addEventListener(air.Event.SELECT, dispatchMenuCommand);

    // Assign application menu (Mac OS X)
    if (air.NativeApplication.supportsMenu) {
      air.NativeApplication.nativeApplication.menu = rootMenu;
    }

    // Assign window menu (MS Windows)
    if (air.NativeWindow.supportsMenu) {
      window.nativeWindow.menu = rootMenu;
    }

    // Assign context (right-click) menu
    contextMenu = createContextMenu();
    contextMenu.addEventListener(air.Event.SELECT, dispatchMenuCommand);

    var iconLoader = new air.Loader();
```

(continued)

Listing 8-1 *(continued)*

```
    iconLoader.contentLoaderInfo.addEventListener(air.Event.COMPLETE,
            iconLoadComplete);

    // Mac OS X dock support
    if (air.NativeApplication.supportsDockIcon) {
      iconLoader.load(new air.URLRequest(«../icons/128.png»));
      air.DockIcon(air.NativeApplication.nativeApplication.icon).menu =
            createDockMenu();
    }

    // Windows system tray support
    if (air.NativeApplication.supportsSystemTrayIcon)  {
      // Load icon image
      iconLoader.load(new air.URLRequest(«../icons/16.png»));
      air.SystemTrayIcon(air.NativeApplication.nativeApplication.icon).menu =
            createDockMenu();
      air.SystemTrayIcon(air.NativeApplication.nativeApplication.icon).tooltip =
            «MenuAIR Command & Control»;
    }
  }

/**
* Context menu event handler
*
*/
function displayContextMenu(event) {
  event.preventDefault();
  contextMenu.display(window.nativeWindow.stage, event.clientX, event.
            clientY);
}

/**
* Fills trayDockIcons with loaded icons
*
*/
function iconLoadComplete(event) {
    trayDockIcon = event.target.content.bitmapData;
    air.NativeApplication.nativeApplication.icon.bitmaps = [trayDockIcon];
  }

/**
* createMenuCommand()
* Creates a «fully loaded» menu command based on parameters
*
*/
function createMenuCommand(menuContainer, itemLabel, itemKey, itemModifiers,
            itemMnemonic,
            selectHandler) {
  var cmd = air.NativeMenu(menuContainer).addItem(new air.
            NativeMenuItem(itemLabel));
  cmd.mnemonicIndex = itemMnemonic;
```

```
  cmd.keyEquivalent = itemKey;
  if (itemModifiers != null ) {
    cmd.keyEquivalentModifiers = itemModifiers;
  }
if (selectHandler != null ) {
  cmd.addEventListener(air.Event.SELECT, selectHandler);
 }
 return cmd;
 }


/**
* createMenuSeparator()
* Creates a menu separator
*/
function createMenuSeparator(menuContainer) {
  var sep = air.NativeMenu(menuContainer).addItem(new air.NativeMenuItem(«sep»,
          true));
  return sep;
 }


/**
* Creates the File menu for app
*/
 function createFileMenu() {
   var mnu = new air.NativeMenu();
   createMenuCommand( mnu, 'New', 'n', null, 0, fileNew);
   createMenuCommand( mnu, 'Open', 'o', null, 0, null);
   createMenuSeparator(mnu);
   createMenuCommand( mnu, 'Save', 's', null, 0, fileSave);
   createMenuSeparator(mnu);
   // If Mac OS X, then use Quit label
   if (air.NativeApplication.supportsMenu) {
     createMenuCommand( mnu, 'Quit', 'q', null, 0, fileExit);
   }
   // If Windows, then use Exit
   else {
     createMenuCommand( mnu, 'Exit', 'x', null, 0, fileExit);
   }
   return mnu;
 }


/**
* Creates the Edit menu for app
*/
function createEditMenu() {
  var mnu = new air.NativeMenu();
  createMenuCommand( mnu, 'Undo', 'z', null, 0, null);
  createMenuCommand( mnu, 'Redo', 'y', null, 0, null);
```

(continued)

Listing 8-1 *(continued)*

```
      createMenuSeparator(mnu);
      createMenuCommand( mnu, 'Cut', 'x', null, 2, null);
      createMenuCommand( mnu, 'Copy', 'c', null, 0, null);
      createMenuCommand( mnu, 'Paste', 'v', null, 0, null);
      return mnu;
   }


   /**
    * Creates the View menu for app
    */
   function createViewMenu() {
     var mnu = new air.NativeMenu();
     var rulerCommand = createMenuCommand( mnu, 'Ruler', 'r', null, 0, null);
     rulerCommand.checked = true;
     var statusBarCommand = createMenuCommand( mnu, 'Status Bar', 's', null, 0,
               null);
     statusBarCommand.checked = true;
     createMenuSeparator(mnu);
     createMenuCommand( mnu, 'Current Status', 'C', [air.Keyboard.ALTERNATE], 0,
               null);
     return mnu;
   }


   /**
    * Creates the Help menu for app
    *
    */
   function createHelpMenu() {
     var mnu = new air.NativeMenu();
     createMenuCommand( mnu, 'Help on MenuAIR', 'h', null, 0, null);
     createMenuSeparator(mnu);
     createMenuCommand( mnu, 'About MenuAIR', '', null, 0, null);
     return mnu;
   }


   /**
    * Creates a context menu for app
    */
   function createContextMenu() {
     var mnu = new air.NativeMenu();
     createMenuCommand( mnu, 'Cut', '', null, 2, null);
     createMenuCommand( mnu, 'Copy', '', null, 0, null);
     createMenuCommand( mnu, 'Paste', '', null, 0, null)
     createMenuSeparator(mnu);
     createMenuCommand( mnu, 'Refresh Status', '', null, 0, null)
     return mnu;
   }


   /**
```

```
 * Creates a dock/system tray icon menu
 *
 */
function createDockMenu() {
  var mnu = new air.NativeMenu();
  createMenuCommand( mnu, 'Current Status', '', null, 0, null);
  createMenuSeparator(mnu);
  createMenuCommand( mnu, 'Refresh', '', null, 0, null)
  return mnu;
}


/**
 * Catch-all menu dispatcher for all menus
 *
 */
function dispatchMenuCommand(event) {
  var menuItem = air.NativeMenuItem(event.target);

  if (!menuItem.hasEventListener('select')) {
    alert(menuItem.label + « has been selected, so don't try to stop it!»);
  }
}

/**
 * Simple handlers for certain menu commands
 *
 */
function fileNew(event) {
  alert( «You created a new document. You must be proud!»);
}

function fileSave(event) {
  alert( «Save that document before this buggy app crashes!»);
}

function fileExit(event) {
  air.NativeApplication.nativeApplication.exit();
}


</script>

</head>
<body oncontextmenu=»displayContextMenu(event)»>
<div style=»font-family: 'Lucida Grande', Verdana, Geneva, Sans-Serif; font-
             size: 10px;
  text-align:center;vertical-align:middle»>
<p style=»-khtml-user-select:none;» oncontextmenu=»displayContextMenu(event);»>M
             enus are more than just for restaurants anymore!</p>
</div>
</body>
</html>
```

MenuAIR: The Flex Edition

Listing 8-2 provides the full source code of the Flex version of MenuAIR.

Listing 8-2:   MenuAIR.mxml

```
<?xml version="1.0" encoding="utf-8"?>
<mx:WindowedApplication xmlns:mx="http://www.adobe.com/2006/mxml"
            layout="absolute" height="218" width="346" applicationComplete="i
            nitWindow()">

 <mx:Script>
  <![CDATA[7

  import flash.display.NativeMenu;
  import flash.display.NativeMenuItem;
  import flash.display.NativeWindow;
  import mx.controls.Alert;

  private var trayDockIcon:BitmapData;

   /**
   * Initializes the app after loading
   *
   */
  private function initWindow():void {

    // Create root menu
    var rootMenu:NativeMenu = new NativeMenu();

    // Create root submenus
    rootMenu.addSubmenu(createFileMenu(),»File»);
    rootMenu.addSubmenu(createEditMenu(),»Edit»);
    rootMenu.addSubmenu(createViewMenu(),»View»);
    rootMenu.addSubmenu(createHelpMenu(),»Help»);

    // Attach event listener routine to root menu
    rootMenu.addEventListener(Event.SELECT, dispatchMenuCommand);

    // Assign application menu (Mac OS X)
    if (NativeApplication.supportsMenu) {
     NativeApplication.nativeApplication.menu = rootMenu;
     }

    // Assign window menu (MS Windows)
    if (NativeWindow.supportsMenu &&
        nativeWindow.systemChrome != NativeWindowSystemChrome.NONE) {
      nativeWindow.menu = rootMenu;
    }

    // Assign pop-up (right-click) menu
    this.contextMenu = createPopupMenu();
```

```actionscript
this.contextMenu.addEventListener(Event.SELECT, dispatchMenuCommand);

// Mac OS X dock support
if (NativeApplication.supportsDockIcon) {
  DockIcon(NativeApplication.nativeApplication.icon).menu = createDockMenu();
}

// Windows system tray support
if (NativeApplication.supportsSystemTrayIcon  &&
  nativeWindow.systemChrome != NativeWindowSystemChrome.NONE)  {

if (NativeApplication.supportsSystemTrayIcon) {
  var iconLoader:Loader = new Loader();
  iconLoader.contentLoaderInfo.addEventListener(Event.COMPLETE,
          iconLoadComplete);
  iconLoader.load(new URLRequest(«../icons/16.png»));
  SystemTrayIcon(NativeApplication.nativeApplication.icon).menu =
          createDockMenu();
  SystemTrayIcon(NativeApplication.nativeApplication.icon).tooltip =
          «MenuAIR Command & Control»;
  SystemTrayIcon(NativeApplication.nativeApplication.icon).
          addEventListener(MouseEvent.CLICK, activateApp);
  stage.nativeWindow.addEventListener(NativeWindowDisplayStateEvent.DISPLAY_
          STATE_CHANGING, diyMinimize);
  }
}

/**
 * Fills trayDockIcons with loaded icons
 *
 */
public function iconLoadComplete(event:Event):void {
  trayDockIcon = event.target.content.bitmapData;
  NativeApplication.nativeApplication.icon.bitmaps = [trayDockIcon];
}

/**
 * Hide app when minimized to system tray  (Windows)
 *
 */
public function minimizeToSystemTray():void {
  stage.nativeWindow.visible = false;
  NativeApplication.nativeApplication.icon.bitmaps = [trayDockIcon];
}

/**
 * Show app again after minimize to system tray (Windows)
 *
 */
public function activateApp(evt:Event):void {
  stage.nativeWindow.visible = true;
```

(continued)

Listing 8-2 *(continued)*

```
        stage.nativeWindow.orderToFront();
        NativeApplication.nativeApplication.icon.bitmaps = [];
    }

    /**
    * Custom minimize event handler (Windows)
    *
    */
    private function diyMinimize(displayStateEvent:NativeWindowDisplayStateEvent)
            :void {
      if(displayStateEvent.afterDisplayState == NativeWindowDisplayState.
            MINIMIZED) {
         displayStateEvent.preventDefault();
         minimizeToSystemTray();
      }
    }


/**
* createMenuCommand()
* Creates a «fully loaded» menu command based on parameters
*
*/
public function createMenuCommand(menuContainer:NativeMenu, itemLabel:String,
            itemKey:String,
  itemModifiers:Array, itemMnemonic:int, selectHandler:Function):
            NativeMenuItem {
 var cmd:NativeMenuItem= NativeMenu(menuContainer).addItem(new
            NativeMenuItem(itemLabel));
 cmd.mnemonicIndex = itemMnemonic;
 cmd.keyEquivalent = itemKey;
 if (itemModifiers != null ) {
    cmd.keyEquivalentModifiers = itemModifiers;
 }
 if (selectHandler != null ) {
   cmd.addEventListener(Event.SELECT, selectHandler);
 }
 return cmd;
}


/**
* createMenuSeparator()
* Creates a menu separator
*/
private function createMenuSeparator(menuContainer:NativeMenu): NativeMenuItem
            {
 var sep:NativeMenuItem= NativeMenu(menuContainer).addItem(new
            NativeMenuItem(«sep», true));
 return sep;
}
```

```
/**
 * Creates the File menu for app
 */
 private function createFileMenu():NativeMenu {
   var mnu:NativeMenu = new NativeMenu();
   createMenuCommand( mnu, 'New', 'n', null, 0, fileNew);
   createMenuCommand( mnu, 'Open', 'o', null, 0, null);
   createMenuSeparator(mnu);
   createMenuCommand( mnu, 'Save', 's', null, 0, fileSave);
   createMenuSeparator(mnu);
   // If Mac OS X, then use Quit label
   if (NativeApplication.supportsMenu) {
     createMenuCommand( mnu, 'Quit', 'q', null, 0, fileExit);
   }
   // If Windows, then use Exit
   else {
     createMenuCommand( mnu, 'Exit', 'x', null, 0, fileExit);
   }
   return mnu;
 }


/**
 * Creates the Edit menu for app
 */
public function createEditMenu():NativeMenu {
  var mnu:NativeMenu = new NativeMenu();
  createMenuCommand( mnu, 'Undo', 'z', null, 0, null);
  createMenuCommand( mnu, 'Redo', 'y', null, 0, null);
  createMenuSeparator(mnu);
  createMenuCommand( mnu, 'Cut', 'x', null, 2, null);
  createMenuCommand( mnu, 'Copy', 'c', null, 0, null);
  createMenuCommand( mnu, 'Paste', 'v', null, 0, null);
  return mnu;
}


/**
 * Creates the View menu for app
 */
public function createViewMenu():NativeMenu {
  var mnu:NativeMenu = new NativeMenu();
  var rulerCommand:NativeMenuItem = createMenuCommand( mnu, 'Ruler', 'r',
             null, 0, null);
  rulerCommand.checked = true;
  var statusBarCommand:NativeMenuItem = createMenuCommand( mnu, 'Status Bar',
             's', null, 0, null);
  statusBarCommand.checked = true;
```

(continued)

Listing 8-2 *(continued)*

```
    createMenuSeparator(mnu);
    createMenuCommand( mnu, 'Current Status', 'C', [Keyboard.ALTERNATE], 0,
            null);
    return mnu;
}


/**
 * Creates the Help menu for app
 *
 */
public function createHelpMenu():NativeMenu {
    var mnu:NativeMenu = new NativeMenu();
    createMenuCommand( mnu, 'Help on MenuAIR', 'h', null, 0, null);
    createMenuSeparator(mnu);
    createMenuCommand( mnu, 'About MenuAIR', '', null, 0, null);
    return mnu;
}


/**
 * Creates a pop-up menu for app
 */
public function createPopupMenu():NativeMenu {
    var mnu:NativeMenu = new NativeMenu();
    createMenuCommand( mnu, 'Cut', '', null, 2, null);
    createMenuCommand( mnu, 'Copy', '', null, 0, null);
    createMenuCommand( mnu, 'Paste', '', null, 0, null)
    createMenuSeparator(mnu);
    createMenuCommand( mnu, 'Refresh Status', '', null, 0, null);
    return mnu;
}


/**
 * Creates a dock/system tray icon menu
 *
 */
public function createDockMenu():NativeMenu {
    var mnu:NativeMenu = new NativeMenu();
    createMenuCommand( mnu, 'Current Status', '', null, 0, null);
    createMenuSeparator(mnu);
    createMenuCommand( mnu, 'Refresh', '', null, 0, null)
    return mnu;
}


/**
```

```
 * Catch-all menu dispatcher for all menus
 *
 */
public function dispatchMenuCommand(evt: Event):void {
  var menuItem:NativeMenuItem = evt.target as NativeMenuItem;

  if (!menuItem.hasEventListener('select')) {
    Alert.show(menuItem.label + " has been selected, so don't try to stop
          it!");
  }
}


/**
 * Simple handlers for certain menu commands
 *
 */
public function fileNew(evt: Event):void {
  Alert.show( "You created a new document. You must be proud!");
}

public function fileSave(evt: Event):void {
  Alert.show( "Save that document before this buggy app crashes!");
}

public function fileExit(evt: Event):void {
  NativeApplication.nativeApplication.exit();
}




  ]]>
 </mx:Script>


<mx:Label id=»lblApp» text=»Menus aren't just for restaurants anymore!»
          verticalCenter=»0» horizontalCenter=»0»/>



</mx:WindowedApplication>
```

When MenuAIR runs under Mac OS X, the main window (see Figure 8-1) is displayed, as you would expect without a window menu. However, the Mac menu bar displays the new application menu. Figures 8-2, 8-3, and 8-4 show the File, View, and Help submenus. Figure 8-5 shows the pop-up menu.

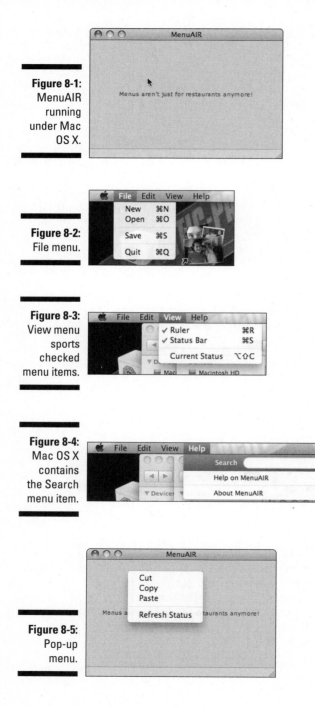

Figure 8-1:
MenuAIR running under Mac OS X.

Figure 8-2:
File menu.

Figure 8-3:
View menu sports checked menu items.

Figure 8-4:
Mac OS X contains the Search menu item.

Figure 8-5:
Pop-up menu.

The MenuAIR Dock icon shows the custom menu items appended to the default menu (see Figure 8-6).

Figure 8-6:
Dock icon
menu.

When MenuAIR runs under Windows, the main window (see Figure 8-7) now comes complete with a window menu. The File menu items, shown in Figure 8-8, provide the Windows-specific shortcut keys.

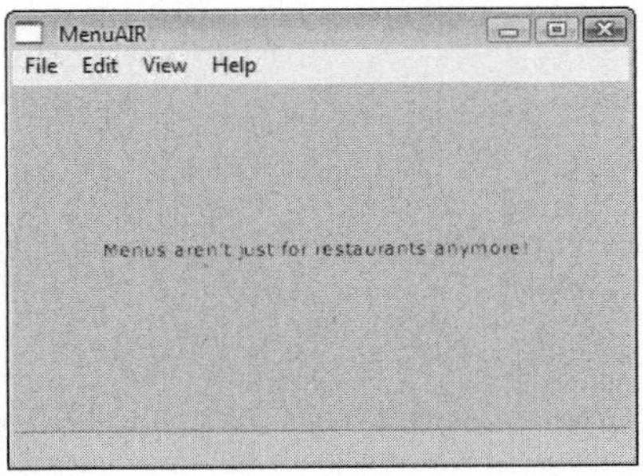

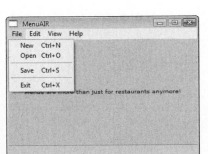

Figure 8-7:
Window
menu.

Figure 8-8:
The File
submenu
is ready for
action.

Figure 8.9 shows the tool tip displayed above the app's taskbar icon, and Figure 8.10 displays the pop-up menu for the taskbar icon.

Figure 8-9:
Tool Tip is
displayed
above the
MenuAIR
taskbar
icon.

Figure 8-10:
Menu
displayed
for the
MenuAIR
taskbar
icon.

Part III
Programming the Adobe AIR API

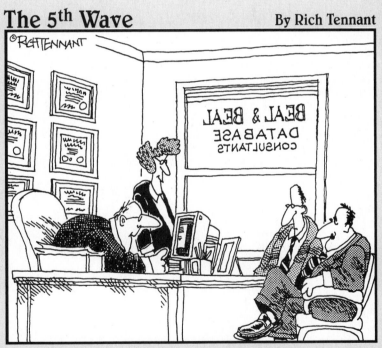

The 5th Wave   By Rich Tennant

"Your database is beyond repair, but before I tell you our backup recommendation, let me ask you a question. How many index cards do you think will fit on the walls of your computer room?"

In this part . . .

In this part, you continue to develop your knowledge of the essentials of AIR application development. You explore how to interact with the local file system. For database applications, I show you how to work with both local and remote data sources. ActionScript developers will want to know how to access their libraries, so I show you how to access libraries in your HTML and Flex apps.

Chapter 9

Don't Be a Drag: Interacting with the Clipboard and Drag-and-Drop

In This Chapter

▶ Exploring how to cut, copy, and paste with the Clipboard

▶ Adding native drag-and-drop to your apps

▶ Working with HTML drag-and-drop functionality

*O*ne of the advantages that AIR has over browser-based apps is the ability to interact with other native applications. Yes, you can do some cool bleeding-edge inter-application communication techniques. However, on a practical, real world basis, you'll find yourself using the Clipboard and drag-and-drop for most inter-application data transfer. In this chapter, you discover how to work with the Clipboard and drag-and-drop within your AIR applications.

Working with the Clipboard

The Clipboard is one part of the OS that is easily taken for granted these days. It's certainly not sexy like drag-and-drop or hip like XML data transfer. Having said that, I hasten to add that the good ol' commands Cut, Copy, and Paste remain the fundamental means of data interchange between desktop apps.

As a citizen of the native OS, Adobe AIR enables you to work with the full capabilities of the Clipboard through the Clipboard object. Although it's easy to think of just Cut/Copy/Paste when working with the Clipboard, the Clipboard is also used for drag-and-drop operations.

What's more, not only can you use the Clipboard to copy and paste text, but you can also work with several different data formats, such as images or a file list. As a result, you can decide which formats your application will support. The [air.]ClipboardFormats class provides the constants for the various data formats supported by AIR. Table 9-1 lists the various formats you can support.

Table 9-1	Clipboard Formats	
Format	**[air.]ClipboardFormats Constant**	*MIME Type*
Text	TEXT_FORMAT	"text/plain"
HTML	HTML_FORMAT	"text/html"
URL	.URL_FORMAT	"text/uri-list"
Bitmap	BITMAP_FORMAT	"image/x-vnd.adobe.air.bitmap"
File list	FILE_LIST_FORMAT	"application/x-vnd.adobe.air.file-list"
Rich Text Format	RICH_TEXT_FORMAT	Not available in HTML context

Data placed in the Clipboard may have multiple formats, which increases the usefulness of the Clipboard data. For example, a fragment of HTML text may be placed in the Clipboard by Dreamweaver as HTML_FORMAT and TEXT_ FORMAT. You can then decide whether to implement support for one or both of these data formats.

You can also implement your own data format for use in the Clipboard to transfer objects as references within the same AIR app or serialized copies between AIR apps. However, note that you can't paste this data into a non-AIR application. For technical details on how to implement custom data formats, visit http:// livedocs.adobe.com/flex/3/html/help.html?content=CopyAndPaste_6.html.

Adding basic cut, copy, and paste functionality

Perhaps the most basic implementation of the Clipboard is to provide services that allow you to cut, copy, and paste text-related data. To add this functionality to an AIR app, I define three functions for this purpose: editCopy(), editCut(), and editPaste().

Copy text to the Clipboard

Copying text to the Clipboard involves the following code. Here's the JavaScript version:

```
editCopy(event) {
  var str = "You're all grown up now, AIR text. You are now heading "
    + "to Clipboardopolis to make a name for yourself.";
  air.Clipboard.generalClipboard.clear();
  air.Clipboard.generalClipboard.setData(air.ClipboardFormats.TEXT_FORMAT, str);
}
```

The `generalClipboard` property is used to access the native OS Clipboard. The `clear()` method clears the Clipboard, followed by a `setData()` command that adds the contents of the `str` variable to the Clipboard, specifying its data format with the first parameter.

Here's an ActionScript version of `editCopy()` that copies the text selection (`TextRange` object) of an `mx:TextArea` to the Clipboard:

```
public function editCopy(evt:Event):void {
    var tr:TextRange = new TextRange(taEditor, true);
    var textToCopy:String = tr.text;
    Clipboard.generalClipboard.clear();
    Clipboard.generalClipboard.setData(ClipboardFormats.TEXT_FORMAT,
        textToCopy);
}
```

Cut text to the Clipboard

From a Clipboard standpoint, cutting text to the Clipboard is the same task as copying it. The only difference is cleaning up the text inside your application. For example, here's an ActionScript version that removes the text inside a selection after the selected text is copied to the Clipboard:

```
public function editCut(evt: Event):void {
    var tr:TextRange = new TextRange(taEditor, true);
    var textToCopy:String = tr.text;
    Clipboard.generalClipboard.clear();
    Clipboard.generalClipboard.setData(ClipboardFormats.TEXT_FORMAT,
        textToCopy, false);
    tr.text = "";
}
```

Paste text from the Clipboard

Retrieving text that is in the Clipboard involves first testing the format of the Clipboard contents and making sure that the format is what you expect. If it is, you can use `getData()` to retrieve the contents. In JavaScript, here's a function that gets Clipboard text and then displays the result in a message box.

```
function editPaste(event) {
if(air.Clipboard.generalClipboard.hasFormat(air.ClipboardFormats.TEXT_FORMAT)){
 var text = air.Clipboard.generalClipboard.getData(ClipboardFormats.TEXT_
            FORMAT);
alert(text);
 }
```

Here's an ActionScript example that pastes text into a text memo:

```
public function editPaste(evt: Event):void {
  var tr:TextRange = new TextRange(taEditor, true);
  if(Clipboard.generalClipboard.hasFormat(ClipboardFormats.TEXT_FORMAT)) {
    var str:String = Clipboard.generalClipboard.getData(ClipboardFormats.TEXT_
            FORMAT) as String;
    tr.text = str;
 }
```

In this example, the Clipboard contents are assigned to the `str` variable, which is then assigned to replace the current text selection (if any).

Using an alternate Clipboard method in HTML environments

The Clipboard object is great for use inside the application sandbox when using ActionScript or JavaScript. However, because of security restrictions, you can't access the AIR Clipboard object outside the sandbox.

Coming to the rescue, AIR provides a basic implementation of cut, copy, and paste if you're using `TextField` or `HTMLLoader` objects or their descendants; it does this by calling the `NativeApplication.nativeApplication` methods `cut()`, `copy()`, and `paste()`. For example:

```
editCopy() {
  air.NativeApplication.nativeApplication.copy();
}

editCut() {
  air.NativeApplication.nativeApplication.cut();
}

editPaste() {
  air.NativeApplication.nativeApplication.paste();
}
```

When one of these functions is called, the command is called for the display object receiving focus. However, the display object needs to be a `TextField` or `HTMLLoader` object (or descendant) or the command is ignored.

Copying and pasting images using ActionScript

The Clipboard can support data formats beyond ordinary text. You can also use it to support other formats, such as images. Here's an example of enabling an AIR application to support the copying and pasting of images. You still use the `Clipboard.generalClipboard.setData()` and `Clipboard.general Clipboard.getData()` methods as before. You just need to specify the different data format to the Clipboard (`ClipboardFormats.BITMAP_ FORMAT`) and convert the data into the format that the OS expects (for example, bitmap data).

Copying an image

To copy an image from your app to the Clipboard, you can't just send an instance of an `Image` object to the Clipboard using `setData()`. That's not in the expected format if you want to use the image in an image editing application, such as Photoshop. Instead, you need to convert the `Image` instance into bitmap data, which is represented by the `BitmapData` class in ActionScript. The following code takes an image (named `srcImage`) and converts it into the more portable `BitmapData` type:

```
var bitmapData:BitmapData = new BitmapData(srcImage.width, srcImage.height);
bitmapData.draw(srcImage);
```

After you've converted the image into the appropriate bitmap format, you're ready to place the image on the Clipboard:

```
Clipboard.generalClipboard.clear();

Clipboard.generalClipboard.setData(ClipboardFormats.BITMAP_FORMAT, bitmapData);
```

The `setData()` method specifies that the `bitmapData` object instance should be classified as `BITMAP_FORMAT`.

Pasting an image

When you paste an image from the Clipboard and put it into a usable format, you essentially want to reverse the process of copying an image — retrieve the bitmap data and convert it into an image that you can then display in your app.

First, you need to use `hasFormat()` to determine whether there is a bitmap to paste in the Clipboard. If there is, then you need to cast the incoming object as `BitmapData`:

```
if(Clipboard.generalClipboard.hasFormat(ClipboardFormats.BITMAP_FORMAT)) {
  var bitmapData:BitmapData =
    Clipboard.generalClipboard.getData(ClipboardFormats.BITMAP_FORMAT) as
            BitmapData;
```

You can't just add `bitmapData` to the stage for display. Instead, you need to add its bitmapped data into an `Image` instance. To do so, you need to use a `Bitmap` instance as an intermediary format:

```
var bitmap:Bitmap = new Bitmap(bitmapData);
var img:Image = new Image();
img.addChild(bitmap);
```

At this point, you just need to determine where to locate the incoming object onto the stage (the visible display area of an AIR app). After setting the x and y properties, you add `img` as a child to a `Canvas` instance:

```
img.x = stage.stageWidth/4;
img.y = stage.stageHeight/4;
canvas.addChild(img);
```

The full source code is shown in Listing 9-1.

Listing 9-1: ImagePaster.mxml

```xml
<?xml version="1.0" encoding="utf-8"?>
<mx:WindowedApplication xmlns:mx="http://www.adobe.com/2006/mxml"
    layout="absolute" width="500" height="400">
<mx:Script>
  <![CDATA[
    import mx.controls.Image;

    public function editCopy(evt:Event):void {
      var bitmapData:BitmapData = new BitmapData(srcImage.width, srcImage.
            height);
      bitmapData.draw(srcImage);
      Clipboard.generalClipboard.clear();
      Clipboard.generalClipboard.setData(ClipboardFormats.BITMAP_FORMAT,
            bitmapData, false);
    }

    public function editPaste(evt:Event):void {
      if(Clipboard.generalClipboard.hasFormat(ClipboardFormats.BITMAP_FORMAT)) {
        var bitmapData:BitmapData = Clipboard.generalClipboard.
            getData(ClipboardFormats.BITMAP_FORMAT) as BitmapData;
        var bitmap:Bitmap = new Bitmap(bitmapData);
        var img:Image = new Image();
        img.addChild(bitmap);
        img.x = stage.stageWidth/4;
        img.y = stage.stageHeight/4;
        canvas.addChild(img);
      }
```

```
      }

  ]]>
</mx:Script>
<mx:Canvas id=»canvas» width=»100%» height=»100%» backgroundColor=»#FFFFFF»>
<mx:Button x=»0» y=»0» label=»Paste» id=»btnPaste» click=»editPaste(event)» />
<mx:Image id=»srcImage» source=»door.png»   x=»40» y=»191»
               click=»editCopy(event)»/>
</mx:Canvas>
</mx:WindowedApplication>
```

Don't Be a Drag: Adding Drag-and-Drop

Just over a decade ago, drag-and-drop gestures were innovative and ground-breaking in UI design — enabling users to perform an action simply by moving their mouse rather than clicking a button or menu item. Although drag-and-drop may not seem to be cutting-edge technology these days, it has proven itself to be far more than a fad or gimmick. With its usefulness and ease of use, drag-and-drop should be something all AIR developers should consider enabling in their application.

You can implement drag-and-drop within your application, such as the ability to move display objects around on your stage. You can also add drag-and-drop support to exchange data between other native apps. Consider a typical scenario. Suppose you want to drag text from a Web page and drop it into your AIR app. When the text is dragged outside the browser, information about the text data is placed into the Clipboard, which is then used by the AIR app during the drag-and-drop process.

For a given drag-and-drop operation, you have two important actors — the drag initiator and the drop target. The *drag initiator* is the source display object selected by the user to be dragged and dropped. The *drop target* is the object on which the user drops the drag initiator. You need to explicitly enable an object to initiate a drag operation or receive a drop.

A drag-and-drop sequence occurs in three distinct actions:

- **Start drag:** A drag sequence begins when a user clicks an object and holds the mouse button down (the drag initiator) and then moves the mouse while continuing to hold the mouse button down.
- **Dragging:** While the mouse button is down, the user drags the clicked object to another part of the app, to another native application, or to the desktop.
- **Drop:** A drag-and-drop sequence ends when a user releases the mouse over a valid drop target.

Most of the AIR functionality I talk about in this book is identical whether you're creating an app using HTML, Flex, or Flash. However, here's one place where you want to implement drag-and-drop differently depending on whether you're working in an HTML, Flash, or Flex environment.

For HTML apps, you use the HTML drag-and-drop API, which is nicely integrated with the Document Object Model (DOM). Technically, you could use the AIR drag-and-drop API calls, but these are less effective than the HTML drag-and-drop API inside the HTML environment.

In Flex and Flash, you want to use the `NativeDragManager` class and work with the `nativeDragEnter`, `nativeDragOver`, and `nativeDragDrop` events when you want to perform drag-and-drop actions with other native apps.

In this section, I show you how to work with drag-and-drop in Flex and Flash, and then in HTML-based apps.

Adding drag-and-drop in Flex and Flash

A typical drag-and-drop action for any native application that works with text is the ability to drag text onto the app and paste the text into the appropriate text control. Another common action is dragging a file from the Windows Explorer or Mac OS X Finder window and dropping it into an app. I show you how to add support for these two drag-and-drop actions in a Flex-based sample AIR app named AIRWrite. (The ActionScript code would be equivalent in a Flash app.)

To make the application serve as a drop target for drag operations, you begin by adding event listeners for the NATIVE_DRAG_ENTER and NATIVE_DRAG_ DROP events. You add these inside an `init()` function that is triggered when the app is done loading:

```
addEventListener(NativeDragEvent.NATIVE_DRAG_ENTER, onDragIn);

addEventListener(NativeDragEvent.NATIVE_DRAG_DROP, onDragDrop);
```

The `onDragIn()` function serves as the event handler for the NATIVE_ DRAG_ENTER event. Its purpose is to determine the drag-and-drop actions that the app will support. For AIRWrite, you want to support text and file drop actions.

The first task is to define the `dropAction`, which could be to either copy, move, or link. The following code chooses copy:

```
NativeDragManager.dropAction = NativeDragActions.COPY;
```

Next, you need to check the format of the Clipboard data. If it is `ClipboardFormats.TEXT_FORMAT`, you want to accept the drag action:

```
if (event.clipboard.hasFormat(ClipboardFormats.TEXT_FORMAT)) {
  NativeDragManager.acceptDragDrop(this);
  }
```

You also want to check to see whether incoming data is of `ClipboardFormats.FILE_LIST_FORMAT`. If it is, you want to accept the drag action. However, because AIRWrite works as an editor only with a single text file, you want to support only one file being dragged in, not multiple ones. Here's the ActionScript code:

```
if (event.clipboard.hasFormat(ClipboardFormats.FILE_LIST_FORMAT ) ) {
        var files:Array = event.clipboard.getData(ClipboardFormats.FILE_LIST_
           FORMAT) as Array;
        if (files.length == 1) {
          NativeDragManager.acceptDragDrop(this);
        }
```

You use the `getData()` method to return the file list as an `Array` type instance. After you do that, you check the length of the array to determine whether to accept the drag action.

The `onDragDrop()` function handles the `NativeDragEvent.NATIVE_DRAG_DROP` events that are dispatched by the app. Depending on the needs of the app, you may need to handle incoming text data. If so, begin by checking to see whether the data being dropped is `ClipboardFormats.TEXT_FORMAT`. If so, you can assign the text to a `String` variable:

```
if (event.clipboard.hasFormat(ClipboardFormats.TEXT_FORMAT)) {
  var txt:String = String(event.clipboard.getData(ClipboardFormats.TEXT_FORMAT,
  ClipboardTransferMode.ORIGINAL_PREFERRED)));
}
```

You then place the contents of `txt` to the drop target in your app.

If you're instead using an `mx:TextArea` for the text editor for AIRWrite, it handles the drop action for text data for you automatically. In other words, you don't even need to deal with text data in the `onDragDrop()` if the built-in drop action suits your needs.

However, you do need to account for `ClipboardFormats.FILE_LIST_FORMAT` and open the file that is being dropped onto the target:

```
if (event.clipboard.hasFormat(ClipboardFormats.FILE_LIST_FORMAT)) {
        var array:Array = event.clipboard.getData(ClipboardFormats.FILE_
           LIST_FORMAT) as Array;
        file = File(array[0]);
        onFileSelect(event);
```

The first item in the file list array is assigned to the `file` variable. The `onFile Select()` function is called, which is AIRWrite's handler for opening text files:

```
public function onFileSelect(evt:Event):void {
    var fs:FileStream = new FileStream();
    fs.openAsync(file, FileMode.READ);
    fs.addEventListener(Event.COMPLETE, onFileRead);
    fs.addEventListener(IOErrorEvent.IO_ERROR, onIOReadError);
    isDirty = false;
    isNewFile = false;
    this.status = "";
    title = "AIRWrite - " + file.name;
    taEditor.setFocus();
}
```

See Chapter 10 for more details on how to read text files.

Figures 9-1 and 9-2 demonstrate the drag action of text data. Figures 9-3 and 9-4 show a file being dragged onto the editor.

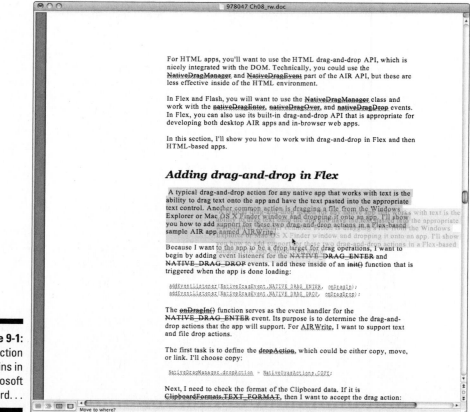

Figure 9-1:
Drag action begins in Microsoft Word. . .

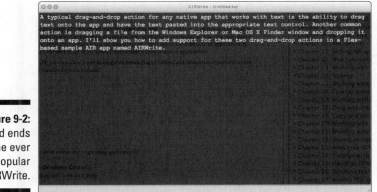

Figure 9-2:
. . .and ends
in the ever
popular
AIRWrite.

Figure 9-3:
File drag
action
begins in
the Mac OS
X Finder. . .

Figure 9-4:
. . .and
AIRWrite
opens the
file dropped
onto the
app.

Listing 9-2 provides the full source code for AIRWrite.mxml.

Listing 9-2: AIRWrite.mxml.

```
<?xml version="1.0" encoding="utf-8"?>
<mx:WindowedApplication xmlns:mx="http://www.adobe.com/2006/mxml"
                layout="absolute" width="764" height="454"
  applicationComplete="init()" styleName="sansChrome"
                backgroundGradientAlphas="[0.3, 0.3]">

  <mx:Style>
  .sansChrome { background-color:"";}
  </mx:Style>



  <mx:Script>
    <![CDATA[
      import mx.controls.Alert;
      import flash.display.NativeMenu;
      import flash.display.NativeMenuItem;
      import mx.events.*;
      import flash.desktop.NativeDragManager;
      import flash.events.NativeDragEvent;
      import flash.desktop.Clipboard;
      import flash.desktop.ClipboardFormats;
      import flash.filesystem.File;
      import flash.filesystem.FileMode;
      import flash.filesystem.FileStream;
      import mx.controls.textClasses.TextRange;

      private var file:File;

      public function onDragIn(event:NativeDragEvent):void {
        // Define drop action - copy, move, link?
        NativeDragManager.dropAction = NativeDragActions.COPY;
        // Check to see if the data is TEXT_FORMAT
        if (event.clipboard.hasFormat(ClipboardFormats.TEXT_FORMAT)) {
          NativeDragManager.acceptDragDrop(this);
          }
         else if (event.clipboard.hasFormat(ClipboardFormats.FILE_LIST_FORMAT )
              ) {
         var files:Array = event.clipboard.getData(ClipboardFormats.FILE_LIST_
             FORMAT) as Array;
         if (files.length == 1) {
           NativeDragManager.acceptDragDrop(this);
         }
         }
      }

      public function onDragDrop(event:NativeDragEvent):void {
        if (event.clipboard.hasFormat(ClipboardFormats.TEXT_FORMAT)) {
```

```
          var text:String = String(event.clipboard.getData(ClipboardFormats.
              TEXT_FORMAT,
            ClipboardTransferMode.ORIGINAL_PREFERRED));
          }
        else if (event.clipboard.hasFormat(ClipboardFormats.FILE_LIST_FORMAT))
            {
          var array:Array = event.clipboard.getData(ClipboardFormats.FILE_
              LIST_FORMAT) as Array;
          file = File(array[0]);
          onFileSelect(event);
        }
      }

  private function init():void {
    file = new File();
    addEventListener(NativeDragEvent.NATIVE_DRAG_ENTER, onDragIn);
    addEventListener(NativeDragEvent.NATIVE_DRAG_DROP, onDragDrop);
  }

  public function onFileSelect(evt:Event):void {
    var fs:FileStream = new FileStream();
    fs.openAsync(file, FileMode.READ);
    fs.addEventListener(Event.COMPLETE, onFileRead);
    fs.addEventListener(IOErrorEvent.IO_ERROR, onIOReadError);
    isDirty = false;
    isNewFile = false;
    this.status = "";
    title = "AIRWrite - " + file.name;
    taEditor.setFocus();
  }

  private function onFileRead(evt:Event):void {
    var fs:FileStream = evt.target as FileStream;
    var str:String = fs.readUTFBytes(fs.bytesAvailable);
    taEditor.text = str;
    fs.close();
  }

  private function onIOReadError(evt:Event):void {
    Alert.show("Something wacky happened. We are unable to open " + file.
        nativePath, "Error", Alert.OK, this);
  }

  private function onIOWriteError(evt:Event):void {
    Alert.show("We are really sorry, but the file cannot be saved. It's not
        our fault...really!", "Error", Alert.OK, this);
  }

]]>
```

(continued)

Listing 9-2 *(continued)*

```
  </mx:Script>

  <mx:TextArea id="taEditor" x="0" y="0" width="100%" height="100%"
               backgroundAlpha="0.8"
     fontFamily="Courier New" fontSize="14" backgroundColor="#000000"
               color="#FFFFFF" />
  <mx:Canvas x="352" y="169" width="200" height="200" backgroundColor="#982A2A"
               label="ddd">
  </mx:Canvas>
</mx:WindowedApplication>
```

If you want to perform drag-and-drop actions with images, you can program your application in much the same manner, with one difference. Although the mx:TextArea and related text controls handle the drag initiator action automatically, you need to explicitly add code to enable drag actions when working with a nontext display object such as mx:Image.

Suppose you'd like to drag an image into other native apps as well as accept new images from outside the application. Here's a very basic UI:

```
<mx:Canvas id="canvas" width="100%" height="100%">
<mx:Image id="doorImage" source="door.png"/>
</mx:Canvas>
```

To begin, you'd want to add event listeners when the app loads, just as you did in the AIRWrite example:

```
private function init():void {

  addEventListener(NativeDragEvent.NATIVE_DRAG_ENTER, onDragIn);
  addEventListener(NativeDragEvent.NATIVE_DRAG_DROP, onDragDrop);

}
```

These event handlers are designed to enable the app as a drop target. The onDragIn() function simply checks to see whether the incoming drop initiator is a bitmap. If it is, it's accepted. The code is as follows:

```
public function onDragIn(event:NativeDragEvent):void {
  NativeDragManager.dropAction = NativeDragActions.COPY;
  if (event.clipboard.hasFormat(ClipboardFormats.BITMAP_FORMAT)) {
    NativeDragManager.acceptDragDrop(this);
  }
}
```

The onDragDrop() function uses getData() to retrieve the bitmap data. A new Image instance is then created using that bitmap data and is added as a child to the Canvas object:

```
public function onDragDrop(event:NativeDragEvent):void {
  if (event.clipboard.hasFormat(ClipboardFormats.BITMAP_FORMAT)) {
    var bitmapData:BitmapData = event.clipboard.getData(ClipboardFormats.
          BITMAP_FORMAT) as BitmapData;
    var bitmap:Bitmap = new Bitmap(bitmapData);
    var img:Image = new Image();
    img.addChild(bitmap);
    img.x = event.localX;
    img.y = event.localY;
    canvas.addChild(img);
  }
}
```

Figures 9-5 and 9-6 demonstrate the drag-and-drop sequence. I start out dragging an image from Photoshop and wind up dropping it onto my AIR app.

Figure 9-5: Image dragged from Photoshop.

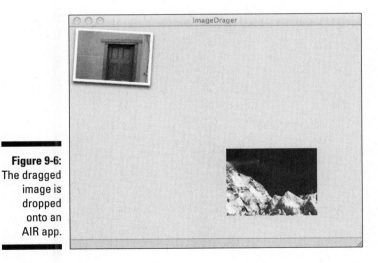

Figure 9-6: The dragged image is dropped onto an AIR app.

To enable the `mx:Image` object as a drag initiator for other native applications, you need to add a handler for the `mouseMove` event:

```
<mx:Image id="doorImage" source="door.png" mouseMove="onMouseMove(event)"/>
```

The onMouseMove() function is defined as follows:

```
private function onMouseMove(event:MouseEvent):void {
    var dragInitiator:Image=Image(event.currentTarget);
    var transferClipboard:Clipboard = new Clipboard();
    var bitmapData:BitmapData = new BitmapData(doorImage.width, doorImage.
            height);
    bitmapData.draw(doorImage);
    transferClipboard.setData(ClipboardFormats.BITMAP_FORMAT, bitmapData);
    NativeDragManager.doDrag(dragInitiator,transferClipboard,bitmapData, new
            Point(-mouseX,-mouseY));
}
```

The image being dragged is assigned to the dragInitiator instance. A Clipboard instance named transferClipboard is created, which serves as the container for the data the app will transfer. The bitmapData instance will store the bitmap image. The image is then added to transferClipboard through its setData() method. Finally, the NativeDragManager. doDrag() method is called to begin the drag and provide this data to outside applications if the mouse moves beyond the window.

Figure 9-7 shows the image being dragged in the AIR app, and Figure 9-8 shows the end result when the image is dropped into Microsoft Word.

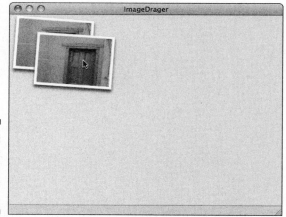

Figure 9-7:
Image dragged from the AIR app.

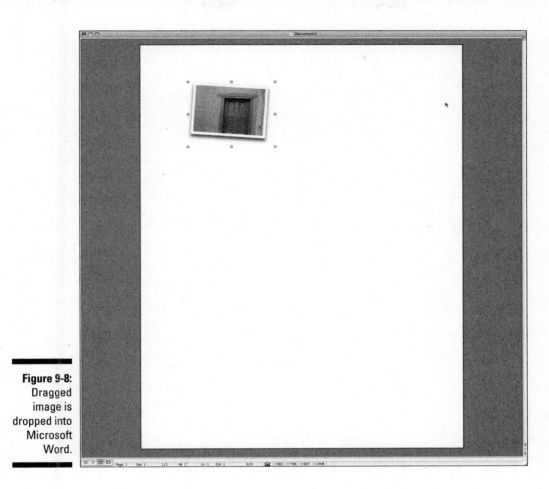

Figure 9-8:
Dragged
image is
dropped into
Microsoft
Word.

Listing 9-3 shows the full source code for this application.

Listing 9-3:   ImageMover.mxml.

```
<?xml version="1.0" encoding="utf-8"?>
<mx:WindowedApplication xmlns:mx="http://www.adobe.com/2006/mxml"
            layout="absolute"
   applicationComplete="init()">

   <mx:Script>
```

(continued)

Listing 9-3 *(continued)*

```
<![CDATA[
  //Import classes so you don't have to use full names.
  import flash.events.MouseEvent;
  import flash.desktop.NativeDragManager;
  import flash.events.NativeDragEvent;

  private function init():void {
    addEventListener(NativeDragEvent.NATIVE_DRAG_ENTER, onDragIn);
    addEventListener(NativeDragEvent.NATIVE_DRAG_DROP, onDragDrop);
  }

  public function onDragIn(event:NativeDragEvent):void {
    NativeDragManager.dropAction = NativeDragActions.MOVE;
    if (event.clipboard.hasFormat(ClipboardFormats.BITMAP_FORMAT)) {
      NativeDragManager.acceptDragDrop(this);
    }
  }

  public function onDragDrop(event:NativeDragEvent):void {
    if (event.clipboard.hasFormat(ClipboardFormats.BITMAP_FORMAT)) {
      var bitmapData:BitmapData = event.clipboard.
    getData(ClipboardFormats.BITMAP_FORMAT) as BitmapData;
      var bitmap:Bitmap = new Bitmap(bitmapData);
      var img:Image = new Image();
      img.addChild(bitmap);
      img.x = event.localX;
      img.y = event.localY;
      canvas.addChild(img);
    }
  }

  private function onMouseMove(event:MouseEvent):void {
      var dragInitiator:Image=Image(event.currentTarget)
      var transferClipboard:Clipboard = new Clipboard();
      var bitmapData:BitmapData = new BitmapData(doorImage.width,
    doorImage.height);
      bitmapData.draw(doorImage);
      transferClipboard.setData(ClipboardFormats.BITMAP_FORMAT,
    bitmapData);
      NativeDragManager.doDrag(dragInitiator,transferClipboard,bitmapDa
    ta, new Point(-mouseX,-mouseY));
  }

  ]]>
</mx:Script>

<!-- The Canvas is the drag target -->
<mx:Canvas id="canvas" width="100%" height="100%" backgroundColor="#DDDDDD"
  dragEnter="onDragEnterCanvas(event);"
```

```
        dragDrop="onDragDropCanvas(event);">

        <!-- The image is the drag initiator. -->
        <mx:Image id="doorImage" source="door.png" mouseMove="onMouseMove(event
            );"/>

    </mx:Canvas>

</mx:WindowedApplication>
```

Adding drag-and-drop functionality in HTML apps

Adobe AIR enables you to take advantage of built-in support for drag-and-drop of key elements within the WebKit environment when creating HTML apps. These elements include text, images, and URLs. However, you can also declare other elements, such as div elements, as draggable by setting the -webkit-user-drag CSS property to element. You still need to determine how you want to use the draggable elements in the drop target, though.

In this section's example, I show you how to make various elements draggable for both inside and outside the AIR app. I then show you how to create a drop zone for working with drag-and-drop data. The HTML file that I start the example with is as follows:

```
<html>
<head>
<title>DragMeDropMe</title>

<style>

  #droptarget {
    float:right;
    background-color: #999999;
    margin: 10px;
    padding: 10px;
    height: 500px;
    width: 300px;
    color: white;
  }

  #draginit-text {
    font-size: 18pt;
  }
```

```
  #draginit-div {
    width: 300px;
    height: 200px;
    text-align:center;
    color: white;
    background-color: #888888;
    border: 1pt solid black;
  }



</style>

<script type=»text/javascript» src=»AIRAliases.js»></
        script>
<script type=»text/javascript»>

function init() {
  // do something, anything
}

</script>
</head>

<body onload=»init()»>

<div id=»droptarget»>Drop Target Zone</div>

<p>
  <span id=»draginit-text»>
    <a href=»http://www.dummies.com»>Draggable text.</a></
        span>
</p>

<img id=»doorImg» alt=»Close the door» src=»door.png»/>


<div id=»draginit-div»>Draggable div</div>


</div>

</body>
</html>
```

The following HTML elements will be enabled as draggable elements: drag
init-text, draginit-div, and doorImg. The droptarget div will be
enabled to serve as a drop target.

Creating draggable elements

The draginit-text and doorImage elements are already enabled for drag-and-drop; however, you need to prepare the draginit-div for this purpose. To do so, add the following CSS rule to its style attribute:

```
<div id="draginit-div" style="-webkit-user-
        drag:element;">Draggable div</div>
```

The ondrag event is the key event that you need to account for. It is dispatched when a user clicks an element and begins to drag. Given that, you're now ready to add ondragstart attributes to the three elements:

```
<p>
  <span id="draginit-text" ondragstart="onDragStartText
        (event);">
    <a href="http://www.dummies.com">Draggable text.</a></
        span>
</p>

<img id="doorImg" alt="Close the door" src="door.png"
        style="-webkit-user-drag:element;" ondragstart=
        "onDragStartImg(event)"/>


<div id="draginit-div" style="-webkit-user-drag:element;"
        ondragstart="onDragStartDiv(event)">Draggable
        div</div>
```

The handler function for the draginit-text element is as follows:

```
function onDragStartText(event) {
  // event.dataTransfer object contains info on the data
        being dragged

  // Determines the "effect" on the data being dragged -
        copied, moved, linked
  // In this case, we're flexible and will let the drag
        target decide
  event.dataTransfer.effectAllowed = "copy";

  // Adds data in one or more formats as specified by the
        mimeType parameter
  event.dataTransfer.setData("text/plain", "Imagine a
        world without drag and drop. What a horrible
        world that would be." );
  event.dataTransfer.setData("text/uri-list", "http://www.
        worldsansdraganddrop.com" );
}
```

The `event.dataTransfer` object is the focus of the drag-and-drop code in the `ondrag` handler. It contains the information on the data being dragged. You first set the `effectAllowed` property to allow for copying of the data from the source to the drop target. The `setData()` method determines the data and its format that you want to transfer using the drag-and-drop operation. Instead of using the `air.ClipboardOperations` constants that you used with the Clipboard examples earlier in the chapter, you need to specify the format by its MIME type. (See Table 9-1 at the start of the chapter for a listing of the MIME types.) You can specify one or more formats, depending on the data you're working with. Because the span contains a link, this example uses both plain text and a URL list.

Here's the `ondrag` handler for the `draginit-div` element:

```
function onDragStartDiv(event) {
   event.dataTransfer.effectAllowed = "copy";
   event.dataTransfer.setData("text/plain", "Divs are
           people, too!");

}
```

The final `ondrag` handler is used for the `doorImg` element. For this example, I demonstrate how to use `setDragImage()`, which enables you to set an image that is displayed when the element is being dragged. The example then uses `setData()` to set the image as the data to be copied:

```
var dragImage = new Image();

dragImage.src = "plaque.png";

function onDragStartImg( event ) {
   event.dataTransfer.effectAllowed = "copy";

   event.dataTransfer.setDragImage( dragImage, 0, 0 );

   var ddImage = document.getElementById("doorImg");
   event.dataTransfer.setData("image/x-vnd.adobe.air.
           bitmap", ddImage);
   var ddFile = new air.File(ddImage.src);
   event.dataTransfer.setData("text/plain", "Close the door
           on your way out");
   event.dataTransfer.setData("application/x-vnd.adobe.air.
           file-list", new Array(ddFile));

}
```

The example also specifies plain text and a file list as alternative formats that will be supported by the app for a drag-and-drop operation.

These three drag initiator elements are now draggable either inside or outside the application. Figure 9-9 shows the elements of the AIR app. For example, if you drag the draggable text, the text and URL are displayed as you move your mouse (see Figure 9-10). Dropping the text into the Mac OS X TextEdit app inserts the text into the current file (see Figure 9-11).

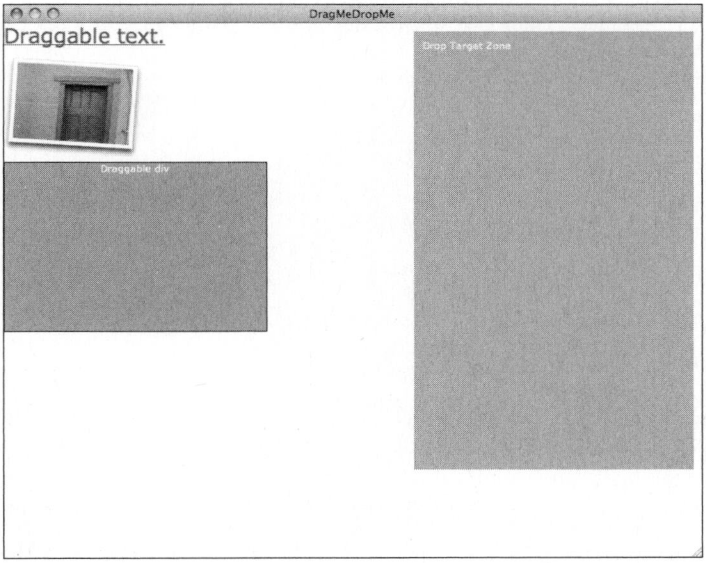

Figure 9-9:
DragMe
DropMe
app.

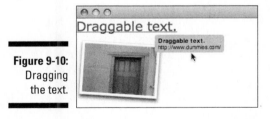

Figure 9-10:
Dragging
the text.

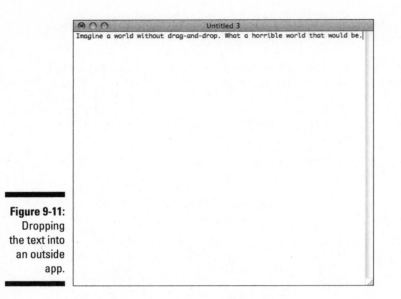

Enabling a drop target

For this sample application, I also want to show you how to create a drop target. I use the `droptarget div` for this great and mighty purpose. To enable the `div` as a drop target, you need to add handlers for the three drop target events:

✔ `ondragenter` dispatches when the mouse enters the element.

✔ `ondragover` is fired continuously while mouse hovers over the element.

Be careful with this event if you have an `ondragenter` event handler, because `ondragover` will quickly override changes you make in that handler unless you disable it with `event.preventDefault()`. Alternatively, you can simply assign the same handler to both events.

✔ `ondrop` is dispatched when the user lifts the mouse button to drop the element on the drop target.

Here's the updated `div` declaration with the event attributes assigned (note that drag event code is bolded):

```
<div id="droptarget" ondragenter="onDragEnter(event);"
  ondragover="onDragOver(event);"
            ondrop="onDrop(event)">Drop Target Zone</div>
```

The `onDragEnter()` function, which follows, indicates that the `div` element will support copy drag-and-drop operations:

```
function onDragEnter(event) {
  event.dataTransfer.dropEffect = "copy";
}
```

The `onDragOver()` function disables the default `ondragover` event:

```
function onDragOver(event) {
  event.preventDefault();
}
```

The `onDrop` event handler is where all the action is for the drop target. For demo purposes, I use `getData()` to retrieve any text, URL, and image data:

```
// Dispatched when the user lifts the mouse button to drop
// the element on the drop target.
function onDrop(event) {
  // Gets the data as specified by the specified mimeType
  var dropText = event.dataTransfer.getData("text/plain");
  var dropUrl = event.dataTransfer.getData("text/uri-
        list");
  var dropImg = event.dataTransfer.getData("image/x-vnd.
        adobe.air.bitmap");
  var targetDiv = document.getElementById('droptarget');
  targetDiv.innerHTML = "<p>Text:" + dropText +  "</p>" +
               "<p>URL:" + dropUrl +  "</p>";

  if ((event.dataTransfer.types.toString()).search("image/
        x-vnd.adobe.air.bitmap") > -1 ) {
    targetDiv.appendChild( dropImg);
  }
}
```

The text and URL data is added as text inside the `div` using `innerHTML`. For a real application, you would obviously want to check to see whether these strings were null. However, I do use the `types` property to check whether bitmap data is being dragged. If its MIME type is found, the image is added as a child element to the `div`.

Figure 9-12 shows the draggable text being dragged over the `droptarget` `div`. Because you specified `copy` as the `dropEffect`, the copy cursor is displayed while the mouse is on top of the `div`. After the text is dropped onto the div, the text and URL info are displayed as text (see Figure 9-13).

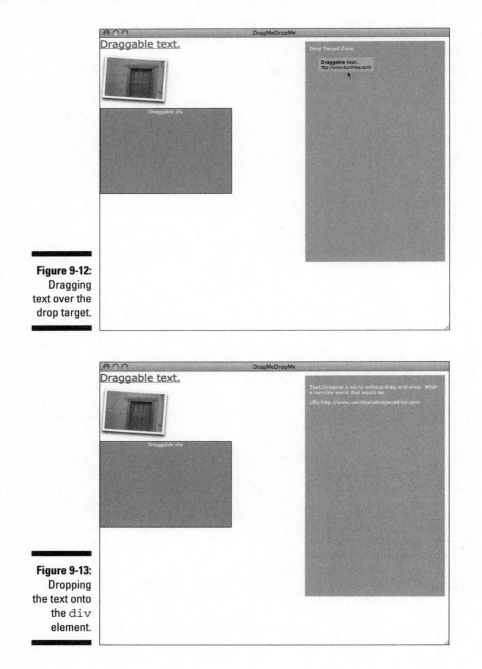

Figure 9-12:
Dragging text over the drop target.

Figure 9-13:
Dropping the text onto the `div` element.

Listing 9-4 displays the full source code for the sample app.

Listing 9-4:   dragmedropme.html.

```html
<html>
<head>
<title>DragMeDropMe</title>

<style>

  #droptarget {
    float:right;
    background-color: #999999;
    margin: 10px;
    padding: 10px;
    height: 500px;
    width: 300px;
    color: white;
  }

  #draginit-text {
    font-size: 18pt;
  }

  #draginit-div {
    width: 300px;
    height: 200px;
    text-align:center;
    color: white;
    background-color: #888888;
    border: 1pt solid black;
  }

</style>

<script type="text/javascript" src="AIRAliases.js"></script>
<script type="text/javascript">

var dragImage;

// Called when app loads
function init() {
  dragImage = new Image();
  dragImage.src = "plaque.png";
}

// ****** Drag initiator event handlers  ******
```

(continued)

Listing 9-4 *(continued)*

```
// Dispatched when the user begins a drag action on the text span
// If you want to disable, then you could use event.preventDefault();
function onDragStartText(event) {
  // event.dataTransfer object contains info on the data being dragged

  // Determines the "effect" on the data being dragged - copied, moved, linked
  // In this case, we're flexible and will let the drag target decide
  event.dataTransfer.effectAllowed = "copy";

  // Adds data in one or more formats as specified by the mimeType parameter
  event.dataTransfer.setData("text/plain", "Imagine a world without drag-and-
             drop. What a horrible world that would be." );
  event.dataTransfer.setData("text/uri-list", "http://www.worldsansdraganddrop.
             com" );
}

// Dispatched when user drags the img
function onDragStartImg( event ) {
  event.dataTransfer.effectAllowed = "copy";
  // Set the drag image
  event.dataTransfer.setDragImage( dragImage, 0, 0 );

  var ddImage = document.getElementById("doorImg");
  event.dataTransfer.setData("image/x-vnd.adobe.air.bitmap", ddImage);
  var ddFile = new air.File(ddImage.src);
  event.dataTransfer.setData("text/plain", "Close the door on your way out");
  event.dataTransfer.setData("application/x-vnd.adobe.air.file-list", new
             Array(ddFile));

}

// Dispatched when users drag the div
function onDragStartDiv( event ) {
  event.dataTransfer.effectAllowed = "copy";
  event.dataTransfer.setData("text/html", "<div id=\"draginit-div\" style=\"-
             webkit-user-drag:element;\" " +
    "ondragstart=\"onDragStartDiv(event)\">Draggable div</div>");
  event.dataTransfer.setData("text/plain", "Divs are people too!");
}

// ***** Drop target event handlers *****

// Dispatched when the mouse enters the element
function onDragEnter(event) {
  // Specifies the copy effect when dropped
  event.dataTransfer.dropEffect = "copy";
//  event.preventDefault();
 }
```

```
// Fires continously while mouse is over the element
// Be careful if you have onDragEnter, since it will quickly
// override changes you make in that handler. Therefore,
// it is a good idea to prevent default handling from taking place
function onDragOver(event) {
  event.preventDefault();
}


// Dispatched when the user lifts the mouse button to drop the
// element on the drop target.
function onDrop(event) {
  s// Gets the data as specified by the specified mimeType
  var dropText = event.dataTransfer.getData("text/plain");
  var dropUrl = event.dataTransfer.getData("text/uri-list");
  var dropImg = event.dataTransfer.getData("image/x-vnd.adobe.air.bitmap");
  var targetDiv = document.getElementById('droptarget');
  targetDiv.innerHTML = "<p>Text:" + dropText +  "</p>" +
                "<p>URL:" + dropUrl +  "</p>";

  if ((event.dataTransfer.types.toString()).search("image/x-vnd.adobe.air.
          bitmap") > -1 ) {
    targetDiv.appendChild( dropImg);
  }
}

</script>
</head>

<body onload="init()">

<div id="droptarget" ondragenter="onDragEnter(event);" ondragover="onDragOver(ev
            ent);"
  ondrop="onDrop(event)">Drop Target Zone</div>

<p>
  <span id=»draginit-text» ondragstart=»onDragStartText(event);»>
    <a href=»http://www.dummies.com»>Draggable text.</a></span>
</p>

<img id=»doorImg» alt=»Close the door» src=»door.png» style=»-webkit-user-
            drag:element;» ondragstart=»onDragStartImg(event)»/>


<div id=»draginit-div» style=»-webkit-user-drag:element;» ondragstart=»onDragSta
            rtDiv(event)»>Draggable div</div>

</body>
</html>
```

Chapter 10

A New Developer Freedom: Working with the Local File System

---

*O*ne of the basic operations of a desktop application is the ability to read and write files and work with the local file system. Adobe AIR opens this functionality to HTML, Flex, and Flash developers. And although you can still access files over the Internet, the ability to work with local files gives you as an application developer considerable flexibility.

In this chapter, I introduce you to how to work with files and directories in your application. You find out how to perform basic file operations, display native OS open and save dialog boxes, and read and write data to a file. I close out the chapter by walking you through the creation of a text editor.

Identifying the File Classes

When you work with native files, you work primarily with three file-related classes:

✔ `File` represents a file or a directory on the local file system. You use a `File` instance for basic file operations (such as copy and delete) and directory-related tasks (such as list files, create directory, and get directory path).

✔ `FileStream` is used for reading and writing to files.

✔ `FileMode` is used by `FileStream` to determine the permissions available during reading and writing operations.

In Flex and Flash, these classes are contained in the `flash.filesystem` package.

Working with Files and Directories

Whether you're working with files or directories, you use a `File` instance to point to a file or directory. As I mention previously in this chapter, the `File` object is used for basic file or directory operations. It doesn't muddy its hands working with the content or data of a file. The `FileStream` object acts on a `File` instance to do that grunt work.

Working with paths

The `File` object can work with an OS-specific path or a URL to point to a directory or file.

Native paths

The `nativePath` property is used for getting or setting a native path. Its path is based on the current running OS. For example, suppose a `File` object points to a user's documents directory. On Windows, the nativePath would be something like `C:\Documents and Settings\`*userName*`\my Documents`. On Mac, it would be `Users\`*userName*`\Documents`.

URLs

The `url` property provides a URL-based way to point to a file. Once again, the formatting of the path is dependent on the current OS. For example, pointing to the user's documents directory, the `url` property would be something like `file:///c:/Documents%20and%20Settings/`*userName*`/My%20Documents` on Windows and `file:///Users/`*userName*`/Documents`.

The `url` property returns the path as in a URI-encoded form. As a result, spaces are substituted with `%20`.

File URLs

The file:/// scheme is the standard URL scheme used for referencing local files. (Yes, that's three forward slashes, not the standard two.)

In addition to file:///, there are two additional schemes that you can use with the url property. These are discussed below.

Application root directory URL

The app: scheme points to the root directory of the application. You can then reference files and directories relative to this folder. For example, to point to an icon image in an icons subdirectory of the root folder, you can use app:/icons/128.png.

Notice that the directory separators of nativePath are based on the native OS: \ for Windows and / for Mac. However, the url property (which is discussed next in the "Application storage directory" section) always uses the / slash.

Application storage directory

The app-storage: scheme points to the application storage directory for your app. The application storage directory is a unique path that the AIR runtime automatically defines for every user of your app. You can use this location to store preferences, user settings, or other files.

On Windows, the path is as follows:

```
C:\Documents and Settings\userName\Application Data\
        applicationID.publisherID\Local Store
```

Here's the path on the Mac:

```
Users/userName/Library/Preferences/applicationID.
        publisherID/Local Store
```

The *applicationID* and *publisherID* values are defined in the application descriptor file. The application ID is defined in the application descriptor file, and is typically structured like this: com.dummies.PrefManager. The publisher ID, on the other hand, is obtained from the certificate used to sign the AIR installation package. You can actually retrieve the publisher ID at runtime through the [air.]NativeApplication.nativeApplication.publisherID property.

When you're testing your app before deployment, you usually don't have a publisher ID defined yet, so the *publisherID* portion of the application storage path is left blank. For example, I'm working with the following path in testing my PrefManager app:

```
Users/rich/Library/Preferences/com.dummies.PrefManager/
        Local Store
```

Pointing to a directory

You can use the `File` object to point to several pre-defined directories, each of which is accessed as properties of the `File` object. For example, to point to the application directory, use the following in JavaScript:

```
var dir = air.File.applicationDirectory;
```

In ActionScript, you use:

```
private var dir:File = File.applicationDirectory;
```

You can then access a subdirectory or file by using the `resolvePath()` method. For example, to point to an `assets` subdirectory:

```
dir = dir.resolvePath("assets");
```

If you want to access a nested subdirectory, be sure to use a forward slash. For example:

```
dir = dir.resolvePath("assets/css");
```

You can also use a shortcut syntax to put all the code in one line. Here's the JavaScript version:

```
var dir = air.File.applicationDirectory.
        resolvePath("assets/css");
```

You can use the `File` object to point to several other predefined directories that are shown in Table 10-1.

Table 10-1	Predefined File System Directories		
Directory	**File Object Property/ Method**	**Windows Path**	**Mac OS X Path**
Application directory	`[air.]File. application Directory`		

Directory	File Object Property/ Method	Windows Path	Mac OS X Path
Application storage	`[air.]File. application Storage Directory`	`C:\ Documents and Settings\ userName\ Application Data\appli cationID. publish erID\Local Store`	`Users/user Name/Library/ Preferences/ applicationID. publisherID/ Local Store`
User's home directory	`[air.]File. user Directory`	`C:\ Documents and Settings\ userName`	`Users/userName`
User's document directory	`[air.]File. documents Directory`	`C:\ Documents and Settings\ userName\My Documents`	`Users/userName/ Documents`
User's desktop directory	`[air.]File. desktop Directory`	`C:\ Documents and Settings\ userName\ Desktop`	`Users/userName/ Desktop`
File system root	`[air.]File. getRootDir ectories()`	Returns `C:` and all other root volumes	Returns the `/` root directory
Temporary directory	`[air.]File. create TempDirec tory();`	`C:\ Documents and Settings\ rich\Local Settings\ Temp\temp DirName`	`/private/var/ tmp/folders. 501/Temporary Items/temp DirName`

In addition to the predefined directories, you can access any arbitrary directory on the file system through the [air.]File.nativePath property. For example, to access a C:\Air directory on a Windows machine in JavaScript:

```
var dir = new air.File();
dir.nativePath = "C:\\Air\";
```

You can use the url property as well. Here's an ActionScript example on a Mac:

```
var dir:File = new File();
var urlString:String = "file:///Users/rich/Books";
dir.url = urlString;
```

Pointing to a file

Big surprise, but the File object also is used to point to specific files.

Using the resolvePath() method, you can point to a specific file. Here's a JavaScript example, pointing to a prefs.xml file in the application storage directory:

```
var prefFile = File.applicationStorageDirectory;
prefFile = prefFile.resolvePath("prefs.xml");
```

Or, in ActionScript:

```
public var prefFile:File = File.
        applicationStorageDirectory;

prefFile = prefFile.resolvePath("prefs.xml");
```

You can also use the nativePath and url properties to point to a specific file. Here's a JavaScript example for a Windows machine:

```
var myFile = new air.File();
myFile.nativePath = "C:\\Air\\text.txt";
```

Here's a second JavaScript example using the url property, which is preferable for working across operating systems:

```
var myFile = new air.File();
myUrl = "file:///C:/Air/text.txt";
myFile.url = myUrl;
```

As a shortcut, you can also pass a path as a parameter to the `File()` constructor function. The following ActionScript example uses both a Windows native path and URL string:

```
var file1:File = new File("C"\\Books\\dummies_toc.txt");
var file2Path:String = "file:///C:/Books/dummies_toc2.
        txt");
var file2:File = new File(file2Path);
```

Allowing Users to Browse For a Directory and Files

The `File` object builds in the functionality to allow users to browse and select a directory, file, or set of files using native OS dialog boxes.

Displaying a Choose Directory dialog box

If you'd like to allow users to browse and pick a directory from inside your application, use the `File.browseForDirectory()` method. When you use this method in conjunction with an `Event.SELECT` event handler, you can capture the directory selected by the user and do something with it.

For example, the following JavaScript snippet displays a Select Directory dialog box. The user then selects the desired directory and clicks OK (or Choose).The directory selected is automatically saved in the `nativePath` and `url` properties. The `selectDirectory()` event handler then does something with the user's path. Here's the code:

```
var folder = air.File.userDirectory;

function showDirBrowser() {
  folder.addEventListener(air.Event.SELECT,
        selectDirectory);
  folder.browseForDirectory("Select your coolest folder");
}

function selectDirectory(evt) {
  var userDreamFolder = folder.nativePath;
  // do something cool here with that cool folder
}
```

Or, in ActionScript:

```
public var folder:File = File.userDirectory;

public function showDirBrowser():void {
    folder.addEventListener(Event.SELECT, selectDirectory);
    folder.browseForDirectory("Select your coolest folder");
}

public function selectDirectory(evt:Event):void {
    var userDreamFolder:String = folder.nativePath;
    // do something cool here with that cool folder

}
```

Figures 10-1 and 10-2 show the dialog box displayed on Windows and Mac, respectively.

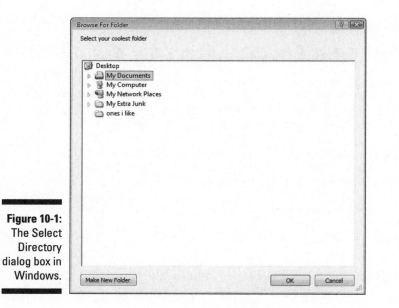

Figure 10-1:
The Select Directory dialog box in Windows.

Displaying a File Open and File Save dialog box

The ubiquitous File Open dialog box can be displayed using the `File.browseForOpen()` method. Its functionality is quite similar to `File.browseForDirectory()`, except you can also define an optional file filter array to specify the types of files you'd like to allow to be selected and opened.

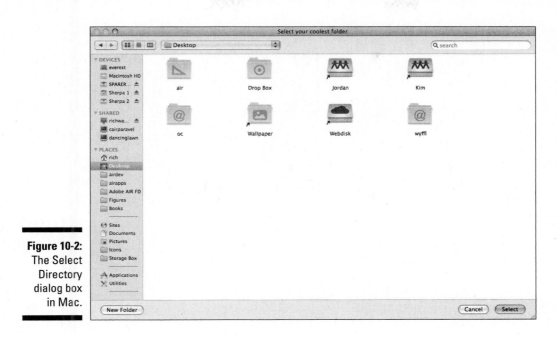

Figure 10-2:
The Select Directory dialog box in Mac.

You define a listener to `Event.SELECT` to do something with the file after the user has selected it. Here's sample JavaScript code:

```
var file = air.File.documentsDirectory;

function fileOpen() {
  var filter:FileFilter = new air.FileFilter("Documents",
        "*.txt;*.html;*.pdf;*.doc;");
  file.addEventListener(air.Event.SELECT,
        fileOpenHandler);
  file.browseForOpen("Select your most awesomest file",
        [filter] );
}

function fileOpenHandler(evt) {
  var openedFile = file.nativePath;
  // do something. anything.
}
```

Or, if you prefer ActionScript, use:

```
public var file:File = File.documentsDirectory;

public function fileOpen():void {
  var filter:FileFilter = new FileFilter("Documents",
        "*.txt;*.html;*.pdf;*.doc;");
  file.addEventListener(Event.SELECT, fileOpenHandler);
```

```
      file.browseForOpen("Select your most awesomest file",
           [filter] );
   }

   public function fileOpenHandler(evt:Event):void {
      var openedFile:String = file.nativePath;
   }
```

Figure 10-3 shows the dialog box in Windows.

Figure 10-3:
File Open
dialog box in
Windows.

You can also use the `File.browseForSave()` method to display a File Save dialog box. It works the same basic way, although no `FileFilter` parameter is available for this method. Here's a JavaScript snippet:

```
var file = air.File.documentsDirectory;

function fileSave() {
   file.addEventListener(air.Event.SELECT,
           fileSaveHandler);
   file.browseForOpen("Save your most precious file now! Or
           else..." );
}

function fileSaveHandler(evt) {
   var savedFile = file.nativePath;
   // I will do something with this var now. Really!
}
```

Displaying a Select Multiple Files dialog box

You may have occasion to allow the user to select multiple files from a dialog box for processing. Rather than call `File.browseForOpen()` multiple times, the friendlier option is to use `File.browseForOpenMultiple()`. This method allows users to select multiple files in the dialog box and returns the selection as an array of filenames.

As with `browseForOpen()`, you can specify an optional `[air.]` `FileFilter` instance to define the types of files you'd like to allow to be selected and opened.

The following JavaScript code attaches an event listener to `air.` `FileListEvent.SELECT_MULTIPLE` and then displays the Select Multiple Files dialog box. When the user selects one or more files, `fileOpenList-Handler()` is called. Here's the code:

```
var file = air.File.documentsDirectory;

function fileOpenFileList() {
  file.addEventListener(air.FileListEvent.SELECT_MULTIPLE,
          fileOpenListHandler);
  file.browseForOpenMultiple("Select your most awesomest
          files");
}


    function fileOpenListHandler(evt) {
      var str = "";
      for (var i=0;i<evt.files.length; i++) {
        str += evt.files[i].nativePath + "\n";
      }
      alert(str);
    }
```

The ActionScript code that follows performs the same basic process, except that the files selected are assigned to the `text` property of an `mx:TextArea` element:

```
public var file:File = File.documentsDirectory;

public function fileOpenFileList():void {
  file.addEventListener(FileListEvent.SELECT_MULTIPLE,
          fileOpenListHandler);
  file.browseForOpenMultiple("Select your most awesomest
          files");
```

```
  }
  public function fileOpenListHandler(evt:FileListEvent):vo
          id {
    var str:String = "";
    for (var i:uint = 0; i < evt.files.length; i++) {
      str += evt.files[i].nativePath + "\n";
    }
    taFavoriteList.text = str;
  }
```

Figure 10-4 shows the `mx:TextArea` control that displays filenames returned from `browseForOpenMultiple()`.

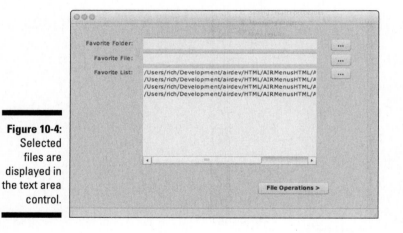

Figure 10-4:
Selected
files are
displayed in
the text area
control.

Listing 10-1 provides the Flex source code of a sample app that illustrates how to use `browseForDirectory()`, `browseForOpen()`, and `browse-ForOpenMultiple()`. The user selection for a dialog box is displayed in a corresponding text control.

Listing 10-1:   Filer.mxml

```
<?xml version="1.0" encoding="utf-8"?>
<mx:WindowedApplication xmlns:mx="http://www.adobe.
          com/2006/mxml" layout="absolute" height="332"
          width="540" alpha="0.67">
<mx:Script>
  <![CDATA[

    public var folder:File = File.userDirectory;
    public var file:File = File.documentsDirectory;

    public function showDirBrowser():void {
```

```
        folder = new File();
        folder.addEventListener(Event.SELECT,
            selectDirectory);
        folder.browseForDirectory("Select your coolest
            folder");
    }

  public function selectDirectory(evt:Event):void {
    tiFavoriteFolder.text = folder.nativePath;
  }

  public function fileOpen():void {
      var filter:FileFilter = new FileFilter("Documents",
          "*.txt;*.html;*.pdf;*.doc;");
      file.addEventListener(Event.SELECT,
          fileOpenHandler);
      file.browseForOpen("Select your most awesomest
          file", [filter] );
  }

  public function fileOpenHandler(evt:Event):void {
    tiFavoriteFile.text = file.nativePath;
  }

  public function fileOpenFileList():void {
      file.addEventListener(FileListEvent.SELECT_MULTIPLE,
          fileOpenListHandler);
      file.browseForOpenMultiple("Select your most
          awesomest files");
  }

  public function fileOpenListHandler(evt:FileListEvent)
          :void {
    var str:String = "";
    for (var i:uint = 0; i < evt.files.length; i++) {
      str += evt.files[i].nativePath + "\n";
    }
    taFavoriteList.text = str;
  }
  ]]>
</mx:Script>
  <mx:Form x="10" y="10" width="464" height="284">
    <mx:FormItem label="Favorite Folder:">
      <mx:TextInput width="320" id="tiFavoriteFolder"
          editable="false" enabled="true"/>
    </mx:FormItem>
    <mx:FormItem label="Favorite File:">
      <mx:TextInput width="320" id="tiFavoriteFile"
          editable="false" enabled="true"/>
    </mx:FormItem>
    <mx:FormItem label="Favorite List:">
```

(continued)

Listing 10-1 *(continued)*

```
        <mx:TextArea id="taFavoriteList" width="320"
            height="187" wordWrap="false" editable="false"
            enabled="true"/>
    </mx:FormItem>
  </mx:Form>
  <mx:Button x="477" y="56" label="..." width="37"
            id="btnOpenFile" click="fileOpen()"/>
  <mx:Button x="477" y="82" label="..."
            width="37" id="btnOpenFileList"
            click="fileOpenFileList()"/>
  <mx:Button label="..." width="37" id="btnSelectFolder"
            click="showDirBrowser()" x="477" y="28"/>
</mx:WindowedApplication>
```

Performing Directory and File Operations

There are several file utility functions that you can perform inside your
Adobe AIR application using the File object. You can use these when you
need, for example, to create a directory, create a temporary file or directory,
or copy a file.

Creating a directory

When you want to create a new directory, use the resolvePath() method
to navigate to the location in which you want the directory to be; then,
follow that up with a call to File.createDirectory(). The File.create
Directory() method first checks to see whether that directory already
exists. If not, then it creates the directory. The following code snippet creates
a wallpaper subdirectory inside the desktop folder. Here's the JavaScript:

```
var folder= air.File.desktopDirectory.
            resolvePath("wallpaper");
folder.createDirectory();
```

Or, in ActionScript:

```
var folder:File = File.desktopDirectory.
            resolvePath("wallpaper");
folder.createDirectory();
```

Creating a temporary directory or file

It's a common need, when you're working with local files and storage, to have a temporary place to store some data. Rather than come up with your own routine to identify and create a unique directory name, you can use `File.createTempDirectory()`. This method creates a unique folder inside the main temporary directory of the operating system. For JavaScript, you use:

```
var tmp = air.File.createTempDirectory();
```

ActionScript looks like this:

```
var tmp:File = File.createTempDirectory();
```

What's more, if you want to create a temporary file, you can use the `File.createTempFile()` method. When called, AIR returns a pointer to a uniquely named temporary file in the temporary directory of the OS. For example:

```
var tmpFile = air.File.createTempFile();
alert(tmpFile.name);
```

AIR does *not* remove the directory automatically when your app closes. Therefore, be sure to add a clean-up routine to execute when the app closes to remove any temporary directories and files that you create.

Copying and moving directories and files

You can synchronously copy a file or the entire contents of one directory to another using the `File.copyTo()` method. Consider the following JavaScript example to see how this works for directories:

```
var sourceFolder = air.File.desktopDirectory.resolvePath("wallpaper");
var targetFolder = air.File.desktopDirectory.resolvePath("son of wallpaper");
sourceFolder.copyTo(targetFolder);
```

In this code, the `wallpaper` directory is copied to a new directory named `son of wallpaper` directory inside of the system's desktop folder.

By default, if the target directory already exists, the operation will fail. However, the `copyTo()` method contains an optional `overwrite` parameter that, if true, will first delete the target directory first and create a new one for this usage.

The following ActionScript sets the `overwrite` parameter to `true`:

```
var sourceFolder:File = File.desktopDirectory.resolvePath("wallpaper");
var targetFolder:File = File.desktopDirectory.resolvePath("son of wallpaper");

sourceFolder.copyTo(targetFolder, true);
```

If you'd prefer to move the directory to a different location rather than copy its contents, use `File.moveTo()`. It takes the same parameters as `copyTo()` but performs a move routine rather than a copy.

Files are synchronously copied and moved in the exact same way. The following JavaScript code copies `text1.txt` to a new file named `text2.txt`:

```
var sourceFile = air.File.desktopDirectory.resolvePath("wallpaper/text1.txt");
var targetFile = air.File.desktopDirectory.resolvePath("wallpaper/text2.txt");
sourceFile.copyTo(targetFile);
```

Both of these methods also have asynchronous versions — `copyToAsync()` and `moveToAsync()` — when you prefer to perform these operations asynchronously. After these operations are completed, they dispatch a `complete` Event (or an `ioError` event if the operation failed). You can add event listeners to these events for processing after the operation completes or fails. Here's an example of copying a directory asynchronously. First, for HTML developers, here is the JavaScript:

```
function createBackupCopy() {

  var sourceFolder = air.File.applicationDirectory.
        resolvePath("Data");
  var targetFolder = air.File.applicationDirectory.
        resolvePath("Data_backup_1");

  sourceFolder.addEventListener(air.Event.COMPLETE,
        onCopyComplete);
  sourceFolder.addEventListener(air.IOErrorEvent.IO_ERROR,
        onCopyError);
  sourceFolder.copyToAsync(targetFolder);

}

function onCopyComplete(evt) {
  alert("Wow, our backup operation actually worked. Is
        that cool or what?");
 }

function onCopyError(evt) {
  alert("Something really, really bad just happened.");
}
```

And, for Flex and Flash developers, here's the ActionScript:

```
import mx.controls.Alert;

    public function createBackupCopy():void {
       var sourceFolder:File = File.applicationDirectory.
          resolvePath("Data");
       var targetFolder:File = File.applicationDirectory.
          resolvePath("Data_backup_01");

       sourceFolder.addEventListener(Event.COMPLETE,
          onCopyComplete);
       sourceFolder.addEventListener(IOErrorEvent.
          IO_ERROR, onCopyError);
       sourceFolder.copyToAsync(targetFolder);
    }

    public function onCopyComplete(evt:Event):void {
       Alert.show("Wow, our backup operation actually
          worked. Is that cool or what?");
    }

    public function onCopyError(evt:IOErrorEvent):void {
       Alert.show("Something really, really bad just
          happened.");
    }
```

Deleting and moving to trash

If you want to delete a file or directory or else just move it to the trash (recycle bin), use one of the following methods:

- ✔ `File.moveToTrash()`
- ✔ `File.moveToTrashAsync()`
- ✔ `File.deleteFile()`
- ✔ `File.deleteFileAsync()`

The following snippet sends a file to the trash:

```
var doomedFile = air.File.applicationStorageDirectory.
         resolvePath("pref.xml");
doomedFile.moveToTrash();
```

If you're using the asynchronous versions of these methods, you can assign a handler to the `complete` event when the process has been finished.

Reading and Writing to Files

After you point to a file using the `File` object, you probably want to do something with it, such as adding or saving data inside it. That's where the `FileStream` object comes in. It takes a `File` instance you've already initialized and allows you to read from or write to it.

Whether you read or write to a file stream, you first need to open it using either the `open()` or `openAsync()` method:

```
fileStream.open(file, fileMode);
fileStream.openAsync(file, fileMode);
```

Both methods have a `fileMode` parameter that specifies the capabilities of the `FileStream` object. There are four possible file modes:

- ✔ `[air.]FileMode.READ` specifies that the file is open for reading only.

- ✔ `[air.]FileMode.WRITE` indicates that the file is open for writing. If the file already exists on the system, the existing contents are deleted. (Use `FileMode.APPEND` if you don't want to overwrite the contents.) If the file does not exist, it is created.

- ✔ `[air.]FileMode.APPEND` tells AIR that the file is open in "append mode," meaning that new data is added to the end of the file instead of replacing existing data. If the file does not exist, the file is created.

- ✔ `[air.]FileMode.UPDATE` specifies that the file is open for both reading and writing. Use this mode when you need random read/write access to the file. When a file is being written to, only the bytes at the current location are overwritten. As you might expect by now, if the file doesn't exist, it is created.

After you've opened a file, you're reading for the two *R*'s — reading and 'riting. (Okay, it's technically an *R* and a *W,* but two *R*'s has a better ring to it.)

If you'd like to see how to asynchronously read/write to a file, skip over to the "AIRWrite: Creating a Simple Text Editor" section, later in this chapter.

Read from a file

You can use several read methods for reading data from a file stream. For general-purpose use with text files, you'll often want to use `readMulti-Byte()` or `readUTFBytes()`. The `readMultiByte()` method reads a mutibyte string from the file stream using a character set you specify. The `readUTFBytes()` method reads data into a string using the UTF-8 character set. (See the "AIRWrite: Creating a Simple Text Editor" section, later in this chapter, for examples of this method.)

To read a file and assign the data to a variable using `readMultiByte()`, you use the following JavaScript code:

```
var file = air.File.desktopDirectory;
file = file.resolvePath("text1.txt");
var fs = new air.FileStream();
fs.open(file, air.FileMode.READ);
var str = fs.readMultiByte(file.size, air.File.
          systemCharset);
// do something with str
fs.close();
```

Here's the ActionScript version:

```
var file:File = File.desktopDirectory;
file = file.resolvePath("text1.txt");
var fs:FileStream = new FileStream();
fs.open(file, FileMode.READ);
var str:String = fs.readMultiByte(file.size, File.
          systemCharset);
// do something with str
fs.close();
```

The `open()` method opens the `file` instance for reading. The second `file-Mode` parameter is used to specify the capabilities of the `FileStream` object. Using `FileMode.READ` enables the `FileStream` instance to read from the file.

The `readMultiByte()` method reads a multibyte string from the file stream using the character set specified by `File.systemCharset` and returns it as a string. The size of the file stream is indicated by the `file.size` property.

When you're done reading, call the `close()` of the `FileStream` instance to close the file stream.

There are also additional reading methods, including `readBytes()` (for assigning to a `ByteArray`) and the lesser used `readUTF()` (for files that have the length of the file's text data precede the data itself).

Write to a file

The write methods used to write to a file stream parallel the read methods. To write to a file using `writeMultiByte()`, here's the JavaScript code:

```
var file = air.File.desktopDirectory;
file = file.resolvePath("text1.txt");
var fs = new air.FileStream();
fs.open(file, air.FileMode.WRITE);
var str = "This is amazing!"
```

```
fs.writeMultiByte(str, air.File.systemCharset);
fs.close();
```

Or, in ActionScript:

```
var file:File= File.desktopDirectory;
file = file.resolvePath("text1.txt");
var fs:FileStream = new FileStream();
fs.open(file, FileMode.WRITE);
var str:String = "This is amazing!"
fs.writeMultiByte(str, File.systemCharset);
fs.close();
```

Check out the following section to discover more techniques related to writing to a file stream.

AIRWrite: Creating a Simple Text Editor

Building a text editor is perhaps the best way to demonstrate the basic read and write capabilities of Adobe AIR. You can then visually see how the read and write operations work inside your own app.

In this part of the chapter, I create both an HTML and Flex version of the editor and walk you through the code of the HTML version. Both versions offer essentially the same functionality.

HTML version

The following sections walk you through the construction of the AIRWrite text editor.

Build the UI

You begin by defining a very simplistic UI — just a single `textarea` element:

```
<p><textarea id="TextEditor"></textarea></p>
```

For this example, make the `textarea` fill the contents of the window and be in monospaced font by adding the following style:

```
#TextEditor {
  width:100%;
  height:100%;
  font-family: "Courier New", Courier, monospace;
  font-size:14px;
}
```

That's all the UI design you need to do for this app, so you're ready to move on to the JavaScript coding.

Add the AIRAliases.js file

Before adding the app specific code, you first need to add the `AIRAliases.js` file, as follows:

```
<script type="text/javascript" src="AIRAliases.js"></script>
```

Add a root menu

Keeping the UI minimal, you can have the users control the file open and save processes through a top-level menu. Add four menu items: New, Open, Save, and Exit/Quit. (See Chapter 8 for the full scoop on working with menus.)

In an `init()` function that executes when the app is loaded (by calling `window.addEventListener("load", init, false)`, you create the `NativeMenu` object that serves as the root menu:

```
var rootMenu = new air.NativeMenu();
rootMenu.addSubmenu(createFileMenu(),"File");

// Mac
if (air.NativeApplication.supportsMenu) {
  air.NativeApplication.nativeApplication.menu = rootMenu;
}
// Windows
if (air.NativeWindow.supportsMenu ) {
  window.nativeWindow.menu = rootMenu;
}
```

The `createFileMenu()` called by the `rootMenu.addSubmenu()` line is defined as follows:

```
/**
 * Creates the File menu for app
 */
  function createFileMenu() {
    var mnu = new air.NativeMenu();
    createMenuCommand( mnu, 'New', 'n', null, 0,
        fileNew);
    createMenuCommand( mnu, 'Open', 'o', null, 0,
        fileOpen);
    createMenuSeparator(mnu);
    createMenuCommand( mnu, 'Save', 's', null, 0,
        fileSave);
    createMenuSeparator(mnu);
    // If Mac OS X, then use Quit label
    if (air.NativeApplication.supportsMenu) {
      createMenuCommand( mnu, 'Quit', 'q', null, 0,
          fileExit);
```

```
    }
    // If Windows, then use Exit
    else {
      createMenuCommand( mnu, 'Exit', 'x', null, 0,
        fileExit);
    }
    return mnu;
}
```

The `createMenuCommand()` and `createMenuSeparator()` functions are helper routines that create a menu command or separator based on the supplied parameters. (These are shown in Listing 10-2, which appears a little later.)

Opening a file asynchronously

When the Open menu item is selected, the following routine is called:

```
function fileOpen(evt) {
  file.addEventListener(air.Event.SELECT, onFileSelect);
  file.browseForOpen("Open");
}
```

The `addEventListener()` method attaches `onFileSelect()` as a handler to process the file that is selected from the dialog box displayed using `browseForOpen()`.

The `onFileSelect` function calls `openAsync()` to open the file asynchronously. When using `openAsynch()`, you need to define handlers to trigger when the reading process has finished or when an error has occurred. Here's the code:

```
function onFileSelect(evt) {
  var fs = new air.FileStream();
  fs.openAsync(file, air.FileMode.READ);
  fs.addEventListener(air.Event.COMPLETE, onFileRead);
  fs.addEventListener(air.IOErrorEvent.IO_ERROR,
          onIOReadError);
  isDirty = false;
  isNewFile = false;
  document.title = "AIRWrite - " + file.name;
}
```

The `isDirty` variable is used to determine whether a file has been modified by the user. The `isNewFile` variable is used to determine whether a file has ever been saved before.

For asynchronous reads, you want to place the file stream reading code inside the `complete` event handler:

```
function onFileRead(evt) {
   var fs = air.FileStream( evt.target );
   var str = fs.readUTFBytes(fs.bytesAvailable);
   document.getElementById("TextEditor").value = str;
   fs.close();
}
```

In this function, the readUTFBytes() routine assigns the contents of the file to the str variable. This value is then set as the value for the textarea element.

In case something goes wrong during the file open process, here's a handler to deal with it:

```
function onIOReadError(evt) {
   alert("Something wacky happened. We are unable to open "
        + file.nativePath);
}
```

Saving a file asynchronously

The Save menu item calls the fileSave() function:

```
function fileSave(evt) {
   if (!isNewFile) {
      var fs = new air.FileStream();
      fs.openAsync(file, air.FileMode.WRITE);
      fs.addEventListener(air.IOErrorEvent.IO_ERROR,
         onIOWriteError);
      var str = document.getElementById
         ("TextEditor").value;
      str = str.replace(/\n/g, air.File.lineEnding);
      fs.writeUTFBytes(str);
      fs.close();
      isDirty = false;
   }
   else {
      fileSaveAs(evt);
   }
}
```

For files that have been previously saved, a file stream is opened for writing using openAsync(). The content of the textarea is then assigned to the str variable. Before writing this string to the file, you replace the new line characters (\n) with a platform specific line ending character (the air. File.lineEnding property). The file stream is written using writeUTF-Bytes() and then closed.

For new files, the `fileSaveAs()` function is called, as follows:

```
function fileSaveAs(evt) {
    file.addEventListener(air.Event.SELECT,
            onFileSaveAsSelect);
    file.browseForSave("Save As");
}
```

This function calls the Save dialog box and sets the handler for the file selection process to `onFileSaveAsSelect()`, as follows:

```
function onFileSaveAsSelect(evt) {
    document.title = "AIRWrite - " + file.name;
    isNewFile = false;
    fileSave(evt);
}
```

By the time this routine nears completion, the file will have a name and be read for saving. As a result, the `fileSave()` function is called again.

Listing 10-2:   AIRWriteHtml.html

```
<html>
<head>
<title>AIRWriteHtml</title>
<style type="text/css">
#TextEditor {
  width:100%;
  height:100%;
  font-family: "Courier New", Courier, monospace;
  font-size:14px;
}
</style>
<script type="text/javascript" src="AIRAliases.js"></
        script>

<script type="text/javascript">

  var file;
  var isDirty= false;
  var isNewFile = false;

  window.addEventListener("load", init, false);


  /**
   * Initializes the app after loading
   *
   */
  function init() {
    file = new air.File();
    var rootMenu = new air.NativeMenu();
```

```
    rootMenu.addSubmenu(createFileMenu(),"File");

    // Mac
    if (air.NativeApplication.supportsMenu) {
      air.NativeApplication.nativeApplication.menu =
          rootMenu;
    }
    // Windows
    if (air.NativeWindow.supportsMenu ) {
        window.nativeWindow.menu = rootMenu;
    }

    // Start out with a blank doc
    fileNew(null);
}

/**
 * Creates new blank file
 */
function fileNew(evt) {
  file = air.File.desktopDirectory;
  file = file.resolvePath("Untitled.txt");
  isDirty = false;
  isNewFile = true;
  document.getElementById("TextEditor").value = "";
  document.title = "AIRWrite - " + file.name;
}

/**
 * Displays File Open dialog box
 */
function fileOpen(evt) {
  file.addEventListener(air.Event.SELECT, onFileSelect);
  file.browseForOpen("Open");
}

/**
 * Opens selected file for editing
 */
function onFileSelect(evt) {
  var fs = new air.FileStream();
  fs.openAsync(file, air.FileMode.READ);
  fs.addEventListener(air.Event.COMPLETE, onFileRead);
  fs.addEventListener(air.IOErrorEvent.IO_ERROR,
        onIOReadError);
  isDirty = false;
  isNewFile = false;
  document.title = "AIRWrite - " + file.name;
}

/**
 * Handler for reading file
```

(continued)

Listing 10-2 *(continued)*

```
*/
function onFileRead(evt) {
  var fs = air.FileStream( evt.target );
  var str = fs.readUTFBytes(fs.bytesAvailable);
  document.getElementById("TextEditor").value = str;
}


/**
* Write file to disc
*/
function fileSave(evt) {
  if (!isNewFile) {
    var fs = new air.FileStream();
    fs.openAsync(file, air.FileMode.WRITE);
    fs.addEventListener(air.IOErrorEvent.IO_ERROR,
        onIOWriteError);
    var str = document.getElementById("TextEditor").
        value;
    str = str.replace(/\r/g, "\n");
    str = str.replace(/\n/g, air.File.lineEnding);
    fs.writeUTFBytes(str);
    fs.close();
    isDirty = false;
  }
  else {
    fileSaveAs(evt);
  }
}


/**
* Displays File Save dialog box
*/
function fileSaveAs(evt) {
  file.addEventListener(air.Event.SELECT,
      onFileSaveAsSelect);
  file.browseForSave("Save As");
}


/**
* Calls FileSave based on dialog box selection
*/
function onFileSaveAsSelect(evt) {
  document.title = "AIRWrite - " + file.name;
  isNewFile = false;
  fileSave(evt);
}


/**
* Exit the app
*/
function fileExit(evt) {
  air.NativeApplication.nativeApplication.exit();
```

```
}

/**
* Error handlers
*/
function onIOReadError(evt) {
  alert("Something wacky happened. We are unable to open
        " + file.nativePath);
}

function onIOWriteError(evt) {
  alert("We are really sorry, but the file cannot be
        saved. It's not our fault...really!");
}

/**
* Creates the File menu for app
*/
 function createFileMenu() {
   var mnu = new air.NativeMenu();
   createMenuCommand( mnu, 'New', 'n', null, 0,
        fileNew);
   createMenuCommand( mnu, 'Open', 'o', null, 0,
        fileOpen);
   createMenuSeparator(mnu);
   createMenuCommand( mnu, 'Save', 's', null, 0,
        fileSave);
   createMenuSeparator(mnu);
   // If Mac OS X, then use Quit label
   if (air.NativeApplication.supportsMenu) {
     createMenuCommand( mnu, 'Quit', 'q', null, 0,
        fileExit);
   }
   // If Windows, then use Exit
   else {
     createMenuCommand( mnu, 'Exit', 'x', null, 0,
        fileExit);
   }
   return mnu;
 }

/**
* Creates a "fully loaded" menu command based on
        parameters
*
*/
function createMenuCommand(menuContainer, itemLabel,
        itemKey, itemModifiers, itemMnemonic,
        selectHandler) {
  var cmd = air.NativeMenu(menuContainer).addItem(new
        air.NativeMenuItem(itemLabel));
  cmd.mnemonicIndex = itemMnemonic;
```

(continued)

Listing 10-2 *(continued)*

```
    cmd.keyEquivalent = itemKey;
    if (itemModifiers != null ) {
      cmd.keyEquivalentModifiers = itemModifiers;
    }

  if (selectHandler != null ) {
    cmd.addEventListener(air.Event.SELECT,
        selectHandler);
  }
  return cmd;
  }


  /**
  * Creates a menu separator
  */
  function createMenuSeparator(menuContainer) {
    var sep = air.NativeMenu(menuContainer).addItem(new
        air.NativeMenuItem("sep", true));
    return sep;
  }


</script>
</head>

<body>
<p><textarea id="TextEditor"></textarea></p>
</body>
</html>
```

Flex version

The Flex version of the AIRWrite editor is shown in Listing 10-3.

Listing 10-3:   AIRWrite.html

```
<?xml version="1.0" encoding="utf-8"?>
<mx:WindowedApplication xmlns:mx="http://www.adobe.
        com/2006/mxml" layout="absolute" width="764"
        height="454"
  applicationComplete="init()" styleName="sansChrome"
        backgroundGradientAlphas="[0.3, 0.3]">

  <mx:Style>
  .sansChrome { background-color:"";}
  </mx:Style>
```

```
<mx:Script>
  <![CDATA[
    import mx.controls.Alert;
    import flash.display.NativeMenu;

    import flash.display.NativeMenuItem;
    import mx.events.*;


    private var file:File;

    public var isDirty:Boolean = false;
    public var isNewFile:Boolean = false;


     /**
     * Initializes the app after loading
     *
     */
    private function init():void {

      file = new File();

      // Create root menu
      var rootMenu:NativeMenu = new NativeMenu();
      rootMenu.addSubmenu(createFileMenu(),"File");

      // Mac
      if (NativeApplication.supportsMenu) {
        NativeApplication.nativeApplication.menu =
        rootMenu;
       }

      // Windows
      if (NativeWindow.supportsMenu) {
        nativeWindow.menu = rootMenu;
      }

      // Start out with a blank doc
      fileNew(null);
    }


    public function fileNew(evt: Event):void {
      file = File.desktopDirectory;
      file = file.resolvePath("Untitled.txt");
      isDirty = false;
      isNewFile = true;
      taEditor.text = "";
      title = "AIRWrite - " + file.name;
      this.status = "";
```

(continued)

Listing 10-3 *(continued)*

```
      taEditor.setFocus();
  }

  public function fileOpen(evt: Event):void {

    file.addEventListener(Event.SELECT, onFileSelect);
    file.browseForOpen("Open");
  }


  public function onFileSelect(evt:Event):void {
    var fs:FileStream = new FileStream();
    fs.openAsync(file, FileMode.READ);
    fs.addEventListener(Event.COMPLETE, onFileRead);
    fs.addEventListener(IOErrorEvent.IO_ERROR,
      onIOReadError);
    isDirty = false;
    isNewFile = false;
    this.status = "";
    title = "AIRWrite - " + file.name;
    taEditor.setFocus();
  }

  private function onFileRead(evt:Event):void {
    var fs:FileStream = evt.target as FileStream;
    var str:String = fs.readUTFBytes(fs.
      bytesAvailable);
    taEditor.text = str;
    fs.close();
  }


  public function fileSave(evt: Event):void {
    if (!isNewFile) {
      var fs:FileStream = new FileStream();
      fs.openAsync(file, FileMode.WRITE);
      fs.addEventListener(IOErrorEvent.IO_ERROR,
       onIOWriteError);
      var str:String = taEditor.text;
      str = str.replace(/\r/g, "\n");
      str = str.replace(/\n/g, File.lineEnding);
      fs.writeUTFBytes(str);
      fs.close();
      isDirty = false;
      this.status = "";
    }
    else {
      fileSaveAs(evt);
    }
  }

  public function fileSaveAs(evt: Event):void {
```

```
    file.addEventListener(Event.SELECT,
        onFileSaveAsSelect);

    file.browseForSave("Save As");
}

public function onFileSaveAsSelect(evt: Event):void
    {
    if (isNewFile) {
        title = "AIRWrite - " + file.name;
        isNewFile = false;
    }
    fileSave(evt);
}

public function fileExit(evt: Event):void {
    NativeApplication.nativeApplication.exit();
}


private function onIOReadError(evt:Event):void {
    Alert.show("Something wacky happened. We are
        unable to open " + file.nativePath, "Error",
        Alert.OK, this);
}

private function onIOWriteError(evt:Event):void {
    Alert.show("We are really sorry, but the file
        cannot be saved. It's not our fault...really!",
        "Error", Alert.OK, this);
}

private function onChange(evt:Event):void {
    this.status = "Modified";
    isDirty = true;
}

/**
* Creates the File menu for app
*/
 private function createFileMenu():NativeMenu {
    var mnu:NativeMenu = new NativeMenu();
    createMenuCommand( mnu, 'New', 'n', null, 0,
        fileNew);
    createMenuCommand( mnu, 'Open', 'o', null, 0,
        fileOpen);
    createMenuSeparator(mnu);
    createMenuCommand( mnu, 'Save', 's', null, 0,
        fileSave);
    createMenuSeparator(mnu);
    // If Mac OS X, then use Quit label
    if (NativeApplication.supportsMenu) {
```

(continued)

Listing 10-3 *(continued)*

```
        createMenuCommand( mnu, 'Quit', 'q', null, 0,
        fileExit);
    }
    // If Windows, then use Exit
    else {
        createMenuCommand( mnu, 'Exit', 'x', null, 0,
        fileExit);
    }
    return mnu;
}

/**
* Creates a "fully loaded" menu command based on
    parameters
*
*/
public function createMenuCommand(menuContainer:
    NativeMenu, itemLabel:String, itemKey:String,
    itemModifiers:Array, itemMnemonic:int,
    selectHandler:Function): NativeMenuItem {
    var cmd:NativeMenuItem= NativeMenu(menuContainer).
    addItem(new NativeMenuItem(itemLabel));
    cmd.mnemonicIndex = itemMnemonic;
    cmd.keyEquivalent = itemKey;
    if (itemModifiers != null ) {
        cmd.keyEquivalentModifiers = itemModifiers;
    }
    if (selectHandler != null ) {
        cmd.addEventListener(Event.SELECT,
        selectHandler);
    }
    return cmd;
}


/**
* Creates a menu separator
*/
private function createMenuSeparator(menuContainer:
    NativeMenu): NativeMenuItem {
    var sep:NativeMenuItem= NativeMenu(menuContainer).
    addItem(new NativeMenuItem("sep", true));
    return sep;
}

]]>
</mx:Script>

<mx:TextArea id="taEditor" x="0" y="0" width="100%"
    height="100%" backgroundAlpha="0.8"
```

```
        fontFamily="Courier New" fontSize="14"
                backgroundColor="#000000" color="#FFFFFF"
                change="onChange(event)"/>
    </mx:WindowedApplication>
```

Figure 10-5 shows the Flex version of the app, which uses custom Flex chrome and features a semitransparent window.

Figure 10-5:
Opening a
text file in
AIRWrite.

Chapter 11

From AIRhead to Datahead: Working with Databases

Databases and Web apps have long been "peas in a pod," two parts of a solution that just work well together. The duo combine to serve as the foundation for the majority of Web apps. Adobe AIR enables you to connect to remote database servers through sockets or HTTP calls. However, it goes one step further: As does a true desktop app, Adobe AIR allows you to store database info in a local SQL database.

In this chapter, I introduce you to the database connectivity of Adobe AIR. I begin by showing you how to connect your app to the SQLLite database engine to store and retrieve local data. I then walk you through various SQL commands to interact with the database. In fact, you could find yourself feeling so productive with databases that you might even begin thinking of yourself as a datahead.

Working with Local Databases

I mention in Chapter 1 that Adobe AIR runtime includes SQLite, a SQL relational database engine that enables you to work with a local database. Here are some facts to keep in mind when working with databases in AIR:

✔ The database file that you work with is a local file with a name and extension you specify (often with a .db extension).

✔ You can connect to multiple databases within the same app.

✔ The AIR API database commands enable you to work local database files, not server-based systems.

A local database provides several added capabilities for your AIR app. You can develop a stand-alone database app that does not require a live connection to the Internet. You can create an application that stores network data as a local copy in the SQLite database, resynching with the main server-side database periodically. You can also use a database to store application-specific data rather than use a local file to store that information.

For info on SQLLite, go to www.sqlite.org.

Introducing the Basics of SQL

All operations you perform on the database are not done with JavaScript or ActionScript. Instead, you use SQL. In case you're not familiar with SQL, the acronym stands for Structured Query Language, which is the standard database access language for interacting with databases. Using SQL, you can create or restructure tables, perform queries, and insert or modify records.

In this section, I give you an overview of the basics of SQL. However, you need to keep in mind that SQL is a complex language. In fact, I could fill an entire *For Dummies* book on the subject. Oh, wait . . . someone already did that. For more on the SQL language, let me point you to *SQL For Dummies,* 6th Edition, by Allen G. Taylor; you might also want to check out *SQL Server 2008 For Dummies,* by Mike Chapple (both published by Wiley).

In human speak, the basic form of a SQL statement is generally the following: *Perform this operation on these fields in this table.* For example, this statement:

```
SELECT * FROM employee
```

means *select all records and all fields from the employee table.* As you can infer, the * means *all.*

Or, you can deal with specific fields:

```
SELECT first_name, last_name FROM contact
```

which means *select all the first name and last name values from the employee table.*

Of course, SQL commands can get much more complex, but these examples give you the basic idea.

In contrast to JavaScript and ActionScript, SQL is not case sensitive. Therefore, both of the following two commands are valid:

```
select order_num from orders
SELECT ORDER_NUM FROM ORDERS
```

To help create readable code, the standard convention is to capitalize reserved words, such as SELECT and FROM, and enter field names and table names as lowercase. I follow this convention in the examples of this chapter.

Let's look at the common SQL commands. I reference the sample database table in Table 11-1 for many of the examples in this chapter.

Table 11-1		Sample Customer Table		
id	*first_name*	*last_name*	*City*	*state*
100	Art	Vandelay	Holden	MA
101	Clark	Kent	Smallville	KS
102	Nelson	Rockenfelder	Jericho	KS
103	Kyle	Exwhy	Lapel	IN
104	Roy	Kent	Jericho	KS
104	Rachel	Armstrong	Boston	MA

Handpicking records with SELECT

The SELECT command is used to retrieve records from a table. The basic syntax is as follows:

```
SELECT field_name(s) FROM table_name
```

The set of records that is returned from the query is called the *result set*.

For example, to return all the records from the customer table, you write:

```
SELECT * FROM customer
```

To return just the first and last names from the customer table, write this instead:

```
SELECT first_name, last_name FROM customer
```

The result set of the preceding query looks like the following:

first_name	last_name
Art	Vandelay
Clark	Kent
Nelson	Rockenfelder
Kyle	Exwhy
Roy	Kent
Rachel	Armstrong

In some cases, fields in a table may contain duplicate values, which can be reflected in your result set. For example, if you want to return the states of the customer table, you can write:

```
SELECT state FROM customer
```

The following result set includes duplicate values:

```
MA
KS
KS
IN
KS
MA
```

However, if you use the `SELECT DISTINCT` statement instead, the result set includes only unique values. Therefore:

```
SELECT DISTINCT state FROM customer
```

returns a result set with no duplicate values:

```
MA
KS
IN
KS
```

Adding conditions with WHERE

The `WHERE` command enables you to specify conditions on the records that you want to return. The syntax is

```
SELECT field_name(s) FROM table_name WHERE field_name operator value
```

For example, if you want to return the names of the customers who live in Kansas, you can use the following statement:

```
SELECT * FROM customer WHERE state='KS'
```

Note that the string value KS is enclosed in single quotation marks. Numeric values, however, are not enclosed in quotation marks. For example:

```
SELECT * FROM customer WHERE id>101
```

You use the greater than sign (>) as the operator in this query. The result set returns all the customer records that have an id value of greater than 101. You have several operators that you can use, as specified in Table 11-2.

Table 11-2	SQL WHERE Operators
Operator	*Description*
=	Equal
<>	Not equal
>	Greater than
<	Less than
>=	Greater than or equal
<=	Less than or equal
BETWEEN	Between an inclusive range
LIKE	Search for a specific pattern

Sorting with ORDER BY

You can specify the sort order of the result set by using the ORDER BY command. Here's the general structure:

```
SELECT field_name(s) FROM table_name ORDER BY field_name(s) ASC|DESC
```

By default, the result is sorted in ascending order (ASC). However, you can instead add the DESC keyword at the end to sort in descending order.

Here's an example of a sort:

```
SELECT first_name, last_name FROM customer ORDER BY last_name, first_name DESC
```

The result set looks like this:

first_name	last_name
Art	Vandelay
Nelson	Rockenfelder
Roy	Kent
Clark	Kent
Kyle	Exwhy
Rachel	Armstrong

Adding records with INSERT INTO

To insert a new record into a database table, you use the INSERT INTO statement. Follow the general syntax shown here:

```
INSERT INTO table_name (field1, field2, field3)
  VALUES ('value1', 'value2', 'value3')
```

As you can see, the field names themselves are not enclosed in quotation marks, but string values are inside the VALUES parentheses.

Here's an example of adding a new record to the customer table:

```
INSERT INTO customer (id, last_name, first_name, city, state)
  VALUES (105, 'Hammer', 'Jack', 'Chicago', 'IL')
```

Modifying records with UPDATE

You can use the UPDATE statement to update existing records in your database table with new values. Check out the structure of a typical UPDATE statement:

```
UPDATE table_name SET field1='value1', field2='value2', ...
  WHERE fieldX='valueY'
```

In most cases, you want to have the WHERE clause on the end of an UPDATE statement to determine which record or set of records to update. If you don't add the WHERE clause, *all* the records in the table are updated to the values specified in the SET clause.

Getting rid of records with DELETE

The DELETE statement removes all the records from a table that match the criteria specified by the WHERE clause. Check out the syntax:

```
DELETE FROM table_name WHERE fieldX='value1' AND fieldY='value2'
```

The following example deletes all customers from MA:

```
DELETE FROM customer WHERE state='MA'
```

Or, if you really, *really* want to, you can delete all records in the table by leaving off the WHERE clause. For example:

```
DELETE FROM customer
```

You can also use the * keyword:

```
DELETE * FROM customer
```

Creating a table with CREATE TABLE

You use the CREATE TABLE statement to create a table in your database. In its simplest form, the syntax is as follows:

```
CREATE TABLE table_name
(
field1 data_type,
field2 data_type,
field3 data_type
}
```

Unsupported SQL Features in Adobe AIR

The following SQL features are not available in Adobe AIR:

- ✔ The triggers FOR EACH STATEMENT and INSTEAD OF, as well as recursive triggers

- ✔ The FOREIGN KEY statement

- ✔ Nested transactions

- ✔ RIGHT OUTER JOIN and FULL OUTER JOIN

- ✔ Updateable VIEW

- ✔ GRANT and REVOKE

Also, most ALTER TABLE options are not supported, including DROP COLUMN, ALTER COLUMN, and ADD CONSTRAINT.

The data type for a given field can be one of the types shown in Table 11-3. When a record is saved, the AIR runtime will attempt to convert the data value from its JavaScript or ActionScript type into the type (more specifically called the *affinity*) of the field you specify. You can specify whether you want to allow NULL values in the field when you define the CREATE TABLE statement.

Table 11-3	Adobe AIR Database Data Types
Type	*Description*
TEXT (or STRING)	Allows normal storage of text.
NUMERIC	Allows you to store real, integer, or null values.
INTEGER	Integer values.
REAL (or NUMBER)	Forces numbers into floating point representation.
BOOLEAN	Contains true or false values.
DATE	Date values.
XML	For storing of XML structures. The ActionScript function XML() is called to convert the incoming data into an XML structure.
XMLLIST	For storing of XML structures. The ActionScript function XMLList() is called to convert the incoming data into an XML list.
OBJECT	For storing JavaScript or ActionScript object instances. Data is serialized in AMF3 format.
NONE	Data is inserted into the field without conversion.

The following statement creates the customer table. Notice the IF NOT EXISTS clause, which tells the database to create the customer table only if the table has not been created before:

```
CREATE TABLE IF NOT EXISTS customer
(
  id INTEGER,
  first_name TEXT,
  last_name TEXT,
  city TEXT,
  state TEXT
)
```

If you want to define a primary key to a field, you add PRIMARY KEY after the desired field:

```
  id INTEGER PRIMARY KEY,
```

A common desire is to have the primary key field be autoincrementing, freeing you from needing to generate a unique field value on your own. For example, suppose you'd like the id field to be autoincrementing. To make it so, you type:

```
id INTEGER PRIMARY KEY AUTOINCREMENT,
```

Following is a full example. If you want the id of your customer table to be autoincrementing, you define the table as follows:

```
CREATE TABLE IF NOT EXISTS customer
(
  id INTEGER PRIMARY KEY AUTOINCREMENT,
  first_name TEXT,
  last_name TEXT,
  city TEXT,
  state TEXT
)
```

Then, when a new record is added, you don't specify the autoincrement field value but instead provide the remaining values:

```
INSERT INTO customer (last_name, first_name, city, state)
  VALUES ('Hammer', 'Jack', 'Chicago', 'IL')
```

Opening a Database Connection

Your first step in performing any database operation is to open a connection to a local database file. Just as with file system files, you can create either synchronous or asynchronous connections. (See Chapter 10 for an explanation of the difference between synchronous and asynchronous connections.)

You create *synchronous connections* using open(), and the commands on the database are performed sequentially in the order in which they occur in the source code. What's more, the app will wait on result of the operation from the database engine before continuing.

For asynchronous connections, you use openAsync() and add a handler to the connection's OPEN event to perform operations on an open connection. When you establish an asynchronous connection, your AIR app hands off a SQL statement to the database engine for processing but doesn't wait for the results. The database engine takes the request and processes it in the background. When the SQL statement has been completed, an event is dispatched in your app.

Perhaps the most practical distinction between `open()` and `openAsynch()` is that `open()` waits to execute any more lines of code until the database open operation finishes. In contrast, `openAsynch()` fires off the database connection call but continues processing lines of code that appear below it. Therefore, if you have code that's dependent on the database connection being established, you want to place that code within the `OPEN` event handler.

When you open a connection, AIR looks for the local file you specify. If that file is not found, a new database file is created for you.

The following JavaScript function establishes a synchronous connection to a database called `rss.db`, located in the `rssfeed` subfolder of the user's documents directory:

```
function connectDatabase() {
  var dbRoot = air.File.documentsDirectory.resolvePath("rssdrop");
  dbRoot.createDirectory();
  dbFile = dbRoot.resolvePath("rss.db");
  sqlConnection = new air.SQLConnection();
  sqlConnection.open(dbFile);
  // do something now
}
```

The `resolvePath()` method assigns the `rssfeed` folder to the `dbRoot` variable. This folder is then created if necessary. The `dbFile` is assigned to the `rss.db`, which is the database file, which is then used as the parameter in the connection's `open()` method.

Here's the ActionScript equivalent:

```
private function connectDatabase():void {
  var dbRoot: File = File.documentsDirectory.resolvePath("rssdrop");
  dbRoot.createDirectory();
  dbFile = dbRoot.resolvePath("rss.db");
  sqlConnection = new SQLConnection();
  sqlConnection.open(dbFile);
  // do something now
}
```

Alternatively, you can open the database asynchronously. To do so in JavaScript, use this code:

```
function connectDatabase() {
  var dbRoot = air.File.documentsDirectory.resolvePath("rssdrop");
  dbRoot.createDirectory();
  dbFile = dbRoot.resolvePath("rss.db");
  sqlConnection = new air.SQLConnection();
  sqlConnection.addEventListener(air.SQLEvent.OPEN, onDatabaseOpen);
  sqlConnection.addEventListener(air.SQLErrorEvent.ERROR, onDatabaseError);
  sqlConnection.openAsync(dbFile);
```

```
}

function onDatabaseOpen(event) {
  // here's where you would do something with the open database
}

private function onDatabaseError(event) {
  alert(event.error.message + " Details: " + event.error.details);
}
```

As you can see, two event listeners are added. They are triggered when the database opens or when a database error occurs. The openAsynch() method is then called to open the rss.db database.

The ActionScript code is as follows:

```
private function connectDatabase(): void {
  var dbRoot: File = File.documentsDirectory.resolvePath('rssdrop');
  dbRoot.createDirectory();
  dbFile = dbRoot.resolvePath(DATABASE_FILE);
  sqlConnection = new SQLConnection();
  sqlConnection.addEventListener(SQLEvent.OPEN, onDatabaseOpen);
  sqlConnection.addEventListener(SQLErrorEvent.ERROR, onDatabaseError);
  sqlConnection.openAsync(dbFile);
}

private function onDatabaseOpen(event:SQLEvent): void {
  // here's where you would do something with the open database
}

private function onDatabaseError(event:SQLErrorEvent): void {
  Alert.show(event.error.message + " Details: " + event.error.details);
}
```

After a database connection is established, you can either create a database table or perform an operation on an existing table.

Performing Database Operations with SQLStatement

You send SQL commands to the database by using a SQLStatement object. The SQLStatement object uses an open database connection to execute a SQL statement on the database. Adobe AIR allows you to work with the results of the SQL statement by attaching a handler to the RESULT event, which is dispatched when the database finishes processing. In case of a problem, you should also add a listener to the ERROR event.

Here's a basic framework for opening a database and executing a SQL command:

```
// Assign File object instance to local database file
database_file = database_path.resolvePath("database.db");
// Create SQL connection
sqlConnection = new air.SQLConnection();
// Open either synchronous or asynchronous connection on the database file
sqlConnection.open(database_file);
// Create SQL statement
var statement = new air.SQLStatement();
// Connect the dots
statement.sqlConnection = sqlConnection;
// Create SQL statement
var sql = "MY SQL STATEMENT GOES HERE"
statement.text = sql;
// Add event handlers
statement.addEventListener(air.SQLEvent.RESULT, onDatabaseCreated);
statement.addEventListener(air.SQLErrorEvent.ERROR, onDatabaseError);
// Execute SQL - process results in the SQLEvent.RESULT handler
statement.execute();
```

The following sections show you how this framework works with a variety of SQL statements.

Creating a Database Table

Unless you are delivering your app with a pre-populated database, your first step will typically be to create one or more tables in which to store data. You do this by passing a CREATE TABLE SQL statement to the database.

The following code assigns an open connection called sqlConnection to the SQLStatement instance's sqlConnection property. A SQL statement is created as a String variable and assigned to the text property of the SQLStatement. This SQL statement is passed to the database engine using execute() for processing. The SQL statement itself tells the database to create a table named rssfeeds if it does not already exist. Event handlers are provided to process the result of the statement.

Check out the JavaScript code:

```
function initializeDatabase() {
  var createStmt = new air.SQLStatement();
  createStmt.sqlConnection = sqlConnection;
```

```
   var sql =
       "CREATE TABLE IF NOT EXISTS rssfeeds (" +
       "    feedId INTEGER PRIMARY KEY AUTOINCREMENT, " +
       "    url TEXT UNIQUE, " +
       "    name TEXT, " +
       "    homeURL TEXT, " +
       "    lastFetched DATE" +
       ")";
   createStmt.text = sql;
   createStmt.addEventListener(air.SQLEvent.RESULT, onDatabaseCreated);
   createStmt.addEventListener(air.SQLErrorEvent.ERROR, onDatabaseError);
   createStmt.execute();
}

function onDatabaseCreated() {
   air.trace("You created your very own database table!!!!!");
}

function onDatabaseError() {
   air.trace("Bummer, something went majorly wrong.");
}
```

Here is the ActionScript code:

```
private function initializeDatabase(): void {
   var createStmt:SQLStatement = new SQLStatement();
   createStmt.sqlConnection = sqlConnection;
   var sql:String =
       "CREATE TABLE IF NOT EXISTS rssfeeds (" +
       "    feedId INTEGER PRIMARY KEY AUTOINCREMENT, " +
       "    url TEXT UNIQUE, " +
       "    name TEXT, " +
       "    homeURL TEXT, " +
       "    lastFetched DATE" +
       ")";
   createStmt.text = sql;
   createStmt.addEventListener(SQLEvent.RESULT, onDatabaseCreated);
   createStmt.addEventListener(SQLErrorEvent.ERROR, onDatabaseError);
   createStmt.execute();
}

private function onDatabaseCreated(event:SQLEvent): void {
   ("You created your very own database table!!!!!");
}

private function onDatabaseError(): void {
   trace("Bummer, something went majorly wrong.");
}
```

Inserting a Record

The following code inserts a database record into the `rssfeed` database. Notice how it uses script variables in the SQL statement.

In JavaScript:

```
function addRecord() {
  var url = "http://www.richwagnerwords.com/rss.xml";
  var name = "Rich Wagner Blog";
  var homeURL = "http://www.richwagnerwords.com";
  var lastFetched = 12/31/2008 as Date;
  insertRecord( url, name, homeURL, lastFetched);
}

function insertRecord( url, name, homeURL, lastFetched) {
  var insertStmt = new air.SQLStatement();
  insertStmt.sqlConnection = sqlConnection;
  var sql:String =
  "INSERT INTO rssfeeds (url, name, homeURL, lastFetched) " +
  "VALUES ('" + url + "', '" + name + "', '" + homeURL + "', " + lastFetched +
          ")";
  insertStmt.text = sql;
  insertStmt.addEventListener(air.SQLEvent.RESULT, onDatabaseInsert);
  insertStmt.addEventListener(air.SQLErrorEvent.ERROR, onDatabaseError);
  insertStmt.execute();
}
```

In ActionScript:

```
private function addRecord() : void {
  var url:String = "http://www.richwagnerwords.com/rss.xml";
  var name:String = "Rich Wagner Blog";
  var homeURL:String = "http://www.richwagnerwords.com";
  var lastFetched:Date = 12/31/2008 as Date;
  insertRecord( url, name, homeURL, lastFetched);
}

private function insertRecord( url:String, name:String, homeURL:String,
    lastFetched:Date): void {
  var insertStmt:SQLStatement = new SQLStatement();
  insertStmt.sqlConnection = sqlConnection;
  var sql:String =
  "INSERT INTO rssfeeds (url, name, homeURL, lastFetched) " +
  "VALUES ('" + url + "', '" + name + "', '" + homeURL + "', " + lastFetched +
          ")";
  insertStmt.text = sql;
  insertStmt.addEventListener(SQLEvent.RESULT, onDatabaseInsert);
  insertStmt.addEventListener(SQLErrorEvent.ERROR, onDatabaseError);
  insertStmt.execute();
}
```

Here's a more complex Flex-based data entry example combining several of these database tasks as well as some other techniques that I discuss in other chapters.

First, this example shows how to develop an app that provides a form-based interface in which to enter information on an RSS feed (see Figure 11-1). This information is then added into the database table.

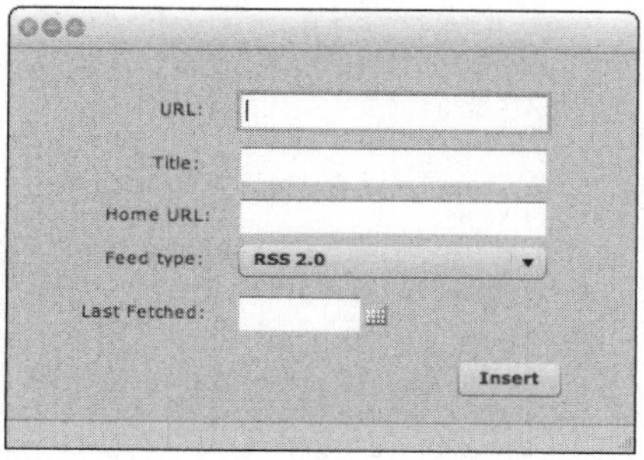

Figure 11-1:
Simple data
entry form.

The MXML layout is as follows:

```
<mx:Text   x="88" y="28" text="URL:&#xd;" textAlign="left"/>
<mx:Text x="84" y="61" text="Title:&#xd;" textAlign="left"/>
<mx:Text   x="56" y="93" text="Home URL:&#xd;" textAlign="left"/>
<mx:Text   x="42" y="155" text="Last Fetched: " textAlign="left"/>
<mx:TextInput id="tiURL" x="138" y="26" width="185"/>
<mx:TextInput id="tiTitle"  x="138" y="59" width="185"/>
<mx:TextInput id="tiHomeURL" x="138" y="91" width="185"/>
<mx:DateField id="dfLastFetched" x="138" y="153"/>
<mx:Button x="270" y="192" label="Insert" click="onInsertClick()"/>
<mx:Text   x="56" y="121" text="Feed type:" textAlign="left"/>
<mx:ComboBox id="cbType" x="138" y="119" width="185">
 <mx:dataProvider>
   <mx:String>RSS 2.0</mx:String>
   <mx:String>RSS 1.0</mx:String>
   <mx:String>Atom</mx:String>
 </mx:dataProvider>
</mx:ComboBox>
```

The following code shows the initialization routine in which the database is opened and the table is created if it does not exist:

```
static private const DATABASE_FILE: String = "rssfeeds.db";

private var dbFile: File;
private var sqlConnection:SQLConnection;
private var feedURL: String;
private var feedTitle: String;
```

```
private var homeURL: String;
private var lastFetched: String;
private var feedType: String;

// Initialize app
private function init() : void
{
  connectDatabase();
}

// Connect to database
private function connectDatabase() : void
{
  var dbRoot: File = File.documentsDirectory.resolvePath('rssdrop');
  dbRoot.createDirectory();
  dbFile = dbRoot.resolvePath(DATABASE_FILE);
  sqlConnection = new SQLConnection();
  sqlConnection.addEventListener(SQLEvent.OPEN, onDatabaseOpen);
  sqlConnection.addEventListener(SQLErrorEvent.ERROR, onDatabaseError);
  sqlConnection.openAsync(dbFile);
}

// Initialize database once the connection is opened
private function onDatabaseOpen(event:SQLEvent) : void
{
  initializeDatabase();
}

// Database error
private function onDatabaseError(event:SQLErrorEvent) : void
{
  Alert.show(event.error.message + " Details: " + event.error.details);
}

// Create database table, if it does not exist
private function initializeDatabase() : void
{
  var createStmt:SQLStatement = new SQLStatement();
  createStmt.sqlConnection = sqlConnection;
  var sql:String =
      "CREATE TABLE IF NOT EXISTS rssfeeds (" +
      "    feedId INTEGER PRIMARY KEY AUTOINCREMENT, " +
      "    url TEXT UNIQUE, " +
      "    title TEXT, " +
      "    feedType TEXT, " +
      "    homeURL TEXT, " +
      "    lastFetched DATE" +
      ")";
  createStmt.text = sql;
```

```
    createStmt.addEventListener(SQLEvent.RESULT, onDatabaseCreated);
    createStmt.addEventListener(SQLErrorEvent.ERROR, onDatabaseError);
    createStmt.execute();
}

// Creation handler
private function onDatabaseCreated(event:SQLEvent) : void
{
    trace("Table created.");
}
```

Note that the `url` field adds a new SQL operator named `UNIQUE`, which ensures that only unique RSS feeds can be added to the system.

Next, when the user clicks the Insert button, the contents of the fields are used in a SQL statement to the open database. Here's the code related to inserting user data into the database:

```
// Insert record into the table
private function insertRecord( url:String, title:String, feedType: String,
        homeURL:String, lastFetched:String) : void
{
    var insertStmt:SQLStatement = new SQLStatement();
    insertStmt.sqlConnection = sqlConnection;
    var lfDate:Date = lastFetched as Date;
    var sql:String =
        "INSERT INTO rssfeeds (url, title, feedType, homeURL, lastFetched) " +
        "VALUES ('" +
            url + "', '" + title + "', '" + feedType + "', '" + homeURL + "', '",
            " + lfDate
        + ")";
    insertStmt.text = sql;
    insertStmt.addEventListener(SQLEvent.RESULT, onDatabaseInsert);
    insertStmt.addEventListener(SQLErrorEvent.ERROR, onDatabaseError);
    insertStmt.execute();
}

// When insert is successful...
private function onDatabaseInsert(event:SQLEvent) : void
{
    Alert.show("Feed successfully inserted!");
    clearFields();
}

// Handler for Insert button click
private function onInsertClick(): void
{
    var d:String = dfLastFetched.selectedDate as String;
```

```
    insertRecord( tiURL.text, tiTitle.text, cbType.text, tiHomeURL.text, d);
}

// Clear all UI fields
private function clearFields() : void
{
  tiURL.text = "";
  tiHomeURL.text = "";
  tiURL.text = "";
  cbType.text = "";
}
```

Figure 11-2 shows the result that appears on-screen.

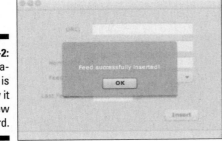

Rather than stop there, you can add one additional way to add data into the database table: through drag-and-drop of an RSS feed onto the app. To do so, you begin by adding two drag-and-drop event listeners to the `init()` function:

```
addEventListener(NativeDragEvent.NATIVE_DRAG_ENTER, onDragIn);
addEventListener(NativeDragEvent.NATIVE_DRAG_DROP, onDragDrop);
```

You then add the two handlers for these events to accept dragged-in URLs:

```
// Drag In handler
public function onDragIn(event:NativeDragEvent) : void
{
  NativeDragManager.dropAction = NativeDragActions.COPY;
  if (event.clipboard.hasFormat(ClipboardFormats.URL_FORMAT))
  {
    NativeDragManager.acceptDragDrop(this);
  }
}

// Drop handler
public function onDragDrop(event:NativeDragEvent) : void
{
```

```
    if (event.clipboard.hasFormat(ClipboardFormats.URL_FORMAT)) {
      feedURL = (event.clipboard.getData(ClipboardFormats.URL_FORMAT,
            ClipboardTransferMode.ORIGINAL_PREFERRED) as String);
      dropFeed(feedURL);
    }
  }
```

The `onDragDrop()` function captures the URL dropped onto the app and passes it to the `dropFeed()` function, which follows:

```
// Retrieve feed info via HTTPService
 public function dropFeed(url:String): void
 {
   CursorManager.setBusyCursor();
   var httpService:HTTPService = new HTTPService();
   httpService.resultFormat = "object";
   httpService.addEventListener(ResultEvent.RESULT, onFetchComplete);
   httpService.addEventListener(FaultEvent.FAULT, onFetchError);
   httpService.url = url;
   httpService.send();
 }
```

See Chapter 9 for more details on drag-and-drop.

Before the app can add the RSS feed as a record into the table, it needs to gather additional field-related info. To have it do so, you can use an `HTTPService` object to retrieve that information directly from the feed itself. (See Chapter 12 for more on connecting to network resources in AIR apps.) Note that the `onFetchComplete()` function is the handler that is triggered when the `HTTPService` object returns a result. Here's the code:

```
// Handler for HTTPService result event
// Retrieve info for record
private function onFetchComplete(event:ResultEvent) : void
{
  // RSS 2.0
  if (event.result.hasOwnProperty("rss"))
  {
    feedTitle = event.result.rss.channel.title as String;
    homeURL = event.result.rss.channel.link as String;
    lastFetched = event.result.rss.channel.lastBuildDate as String;
    feedType = "RSS 2.0";
  }
  // RSS 1.0
  else if (event.result.hasOwnProperty("RDF"))
  {
    feedTitle = event.result.RDF.channel.title as String;
    homeURL = event.result.RDF.channel.link as String;
    lastFetched = event.result.RDF.channel.lastBuildDate as String;
    feedType = "RSS 1.0";
  }
  // Atom
```

```
      else if (event.result.hasOwnProperty("feed"))
      {
        feedTitle = event.result.feed.title as String;
        homeURL = event.result.feed.link[0] as String;
        lastFetched = event.result.feed.updated as String;
        lastFetched = lastFetched.replace(/-/g, "/");
        lastFetched = lastFetched.replace("T", " ");
        lastFetched = lastFetched.replace("Z", " GMT-0000");
        feedType = "Atom";
      }
      // Unsupported
      else
      {
        trace("Unable to retrieve RSS feed: Unsupported format.");
        return;
      }

      clearFields();
      insertRecord( feedURL, feedTitle, feedType, homeURL, lastFetched);
      CursorManager.removeBusyCursor();
   }

   // Error handler for HTTPService
   private function onFetchError(event:FaultEvent) : void
   {
     CursorManager.removeBusyCursor();
     trace("The following error occurred when fetching the RSS feed: " + event.
           message);
   }
```

Listing 11-1 provides the full source code for this app.

Listing 11-1: rssdrop.mxml

```
<?xml version="1.0" encoding="utf-8"?>
<mx:WindowedApplication xmlns:mx="http://www.adobe.com/2006/mxml"
            layout="absolute"
  applicationComplete="init()" height="276" width="378">

<mx:Script>
  <![CDATA[
    import mx.rpc.http.HTTPService;
    import flash.data.SQLConnection;
    import flash.data.SQLStatement;
    import flash.events.SQLErrorEvent;
    import flash.events.SQLEvent;
    import mx.controls.Alert;
    import mx.collections.ArrayCollection;
    import mx.managers.CursorManager;
    import mx.rpc.events.FaultEvent;
```

```
import mx.rpc.events.ResultEvent;


static private const DATABASE_FILE: String = "rssfeeds.db";

private var dbFile: File;
private var sqlConnection:SQLConnection;
private var feedURL: String;
private var feedTitle: String;
private var homeURL: String;
private var lastFetched: String;
private var feedType: String;

// Initialize app
private function init() : void
{
  connectDatabase();
  addEventListener(NativeDragEvent.NATIVE_DRAG_ENTER, onDragIn);
  addEventListener(NativeDragEvent.NATIVE_DRAG_DROP, onDragDrop);
}

// Connect to database
private function connectDatabase() : void
{
  var dbRoot: File = File.documentsDirectory.resolvePath('rssdrop');
  dbRoot.createDirectory();
  dbFile = dbRoot.resolvePath(DATABASE_FILE);
  sqlConnection = new SQLConnection();
  sqlConnection.addEventListener(SQLEvent.OPEN, onDatabaseOpen);
  sqlConnection.addEventListener(SQLErrorEvent.ERROR, onDatabaseError);
  sqlConnection.openAsync(dbFile);
}

// Initialize database once the connection is opened
private function onDatabaseOpen(event:SQLEvent) : void
{
  initializeDatabase();
}

// Database error
private function onDatabaseError(event:SQLErrorEvent) : void
{
  Alert.show(event.error.message + " Details: " + event.error.details);
}

// Create database table, if it does not exist
private function initializeDatabase() : void
{
  var createStmt:SQLStatement = new SQLStatement();
```

(continued)

Listing 11-1 *(continued)*

```
    createStmt.sqlConnection = sqlConnection;
    var sql:String =
        "CREATE TABLE IF NOT EXISTS rssfeeds (" +
        "   feedId INTEGER PRIMARY KEY AUTOINCREMENT, " +
        "   url TEXT UNIQUE, " +
        "   title TEXT, " +
        "   feedType TEXT, " +
        "   homeURL TEXT, " +
        "   lastFetched DATE" +
        ")";
    createStmt.text = sql;
    createStmt.addEventListener(SQLEvent.RESULT, onDatabaseCreated);
    createStmt.addEventListener(SQLErrorEvent.ERROR, onDatabaseError);
    createStmt.execute();
}

// Creation handler
private function onDatabaseCreated(event:SQLEvent) : void
{
    trace("Table created.");
}

// Insert record into the table
private function insertRecord( url:String, title:String, feedType: String,
        homeURL:String, lastFetched:String) : void
{
    var insertStmt:SQLStatement = new SQLStatement();
    insertStmt.sqlConnection = sqlConnection;
    var lfDate:Date = lastFetched as Date;
    var sql:String =
        "INSERT INTO rssfeeds (url, title, feedType, homeURL, lastFetched) " +
        "VALUES ('" +
            url + "', '" + title + "', '" + feedType + "', '" + homeURL + "', " +
            " + lfDate
        + ")";
    insertStmt.text = sql;
    insertStmt.addEventListener(SQLEvent.RESULT, onDatabaseInsert);
    insertStmt.addEventListener(SQLErrorEvent.ERROR, onDatabaseError);
    insertStmt.execute();
}

// When insert is successful...
private function onDatabaseInsert(event:SQLEvent) : void
{
    Alert.show("Feed successfully inserted!");
    clearFields();
}

// Handler for Insert button click
private function onInsertClick(): void
{
    var d:String = dfLastFetched.selectedDate as String;
```

```
        insertRecord( tiURL.text, tiTitle.text, cbType.text, tiHomeURL.text, d);
    }

    // Clear all UI fields
    private function clearFields() : void
    {
        tiURL.text = "";
        tiHomeURL.text = "";
        tiURL.text = "";
        cbType.text = "";
    }

    // Drag In handler
    public function onDragIn(event:NativeDragEvent) : void
    {
        NativeDragManager.dropAction = NativeDragActions.COPY;
        if (event.clipboard.hasFormat(ClipboardFormats.URL_FORMAT))
        {
            NativeDragManager.acceptDragDrop(this);
        }
    }

    // Drop handler
    public function onDragDrop(event:NativeDragEvent) : void
    {
        if (event.clipboard.hasFormat(ClipboardFormats.URL_FORMAT)) {
            feedURL = (event.clipboard.getData(ClipboardFormats.URL_FORMAT,
                    ClipboardTransferMode.ORIGINAL_PREFERRED) as String);
            dropFeed(feedURL);
        }
    }

// Retrieve feed info via HTTPService
    public function dropFeed(url:String): void
    {
        CursorManager.setBusyCursor();
        var httpService:HTTPService = new HTTPService();
        httpService.resultFormat = "object";
        httpService.addEventListener(ResultEvent.RESULT, onFetchComplete);
        httpService.addEventListener(FaultEvent.FAULT, onFetchError);
        httpService.url =  url;
        httpService.send();
    }

    // Handler for HTTPService result event
    // Retrieve info for record
    private function onFetchComplete(event:ResultEvent) : void
    {
        // RSS 2.0
        if (event.result.hasOwnProperty("rss"))
        {
```

(continued)

Listing 11-1 *(continued)*

```
      feedTitle = event.result.rss.channel.title as String;
      homeURL = event.result.rss.channel.link as String;
      lastFetched = event.result.rss.channel.lastBuildDate as String;
      feedType = "RSS 2.0";
    }
    // RSS 1.0
    else if (event.result.hasOwnProperty("RDF"))
    {
      feedTitle = event.result.RDF.channel.title as String;
      homeURL = event.result.RDF.channel.link as String;
      lastFetched = event.result.RDF.channel.lastBuildDate as String;
      feedType = "RSS 1.0";
    }
    // Atom
    else if (event.result.hasOwnProperty("feed"))
    {
      feedTitle = event.result.feed.title as String;
      homeURL = event.result.feed.link[0] as String;
      lastFetched = event.result.feed.updated as String;
      lastFetched = lastFetched.replace(/-/g, "/");
      lastFetched = lastFetched.replace("T", " ");
      lastFetched = lastFetched.replace("Z", " GMT-0000");
      feedType = "Atom";
    }
    // Unsupported
    else
    {
      trace("Unable to retrieve RSS feed: Unsupported format.");
      return;
    }

    clearFields();
    insertRecord( feedURL, feedTitle, feedType, homeURL, lastFetched);
    CursorManager.removeBusyCursor();
  }

  // Error handler for HTTPService
  private function onFetchError(event:FaultEvent) : void
  {
    CursorManager.removeBusyCursor();
    trace("The following error occurred when fetching the RSS feed: " + event.
          message);
  }

]]>
</mx:Script>
<mx:Text  x="88" y="28" text="URL:&#xd;" textAlign="left"/>
<mx:Text x="84" y="61" text="Title:&#xd;" textAlign="left"/>
<mx:Text  x="56" y="93" text="Home URL:&#xd;" textAlign="left"/>
<mx:Text  x="42" y="155" text="Last Fetched: " textAlign="left"/>
<mx:TextInput id="tiURL" x="138" y="26" width="185"/>
<mx:TextInput id="tiTitle"  x="138" y="59" width="185"/>
```

```
<mx:TextInput id="tiHomeURL" x="138" y="91" width="185"/>
<mx:DateField id="dfLastFetched" x="138" y="153"/>
<mx:Button x="270" y="192" label="Insert" click="onInsertClick()"/>
<mx:Text   x="56" y="121" text="Feed type:" textAlign="left"/>
<mx:ComboBox id="cbType" x="138" y="119" width="185">
 <mx:dataProvider>
   <mx:String>RSS 2.0</mx:String>
   <mx:String>RSS 1.0</mx:String>
   <mx:String>Atom</mx:String>
 </mx:dataProvider>
 </mx:ComboBox>

</mx:WindowedApplication>
```

Requesting Data from a Table

When you perform a SELECT query on a table, you execute the SQL statement in much the same way as you do the CREATE NEW and INSERT examples shown in the previous sections. However, the key aspect of a SELECT statement is processing the result set that is returned to you from the database.

Consider the following HTML/JavaScript example that demonstrates how to work with the result set of the rssfeed.db database that is created earlier in this chapter. The app is simple (see Figure 11-3); it consists of a single button that, when clicked, queries the database and returns all the records from the rssfeeds table. The title and URL of the RSS feed are then displayed in a bulleted list.

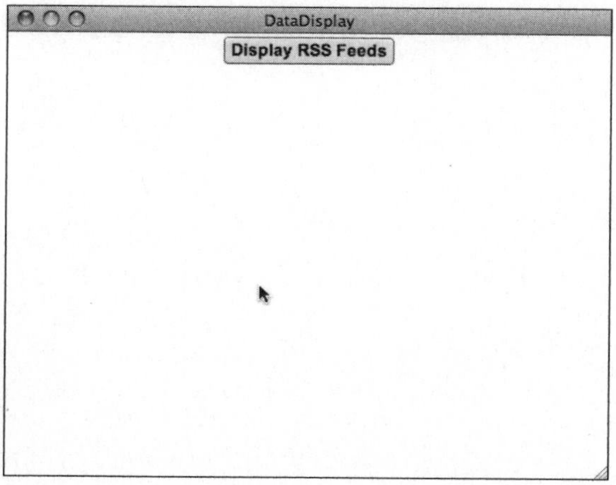

Figure 11-3:
Ready to get
a list of RSS
feeds with
the push of
a button.

Here is the initial HTML file:

```html
<html>
<head>
<title>DataDisplay</title>

<link href="style.css" rel="stylesheet" type="text/css"/>
<script type="text/javascript" src="AIRAliases.js"></script>

<script type="text/javascript">

</script>
</head>
<body>


<div id="container">
<p style="text-align:center">
<button type="button">Display RSS Feeds</button></p>

</div>
</body>
</html>
```

After this document shell is created, you're ready to establish a connection to the database file when the app opens. Here's the code:

```javascript
// Add event listener when app loads
window.addEventListener("load", init, false);

// Global vars
var DATABASE_FILE = "rssfeeds.db";
var sqlConnection;

// Initialize app
function init()
{
  connectDatabase();
}

// Connect to database
function connectDatabase()
{
  var dbRoot = air.File.documentsDirectory.resolvePath('rssdrop');
  dbRoot.createDirectory();
  dbFile = dbRoot.resolvePath(DATABASE_FILE);
  sqlConnection = new air.SQLConnection();
  sqlConnection.addEventListener(air.SQLEvent.OPEN, onDatabaseOpen);
  sqlConnection.addEventListener(air.SQLErrorEvent.ERROR, onDatabaseError);
  sqlConnection.openAsync(dbFile);
}

// Initialize database once the connection is opened
```

```
function onDatabaseOpen(event)
{
  air.trace( "Database connection is opened." );
}

// Database error
function onDatabaseError(event)
{
  alert(event.error.message + " Details: " + event.error.details);
}
```

The init() function is executed when the app loads and then calls the connectDatabase() function. If you read the earlier section on connecting to a database, this code should look familiar.

The database connection is now open and ready for action.

Next, you add an onclick event handler for the HTML button named selectFromDatabase(). This function is responsible for calling the SQL query on the rssfeeds table:

```
// Insert record into the table
function selectFromDatabase()
{
  selectStmt = new air.SQLStatement();
  selectStmt.sqlConnection = sqlConnection;
  var sql = "SELECT * FROM rssfeeds";
  selectStmt.text = sql;
  selectStmt.addEventListener(air.SQLEvent.RESULT, onSelectResult);
  selectStmt.addEventListener(air.SQLErrorEvent.ERROR, onDatabaseError);
  selectStmt.execute();
}
```

In this function, the SELECT SQL statement is passed onto the database engine for processing. The onSelectResult() function is assigned to be the handler for the RESULT event, which is triggered when the SQL query finishes.

The selectStmt is defined globally so that it can be accessed from the onSelectResult() function.

Here's the onSelectResult() function, which takes the results and adds the content to the DOM:

```
function onSelectResult(event)
{
  var result = selectStmt.getResult();
  var len = result.data.length;
  for (i = 0; i < len; i++)
  {
```

```
    var record = result.data[i];

     var c = document.getElementById('container');
    var ul_tag = document.createElement('ul');
    c.appendChild(ul_tag);
    var li_tag = document.createElement('li');
   li_tag.appendChild(document.createTextNode(record.title + " (" + record.url
           + ")" ));
    ul_tag.appendChild(li_tag);
  }
}
```

Figure 11-4 shows the results when this code is performed on the `rssfeeds` database table.

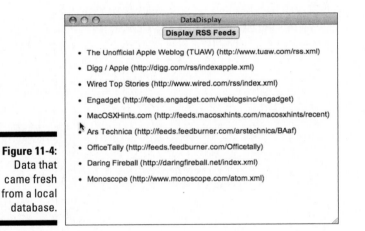

Figure 11-4:
Data that came fresh from a local database.

Listing 11-2 provides a full listing of the HTML/JavaScript source code.

Listing 11-2: DataDisplay.html

```html
<html>
<head>
<title>DataDisplay</title>

<script type="text/javascript" src="AIRAliases.js"></script>

<script type="text/javascript">

  // Add event listener when app loads
  window.addEventListener("load", init, false);

  // Global vars
  var DATABASE_FILE = "rssfeeds.db";
```

```
var sqlConnection;
var selectStmt;

// Initialize app
function init()
{
  connectDatabase();
}

// Connect to database
function connectDatabase()
{
  var dbRoot = air.File.documentsDirectory.resolvePath('rssdrop');
  dbRoot.createDirectory();
  dbFile = dbRoot.resolvePath(DATABASE_FILE);
  sqlConnection = new air.SQLConnection();
  sqlConnection.addEventListener(air.SQLEvent.OPEN, onDatabaseOpen);
  sqlConnection.addEventListener(air.SQLErrorEvent.ERROR, onDatabaseError);
  sqlConnection.openAsync(dbFile);
}

// Initialize database once the connection is opened
function onDatabaseOpen(event)
{
  air.trace( "Database connection is opened." );
}

// Database error
function onDatabaseError(event)
{
  alert(event.error.message + " Details: " + event.error.details);
}


// Insert record into the table
function selectFromDatabase()
{
  selectStmt = new air.SQLStatement();
  selectStmt.sqlConnection = sqlConnection;
  var sql = "SELECT * FROM rssfeeds";
  selectStmt.text = sql;
  selectStmt.addEventListener(air.SQLEvent.RESULT, onSelectResult);
  selectStmt.addEventListener(air.SQLErrorEvent.ERROR, onDatabaseError);
  selectStmt.execute();
}

// When insert is successful...
function onSelectResult(event)
{
  var result = selectStmt.getResult();
  var len = result.data.length;
```

(continued)

Listing 11-2 *(continued)*

```
    for (i = 0; i < len; i++)
    {
      var record = result.data[i];

       var c = document.getElementById('container');
      var ul_tag = document.createElement('ul');
      c.appendChild(ul_tag);
      var li_tag = document.createElement('li');
      li_tag.appendChild(document.createTextNode(record.title + " (" + record.
             url + ")" ));
      ul_tag.appendChild(li_tag);
    }
  }

</script>
</head>
<body>
<div id="container">
<p style="text-align:center"><button type="button" onclick="selectFromDatabase()
             ;">Display RSS Feeds</button></p>

</div>
</body>
</html>
```

Chapter 12

Surfing the AIRwaves: Net Connectivity

As I say at the start of this book, Adobe AIR is designed to create rich Internet applications (RIAs). Given that "Internet" is the middle word of that acronym, it's natural that AIR would provide network support.

In this chapter, I introduce you to some key network capabilities of AIR that you'll find yourself wanting to incorporate into your app. You can discover how to detect whether the app has access to the Internet. You also explore how to communicate with a server using XML sockets. Finally, I round out the discussion by showing you how to push data from a server right into your AIR app.

Detecting Network Connectivity

If you're developing a traditional Web application, you can assume the need for Internet connectivity for your app when you're building it. After all, if users do not have a connection, they'll either be unable to access it at all or they won't be able to complete a task because a server is required.

An Adobe AIR application, however, is different. A live connection when running in a desktop environment may or may not be available. As a result, AIR enables you to detect changes to Internet connectivity in two ways. First, you can detect basic changes by trapping for the event of the `nativeApplication` object. Second, if you want to detect changes to a specific network resource, such as an IP address or Web site, you can use a service monitor. (For information on remote service monitoring, see the upcoming "Monitoring Remote Network Services" section.)

If you'd simply like to know whether a change has occurred in the connection status of your app, add an event listener to the NETWORK_CHANGE event of the application. In JavaScript, you can add the following code:

```
// Add event listener to init() function
air.NativeApplication.nativeApplication.addEventListener
        (air.Event.NETWORK_CHANGE, onNetworkChange);


function onNetworkChange(event){
  Alert("Network change detected. Seek shelter immediately.");
}
```

The ActionScript equivalent is the following:

```
// Add event listener to init() function
NativeApplication.nativeApplication.addEventListener(Event.NETWORK_CHANGE,
            onNetworkChange);

public function onNetworkChange(evt:Event):void {
  mx.controls.Alert.show("Network change detected. Seek shelter immediately.");
}
```

Suppose you run an app with this code in it and unplug your network cable to disconnect your laptop from your home network. The app would quickly notice that a change occurred and show the alert message. Then, when you reconnected to the Internet using WIFI, the alert message would trigger once again.

You can't use this event to detect the exact nature of the network change, only that some sort of connection change occurred.

Monitoring Remote Network Services

Although the application's NETWORK_CHANGE event can be helpful, it also can be incomplete. Specifically, in a real world situation, when you want to determine whether you've experienced a connectivity change, what you *really* want to know is whether a change in connection has occurred with a specific network resource your application needs.

Adobe AIR provides network service monitoring capabilities to detect changes in connectivity to a given HTTP or socket connection. For HTTP URLs, you use the URLMonitor class, whereas socket connections require you to use SocketMonitor. Both URLMonitor and SocketMonitor are children of the ServiceMonitor base class.

The ServiceMonitor class and its children use an event-based approach to respond to network connectivity changes. To do so, they dispatch a STATUS event whenever a change in network connection is discovered. You can then add an event listener to do something based on the change.

To activate an instance of ServiceMonitor, call its start() method.

By default, a service monitor kicks in and polls the specified network resource only after the start() method is called and when the network status changes (from the application's NETWORK_CHANGE event). However, by setting its pollInterval property to a specified number of milliseconds, you can have the service monitor check periodically independent of the application's NETWORK_CHANGE event.

Enabling HTML apps for service monitoring

For HTML apps, network service monitoring is outside the normal AIR application framework that you're used to working with by now. As a result, you need to perform two tasks to enable your app for monitoring:

1. **Copy the** servicemonitor.swf **file from the frameworks subdirectory of the Adobe AIR SDK into your root application directory.**

   This gives you access to ServiceMonitor and its descendents.

2. **Add the following script reference to your document head to include** servicemonitor.swf **in your app:**

   ```
   <script source="servicemonitor.swf" type="application/x-shockwave-flash"/>
   ```

After you've added this reference, you're ready to go perform network monitoring to your heart's content.

Monitoring connectivity to a Web site

The URLMonitor object comes in handy when you need to check on the connectivity to make HTTP or HTTPS requests to a given URL. The URLMonitor object is designed for checking connectivity at port 80, the standard port for HTTP communication.

The typical way to use `URLMonitor` is to create an instance of the class, assign a URL to it, and attach an event listener to it when the connection status changes.

For example, use the following HTML/JavaScript code to detect connectivity to `google.com`:

```
<script src="servicemonitor.swf" type="application/x-shockwave-flash" />

<script>
var urlMonitor;

function init() {
  urlMonitor = new air.URLMonitor(new air.URLRequest('http://www.google.com'));
  urlMonitor.addEventListener(air.StatusEvent.STATUS, onStatusChange);
  urlMonitor.start();
}

function onStatusChange(event) {
 if (urlMonitor.available) {
   alert("The current network status is A-OK!");
 }
 else
   alert("The current network status is BAD, AWFUL, and OTHERWISE TERRIBLE.");
 }
}
</script>
```

As you can see, the `URLMonitor` instance uses a URLRequest instance in its constructor to determine the exact resource to monitor. After assigning a listener to the `STATUS` event, the `onStatusChange` handler tests the `URLMonitor`'s `available` property to determine whether the resource is available.

Here's a similar example using ActionScript:

```
import air.net.SocketMonitor;
import mx.controls.Alert;
import air.net.URLMonitor;
import flash.net.URLRequest;
import flash.events.StatusEvent;

private static const TEST_URL:String = 'http://www.dummies.com';
private static const CODE_UNAVAILABLE:String = "Service.unavailable";
private static const CODE_OK:String = "Service.available";
private static const  MSG_OK:String = "Site is accessible";
private static const MSG_UNAVAILABLE = "Site is unavailable. Please check
          your internet connection.";

public function init():void {
  var urlMonitor:URLMonitor;
```

```
    var socketMonitor:SocketMonitor;

    urlMonitor = new URLMonitor(new URLRequest(TEST_URL));
    urlMonitor.addEventListener(StatusEvent.STATUS, onConnectionStatusChange);
    urlMonitor.start();
}

public function onConnectionStatusChange(evt:StatusEvent):void {
    if (evt.code == CODE_OK) {
        Alert.show(MSG_OK);
    }
    else if (evt.code == CODE_UNAVAILABLE) {
        Alert.show(MSG_UNAVAILABLE);
    }
}
```

Notice the `code` property of the `StatusEvent` instance in the `onConnection StatusChange` handler. You can use it to determine whether the service is available. It has two values:

✔ `Service.available`
✔ `Service.unavailable`

However, in general, it is considered better practice to use the `available` property of the `ServiceMonitor` instance rather than the event code.

Monitoring socket connections

The `SocketMonitor` object provides the same functionality as `URLMonitor` does when you need to work with socket connections to ports other than 80. Here is a JavaScript example that connects to an FTP server:

```
<script src="servicemonitor.swf" type="application/x-shockwave-flash"/>

<script>
var socketMonitor;

function init() {
  socketMonitor= new air.SocketMonitor(new air.URLRequest('ftp://ftp.dummies.
            com', 21));
  socketMonitor.addEventListener(air.StatusEvent.STATUS, onStatusChange);
  socketMonitor.start();
}

function onStatusChange(event) {
  if (socketMonitor.available) {
    alert("The current socket connection is working!");
  }
```

```
  else
    alert("Houston, we have a socket problem.");
  }
}
</script>
```

Making an XML Socket Connection

Adobe AIR provides a framework for creating both XML and binary socket connections with a server. An XML socket is useful when you want to keep a live connection open between your app and a server for exchanging data. So, not only can your app request data from or upload data to a server, but you can also have a server push information down to your app without user intervention. An XML socket, implemented through the XMLSocket class, is intended for XML data, but AIR does actually enforce an XML structure in the data you interchange.

Establishing TCP/IP socket connection is a two-sided project. First, you need to enable your AIR client app for the data interchange. Second, a server-side process must be able to monitor the port and then process the data or instructions of your app when a connection is established. The server side app can be written in any traditional app server language, such as Java, PHP, Cold Fusion, Python, and so on.

Keep in mind a couple of security restrictions when working with XML sockets. First, you can't connect to any port you want with XMLSocket. Because lower number ports are reserved for core services such as FTP, POP3, or HTTP, you can connect only to a port greater than or equal to 1024. Second, nonsandboxed content can connect to a server only in the same domain as the one in which the content resides.

To show you how to create a socket connection, I first show you how to create a very basic Java server to handle your socket connection. I then walk you through creating the socket connection in your AIR app.

Creating a basic socket server

A socket connection is much like a phone line. You can have the coolest phone in the world, but if no one is on the other end of the phone line to talk with you, what's the point? In the same way, if your AIR application is going to be able to converse with a remote server using a socket connection, then you need to have a backend server to talk to.

With that in mind, in this section I show you how to create a very simplistic Java server for this task. The server's job is simply to listen for a socket connection at a specified port, and when a conversation is started, the server simply prints that text to a console window. Because this book is about Adobe AIR and not Java or any other server-side technology, I don't dwell on many of the details concerning how the server works. At a minimum, you can read the source code comments to get a better idea of what the Java server does. But if you'd like to know more about Java or how to create Java servers, I recommend checking out *Java For Dummies,* 4th Edition, by Barry Burd (Wiley Publishing).

If you expect to spend any time at all working with a Java server, I strongly recommend downloading the Eclipse IDE at `http://eclipse.org`. It's a free download and is an excellent way to work with and debug the Java server, even if you're a Java newbie. If not, find yourself a text editor and command prompt.

1. **If necessary, install the JDK (Java SE Developer's Kit).**

   Before proceeding, you need to have the JDK installed. Mac OS X users already have this on their system. Windows users need to download and install from `http://java.sun.com/javase/downloads/index.jsp`.

2. **Create or download** `ReallySimpleServer.java`.

   Listing 12-1, which follows these steps, shows the Java code for the simple server. You can type this code into a new text-based file and save it as `ReallySimpleServer.java`.

   Or, much easier, simply download `ReallySimpleServer.java` from this book's Web site at `www.dummies.com/go/adobeairfd`.

3. **Open a command-line window and change the directory to the location of the** `ReallySimpleServer.java` **file.**

4. **From a command-line window, enter the following instruction from the same directory that the** `.java` **file is in:**

   ```
   javac ReallySimpleServer.java
   ```

   This command compiles the source code and generates a `ReallySimpleServer.class` file.

   If `javac` is unrecognized, make sure that the JDK path is in your path.

5. **Run the Java server by typing the following command in a command-line window:**

   ```
   java -classpath . ReallySimpleServer
   ```

If you're using Eclipse, you can compile and run the server right from within the IDE.

Listing 12-1: **ReallySimpleServer.java.**

```java
import java.io.*;
import java.net.*;

class ReallySimpleServer {
 private static ReallySimpleServer server;
 ServerSocket socket;
 Socket incomingSocket;
 BufferedReader inputReader;
 PrintStream outputStream;

 // Called when ReallySimpleServer is launched
 public static void main(String[] args) {
   int port = 6101;
     try {
       port = Integer.parseInt(args[0]);
     }
     catch (ArrayIndexOutOfBoundsException e) {
       // Catch exception
     }
     // Create new server socket listener at specified port
     server = new ReallySimpleServer(port);
 }

 private ReallySimpleServer(int port) {
   System.out.println(«>>>>>>> Starting ReallySimpleServer - the Server to the
           Masses...Really!»);
   System.out.println(«Hey ya - talk to me. When you are done, send me a
           <closeConnection/> to quit.»);
   try {
     // Listen for socket connections
     socket = new ServerSocket(port);
     incomingSocket = socket.accept();
     // Incoming text
     inputReader = new BufferedReader(new InputStreamReader(incomingSocket.
           getInputStream()));
     outputStream = new PrintStream(incomingSocket.getOutputStream());
     boolean completed = false;

     while (!completed) {
       String str = inputReader.readLine();
       // If incoming text is null
       if (str == null) {
         printOut( «NULL VALUE: Hey, gimme a break. You gave me nothing!» );
         completed = true;
       }
       // If all goes well, here's where the code will go to
       else {
         printOut(«Here's what you wrote: « + str + «\r»);
         // If client closes connection, mark flag as true to leave loop
         if(str.trim().equals(«<closeConnection/>»)) {
```

```
        completed = true;
      }
    }
    incomingSocket.close();
  }
}
catch (Exception e)  {
  System.out.println(e);
}
}

// Prints output
private void printOut(String str) {
outputStream.println(str);
  System.out.println(str);
}
}
```

Adding a socket connection

With the Java server waiting patiently for someone to talk to, it's time to
develop a simple AIR app that sends data to it. After you have created the
application shell in HTML, Flex, or Flash, you want to establish a socket connection to the server using the XMLSocket object.

Begin by creating an instance of XMLSocket. Here's the code in JavaScript:

```
var xmlSocket = new air.XMLSocket();
```

In ActionScript:

```
var xmlSocket:XMLSocket = new XMLSocket();
```

You want to add event listeners to xmlSocket. For a simple conversation,
you're concerned only with listening to CONNECT and IO_ERROR events:

```
xmlSocket.addEventListener([air.]Event.CONNECT, onConnect);
xmlSocket.addEventListener([air.]IOErrorEvent.IO_ERROR, OnIOError);
```

With that groundwork laid, you're ready to connect to the socket. For this
demo, you're connecting to localhost at port 6101.

```
xmlSocket.connect("localhost", 6101);
```

After a connection is made, the server can accept XML data from the AIR app. To enable the server to do so, you use the `send()` method.

However, keep in mind a couple of important points on sending data:

- Each string you send over the socket connection needs to be terminated with a `\n` character combo.
- Be sure to place `send()` statements in the `onConnect` handler. If you place them just after a `connect()` statement, they could be called before the connection has been established.

Here's the code in JavaScript:

```
function onConnect(evt){
  var cmdConnect = "<connect/> \n";
  var cmdLogin = "<login username=\"ivan\" password=\"noneofurbiz\"/>\n";
  var cmdClose = "<closeConnection/>\n";
  xmlSocket.send(cmdConnect);
  xmlSocket.send(cmdLogin);
  xmlSocket.send(cmdClose);
}
```

And in ActionScript:

```
private function onConnect(evt:Event):void {
  var cmdConnect:String = "<connect/> \n";
  var cmdLogin:String =
      "<login username=\"ivan\" password=\"noneofurbiz\"/>\n";
  var cmdClose:String = "<closeConnection/>\n";
  xmlSocket.send(cmdConnect);
  xmlSocket.send(cmdLogin);
  xmlSocket.send(cmdClose);
}
```

When the AIR app runs, the following output is generated by the server:

```
>>>>>>> Starting ReallySimpleServer - the Server to the Masses...Really!
Hey ya - talk to me. When you are done, send me a <closeConnection/> to quit.
Here's what you wrote: <connect/>
Here's what you wrote: <login username="ivan" password="noneofurbiz"/>
Here's what you wrote: <closeConnection/>
```

Listings 12-2 and 12-3 show the full source code for this example.

Listing 12-2: SockIt2Me.html.

```
<?xml version="1.0" encoding="utf-8"?>
<html>
<head>
<title>SockIt2Me</title>
<script type="text/javascript" src="AIRAliases.js"></script>

<script type="text/javascript">
    private var xmlSocket;

    function init(){
      xmlSocket = new air.XMLSocket();
      xmlSocket.addEventListener(air.Event.CONNECT, onConnect);
      xmlSocket.addEventListener(air.IOErrorEvent.IO_ERROR, onIOError);
      xmlSocket.connect("localhost", 6101);
    }

    function onConnect(evt){
      var cmdConnect = "<connect/> \n";
      var cmdLogin = "<login username=\"ivan\" password=\"noneofurbiz\"/> \n";
      var cmdClose = "<closeConnection/>\n";
      xmlSocket.send(cmdConnect);
      xmlSocket.send(cmdLogin);
      xmlSocket.send(cmdClose);
    }

    function onIOError(evt){
       alert("Error: " + evt);
    }
</script>
</head>
<body>
<p>XMLSocket's Done Right!</p>
</body>
</html>
```

Listing 12-3: SockIt2Me.mxml.

```
<?xml version="1.0" encoding="utf-8"?>
<mx:WindowedApplication xmlns:mx="http://www.adobe.com/2006/mxml"
             layout="absolute" applicationComplete="init()">
 <mx:Script>
  <![CDATA[
    import flash.events.*;
    import flash.net.XMLSocket;
```

(continued)

Listing 12-3 *(continued)*

```
    private var xmlSocket:XMLSocket;

    public function init():void{
      xmlSocket = new XMLSocket();
      xmlSocket.addEventListener(Event.CONNECT, onConnect);
      xmlSocket.addEventListener(IOErrorEvent.IO_ERROR, onIOError);
      xmlSocket.connect("localhost", 6101);
    }

    private function onConnect(evt:Event):void {
      var cmdConnect:String = "<connect/> \n";
      var cmdLogin:String = "<login username=\"ivan\" password=\"noneofurbiz\"/>
             \n";
      var cmdClose:String = "<closeConnection/>\n";
      xmlSocket.send(cmdConnect);
      xmlSocket.send(cmdLogin);
      xmlSocket.send(cmdClose);
    }
    private function onIOError(evt:IOErrorEvent):void {
        trace("Error: " + evt);
    }
  ]]>
</mx:Script>
</mx:WindowedApplication>
```

Creating a "Server Push" Socket Connection

In the previous section, I walk you through the process of establishing an XML socket connection to a server and sending information to it. However, in this section, I expand on this basic functionality and allow the server to push data to the AIR client application and have the AIR app handle the incoming data.

The major advantage to server push is that it eliminates the need for multiple clients to continually poll the server to look for new information. Clients simply remain in listen mode and wait for the server to come to them. Your AIR app is thus easier to implement, and it lessens the load on the server.

However, because a server push solution is driven and controlled by the server-side process, much of the development effort will be on the server side. (For example, the server will need to be multithreaded, devoting a thread for each client that connects to it.)

The server side part of the server push solution is beyond the scope of this book. However, to give you a kick start, you can download the Java `SimplePushServer.class` from `www.dummies.com/go/adobeairfd` and use it for initial testing and experimenting with your AIR app.

In this example, I show you how to create a status monitor for a fictional company that displays status info (OK or NOT OK) for its local branches when the server pushes that info to it. (I'm not sure what, exactly, the status refers to, but you can be sure that it's of national importance!)

The connection to the server happens much in the same way as how I walk you through it in the "Making an XML Socket Connection" section, earlier in this chapter. However, you need to add a DATA event handler to handle the incoming data.

This example focuses on Flex to take advantage of its data-binding capabilities. However, the same logic applies to an HTML app as well.

To begin, you define a basic grid UI to display status info. The data grid is linked to an `ArrayCollection` object called `cities`:

```
<mx:VBox>
  <mx:DataGrid width="100%" height="100%" dataProvider="{cities}">
    <mx:columns>
      <mx:Array>
        <mx:DataGridColumn headerText="Test ID" dataField="id"/>
        <mx:DataGridColumn headerText="City" dataField="city"/>
        <mx:DataGridColumn headerText="Time" dataField="time"/>
        <mx:DataGridColumn headerText="Status" dataField="status"/>
      </mx:Array>
    </mx:columns>
  </mx:DataGrid>
</mx:VBox>
```

Next, you add the initial code:

```
private var xmlSocket:XMLSocket;
[Bindable] private var cities:ArrayCollection = new ArrayCollection();


private function init():void {
  connectToServer();
}

private function connectToServer():void {
  xmlSocket = new XMLSocket();
  xmlSocket.addEventListener(Event.CONNECT, onConnect);
  xmlSocket.addEventListener(IOErrorEvent.IO_ERROR, onConnectError);
  xmlSocket.addEventListener(DataEvent.DATA, onDataReceived);
  xmlSocket.connect("localhost", 6102);
}
```

The `citiesCollection` array is created as bindable. The `init()` function is called when the page loads. It calls the `connectToServer()` function to establish the XML socket connection to the server.

You then add handlers for the `CONNECT` and `IO_ERROR` events. Here's the ActionScript code:

```
private function onConnect(evt:Event):void {
  subscribe("Denver");
  subscribe("Seattle");
  subscribe("Boston");
}

private function subscribe(cityName:String):void {
  var cmd:String = "<subscribe event=\"" + cityName + "\"/>\n";
  xmlSocket.send(cmd);
}

private function onIOError( evt: IOErrorEvent ): void {
  mx.controls.Alert.show( "Error. Unable to connect to server." );
}
```

The `onConnect()` handler is called when a connection is established. It calls the `subscribe()` function, which sends an XML fragment to the server using `send()`.

The key event handler for dealing with server push is defined as `onData Received()`:

```
public function onDataReceived(evt:DataEvent):void {
  var xml:XML = new XML(evt.data);
  var element:String = xml.name().toString();

  if (element == "city") {
    var obj:Object = new Object();
    obj.id = nextId++;
    obj.city = xml.@name;
    obj.time = xml.property.@time;
    obj.status =xml.property.@status;
    cities.addItem(obj);
  }
}
```

This function is called each time data is pushed from the server in the XML socket. In this simple example, you need to account only for `city` elements, but a real-world app could account for many different messages from the server by testing the value of the incoming element.

When a `city` element is received, the XML structure looks like the following:

```
<city name="Denver">
<property time="12/01/2008 11:20:12PM" status="OK"/>
</city>
```

The values from the XML document are then placed into an object, which is added to the `cities` array.

The final task is to close the connection with the server when the app closes. To do so, you add a listener for the `EXITING` event:

```
NativeApplication.nativeApplication.addEventListener(Event.EXITING, onAppExit);
```

Here's the handler:

```
private function onAppExit(evt:Event):void {

  disconnectFromServer();

}

private function disconnectFromServer():void {

  var cmd:String = "<closeConnection />\n";

  xmlSocket.send(cmd);

}
```

The `disconnectFromServer()` function sends a `<closeConnection/>` element to the server, telling it to close the socket connection and end the conversation.

Figure 12-1 shows the AIR client with data provided from the server.

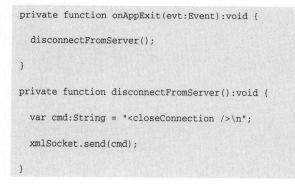

Test ID	City	Time	Status
0	Boston	Mon Sep 08 22:35:28 EDT 2008	OK
1	Denver	Mon Sep 08 22:35:37 EDT 2008	OK
2	Boston	Mon Sep 08 22:35:40 EDT 2008	OK
3	Denver	Mon Sep 08 22:35:43 EDT 2008	OK
4	Seattle	Mon Sep 08 22:35:46 EDT 2008	OK
5	Seattle	Mon Sep 08 22:35:52 EDT 2008	OK
6	Boston	Mon Sep 08 22:35:55 EDT 2008	OK
7	Denver	Mon Sep 08 22:36:01 EDT 2008	OK
8	Boston	Mon Sep 08 22:36:04 EDT 2008	OK
9	Denver	Mon Sep 08 22:36:13 EDT 2008	OK
10	Denver	Mon Sep 08 22:36:16 EDT 2008	OK
11	Seattle	Mon Sep 08 22:36:28 EDT 2008	OK
12	Boston	Mon Sep 08 22:36:37 EDT 2008	OK

Figure 12-1: Data pushed from the server.

Listing 12-4 shows the full source code for this section's example app.

Listing 12-4: TwoSocks.mxml.

```
<?xml version="1.0" encoding="utf-8"?>
<mx:WindowedApplication xmlns:mx="http://www.adobe.com/2006/mxml"
            layout="vertical"
  applicationComplete="init()">

  <mx:Script>
    <![CDATA[
      import mx.controls.Alert;
      import mx.collections.ArrayCollection;

      private var xmlSocket:XMLSocket;
      private var nextId:int;

      [Bindable] private var cities:ArrayCollection = new ArrayCollection();

      private function init():void {
        connectToServer();
        NativeApplication.nativeApplication.addEventListener(Event.EXITING,
            onAppExit);
      }

      private function onAppExit(evt:Event):void {
        disconnectFromServer();
      }

      private function connectToServer():void {
        xmlSocket = new XMLSocket();
        xmlSocket.addEventListener(Event.CONNECT, onConnect);
        xmlSocket.addEventListener(DataEvent.DATA, onDataReceived);
        xmlSocket.addEventListener(IOErrorEvent.IO_ERROR, onIOError);
        xmlSocket.connect("localhost", 6102);
      }


      private function onIOError( evt: IOErrorEvent ): void {
        mx.controls.Alert.show( "Error. Unable to connect to server." );
      }

      private function subscribe(cityName:String):void {
        var cmd:String = "<subscribe event=\"" + cityName + "\"/>\n";
        xmlSocket.send(cmd);
      }

      public function onDataReceived(evt:DataEvent):void {
        var xml:XML = new XML(evt.data);
```

```
            var element:String = xml.name().toString();

            if(element == "response") {
              // do something
            }
            else if (element == "city") {
              var obj:Object = new Object();
              obj.id = nextId++;
              obj.city = xml.@name;
              obj.time = xml.property.@value;
              obj.status =xml.property.@status;
              cities.addItem(obj);
            }
          }

          private function onConnect(evt:Event):void {
            subscribe("Denver");
            subscribe("Seattle");
            subscribe("Boston");
          }

          private function disconnectFromServer():void {
            var cmd:String = "<closeConnection />\n";
            xmlSocket.send(cmd);
          }
      ]]>
    </mx:Script>

  <mx:VBox>
    <mx:DataGrid width="100%" height="100%" dataProvider="{cities}">
      <mx:columns>
        <mx:Array>
          <mx:DataGridColumn headerText="Test ID" dataField="id"/>
          <mx:DataGridColumn headerText="City" dataField="city"/>
          <mx:DataGridColumn headerText="Time" dataField="time"/>
          <mx:DataGridColumn headerText="Status" dataField="status"/>
        </mx:Array>
      </mx:columns>
    </mx:DataGrid>
  </mx:VBox>

</mx:WindowedApplication>
```

Chapter 13

Working with Audio

*W*hether you want to create a full-fledged media player or simply add sound effects, you can include AIR's sound capabilities inside your application.

Adobe AIR allows you to take advantage of Flash's capabilities to work with audio inside your apps. What's more, AIR enables you to connect with and use a computer's microphone.

In this chapter, I take you into the world of audio. No longer will your AIR apps be forced into library-like silence. Instead, you can discover how to add sounds to respond to events in your apps. I also walk you through how to work with a microphone.

Working with Sounds

Adobe AIR allows you to work with sound files in your app through the Sound class. Each instance of Sound is used for playing a specific sound file inside your app directory, local file, or a network resource. However, several related classes can also act upon these sounds. Table 13-1 lists these classes.

Table 13-1	Sound-Related Classes
Class	*Description*
`[air.]Sound`	Manages basic sound load and playback.
`[air.]SoundChannel`	Controls the playback of a particular Sound instance, including the volume of left/right channels. Each Sound instance has a companion SoundChannel.
`[air.]SoundMixer`	Manages the playback and security properties to all sounds in an app.
`[air.]SoundTransform`	Controls volume and panning for a specific SoundChannel, the SoundMixer object, or the Microphone object.
`[air.] SoundLoaderContext`	Manages buffering time and policy permissions during sound loading.
`[air.]Microphone`	Controls the computer microphone and its audio stream properties.
`[air.]ID3Info`	Provides access to the ID3 metadata of an MP3 file.

Playing a sound file

If you're simply playing a sound file, you just need to create a `Sound` instance, load the URL, and then play it. Here's how it looks using JavaScript:

```
function playSound() {
  var soundFile = new air.URLRequest
          ("app:/assets/iphone.mp3");
  var snd = new air.Sound();
  snd.load(soundFile);
  snd.play();
}
```

Or, in ActionScript:

```
private function playSound():void {
  var soundFile:URLRequest = new URLRequest
          ("app:/assets/iphone.mp3");
  var snd:Sound = new Sound();
  snd.load(soundFile);
  snd.play();
}
```

In this example, the `snd` instance of `Sound` loads the sound file referenced by `soundFile`. After it's loaded, it's played using `play()`.

This example is fine for small or local sound files, but you typically want to account for possible delays in the loading process before you attempt to play a sound back. Therefore, it's good practice to add an event listener to the `[air.]Event.COMPLETE` event to start playback after the resource has been loaded. Note the bolded lines of JavaScript code, which connect the event listener:

```
function playSound() {
  var soundFile = new air.URLRequest
         ("app:/assets/iphone.mp3");
  var snd = new air.Sound();
  snd.addEventListener(air.Event.
         COMPLETE, onSoundLoaded);
  snd.load(soundFile);
}

function onSoundLoaded(event) {
  loadedSound = event.target;
  loadedSound.play();
}
```

Here's the ActionScript version:

```
private function playSound():void {
  var soundFile:URLRequest = new URLRequest("app:/assets/
         iphone.mp3");
  var snd:Sound = new Sound();
  snd.addEventListener(Event.COMPLETE, onSoundLoaded);
  snd.load(soundFile);
}

private function onSoundLoaded(event):void {
  var loadedSound:Sound = event.target as Sound;
  loadedSound.play();
}
```

What's more, if you're loading a large audio file from the Web, you can use the `[air.]ProgressEvent.PROGRESS` to monitor and display the progress of the loading process. When you trap for this event, you can access the `bytesLoaded` and `bytesTotal` properties of the event.

As always, you should also trap for loading errors by listening to the `[air.]IOErrorEvent.IO_Error`.

Here's an updated version of the sound-playing example with these two event handlers. Note that the new event handlers are shown in bold. The JavaScript code is shown first.

```
function playSound() {
  var soundFile = new air.URLRequest("http://www.
          richwagnerwords.com/really-long.mp3");
  var snd = new air.Sound();
  snd.addEventListener(air.Event.COMPLETE, onSoundLoaded);
  snd.addEventListener(air.ProgressEvent.PROGRESS,
          onLoadProgress);
  snd.addEventListener(air.IOErrorEvent.IO_ERROR,
          onLoadError);
  snd.load(soundFile);
}

function onSoundLoaded(event) {
  loadedSound = event.target;
  loadedSound.play();
}

function onLoadProgress(event) {
  var myText = event.bytesLoaded + " of " + event.
          bytesTotal " loaded.";
}

function onLoadError(event) {
  alert( "The request sound file could not be loaded. But
          thanks for trying!");
}
```

And here's the ActionScript code:

```
private function playSound():void {
  var soundFile:URLRequest = new URLRequest
          ("app:/assets/iphone.mp3");
  var snd:Sound = new Sound();
  snd.addEventListener(Event.COMPLETE, onSoundLoaded);
  snd.addEventListener(ProgressEvent.PROGRESS,
          onLoadProgress);
  snd.addEventListener(IOErrorEvent.IO_ERROR,
          onLoadError);
  snd.load(soundFile);
}

private function onSoundLoaded(event):void {
  var loadedSound:Sound = event.target as Sound;
  loadedSound.play();
}

private function onLoadProgress(event:ProgressEvent):
```

```
          void {
  statusUpdate.text = String( event.bytesLoaded ) + " of "
            + String( event.bytesTotal) + " loaded.";
}


private function onLoadError(event:IOErrorEvent):void {
  alert( "The request sound file could not be loaded. But
          thanks for trying!");
}
```

Pausing and resuming playback

Although the `play()` method is sufficient for working with short sound effects or clips, you probably want to allow users to pause or stop the playback of longer audio files. To do so, use the `SoundChannel` object (which is assigned to every `Sound` object) to provide this additional layer of control. This section shows you how to set up this functionality.

Begin by declaring the `Sound` variable and creating the instance inside the `init()` function. You need to refer to its accompanying `SoundChannel` object, so you can declare that now as well. The JavaScript code looks like this:

```
var snd;
var soundChannel;

function init() {
  snd = new air.Sound(new air.URLRequest("app:/assets/you-
          could-be-happy.mp3"));
}
```

Or, in ActionScript:

```
private var snd:Sound;
private var soundChannel:SoundChannel;

private function init():void {

  snd = new Sound(new URLRequest("app:/assets/you-could-
          be-happy.mp3"));
}
```

The sound file is ready to roll when you're ready to play it.

The key to creating pause/resume functionality is the ability to track the current position of the playback as it plays. You use the `position` property of the `SoundChannel` for this purpose. You can use the variable `playback Position` to store the latest position.

Here's the code in JavaScript:

```
var playbackPosition  = 0;
```

And in ActionScript:

```
var playbackPosition:int = 0;
```

Then, when you play the sound file, you want to use `playbackPosition` as the `startTime` parameter for `play()`. Here's the JavaScript:

```
function playSong() {
   soundChannel = snd.play(playbackPosition);
 }
```

Or, in ActionScript:

```
private function playSong():void {
   soundChannel = snd.play(playbackPosition);
 }
```

To pause playback, you use the `stop()` method of the `SoundChannel`. However, before doing so, you capture the current playback position:

Here's the code in JavaScript:

```
function pauseSong() {
  playbackPosition = soundChannel.position;
  soundChannel.stop();
 }
```

And in ActionScript:

```
private function pauseSong(): void {
  playbackPosition = soundChannel.position;
  soundChannel.stop();
 }
```

The entire JavaScript code is as follows:

```
var snd;
var soundChannel;
var playbackPosition  = 0;
// Called on document load
function init() {
  snd = new air.Sound(new air.URLRequest("app:/assets/you-
         could-be-happy.mp3"));
 }

function playSong() {
```

```
      soundChannel = snd.play(playbackPosition);
}
function pauseSong() {
  playbackPosition = soundChannel.position;
  soundChannel.stop();
}
```

Not to be forgotten is the ActionScript code:

```
import flash.events.Event;
import flash.media.Sound;
import flash.media.SoundChannel;

private var snd:Sound;
private var soundChannel:SoundChannel;
private var playbackPosition:int = 0;

// Called when application loading is complete
private function init():void {
  snd = new Sound(new URLRequest("app:/assets/you-could-
        be-happy.mp3"));
}

private function playSong():void {
  soundChannel = snd.play(playbackPosition);
}

private function pauseSong():void {
  playbackPosition = soundChannel.position;
  soundChannel.stop();
}
```

Adding sound effects

You can use the SoundTransform class to control volume and panning (the relative balance between left and right speakers) of a sound channel. Using SoundTransform on a channel can give you some interesting effects. Here's an example of using SoundTransform to create a swirl-like effect across the speakers as the sound file plays.

You begin by declaring Sound, SoundChannel, and SoundTransform variables. You also declare a counter variable, which I use in the example. Here's the code in JavaScript:

```
var snd;
var counter = 0;
var channel;
var transformerSoundTransform;
```

And here's the code in ActionScript:

```
private var snd:Sound;
private var counter:Number = 0;
private var channel:SoundChannel;
private var transformer:SoundTransform;
```

A playSound() function begins by loading the file.

Use this code in JavaScript:

```
function playSound() {
   var soundFile = new air.URLRequest("app:/assets/
         iphone.mp3");
   var snd = new air.Sound();
   snd.load(soundFile);
}
```

Or, in ActionScript:

```
private function playSound():void {
   var soundFile:URLRequest = new URLRequest("app:/assets/
         iphone.mp3");
   var snd:Sound = new Sound();
   snd.load(soundFile);
}
```

After the sound file is loaded, you need to create a new SoundTransform instance. The first parameter specifies the volume level and the second specifies the panning (–1.0 is all left, 1.0 is all right, 0 is a balance). The play() method uses the SoundTransform instance. One last task: You need to attach event handlers to the SoundChannel COMPLETE event and ENTER_ FRAME events. Here's the JavaScript code:

```
transformer = new SoundTransform(0.5, 1.0);
 channel = snd.play(0, 1, transformer);
 channel.addEventListener(Event.SOUND_COMPLETE,
       onPlaybackComplete);
 channel.addEventListener(Event.ENTER_FRAME,
       onEnterFrame);
```

The full ActionScript function looks like this:

```
private function playSound():void {
   var soundFile:URLRequest = new URLRequest("app:/assets/
         iphone.mp3");
   var snd:Sound = new Sound();
   snd.load(soundFile);
   transformer = new SoundTransform(0.5, 1.0);
   channel = snd.play(0, 1, transformer);
```

```
        channel.addEventListener(Event.SOUND_COMPLETE,
                onPlaybackComplete);
      channel.addEventListener(Event.ENTER_FRAME,
                onEnterFrame);
    }
```

The event handlers for the `SoundChannel` events are as follows, beginning with the JavaScript:

```
function onEnterFrame(event) {
    transformer.pan = Math.sin(counter);
    channel.soundTransform = transformer;
    counter += 0.05;
}

function onPlaybackComplete(event) {
    removeEventListener(air.Event.ENTER_FRAME,
            onEnterFrame);
}
```

Now for the ActionScript code:

```
private function onEnterFrame(event:Event):void {
    transformer.pan = Math.sin(counter);
    channel.soundTransform = transformer;
    counter += 0.05;
}

private function onPlaybackComplete(event:Event):void {
    removeEventListener(Event.ENTER_FRAME, onEnterFrame);
}
```

Mike Me Up: Working with the Microphone

Adobe AIR enables access to the microphone or other input device of a computer. Here's an example of accessing the microphone and adjusting several of the sound properties. In JavaScript, use this code:

```
var mic = air.Microphone.getMicrophone();

mic.setUseEchoSuppression(true);
mic.setLoopBack(true);
mic.gain = 30;
mic.rate = 11;
```

Here's the ActionScript equivalent:

```
var mic:Microphone = Microphone.getMicrophone();

mic.setUseEchoSuppression(true);
mic.setLoopBack(true);
mic.gain = 30;
mic.rate = 11;
```

Of special note, the `setLoopBack(true)` method sends incoming audio to the local speakers.

Chapter 14

Quick and Easy: Instant Downloading and Auto-Updating

....

In This Chapter

▶ Using `badge.swf` for easy downloads of your app

▶ Adding auto-update functionality to your app

....

S ome of the best aspects of normal Web applications are that installation and maintenance issues are a breeze to deal with. Because the app resides on a server you control, you simply copy a new version of the app, and all the users accessing it from their browser instantly receive the latest version.

Not so with traditional desktop apps. Because the app exists on hundreds, if not thousands, of computers, the issues of installation and app updates become quite problematic.

Fortunately, Adobe thought about this problem in the construction of Adobe AIR. In fact, AIR offers point-and-click install and no-hassle updates as two built-in capabilities of Adobe AIR that AIR developers can take advantage of. In this chapter, I walk you through how to add these capabilities to your app, putting on that finishing touch that makes your app usable and professional looking.

Seamlessly Installing an AIR App with badge.swf

The AIR SDK comes with the badge.swf file (located in the samples/badge subdirectory) that enables you to provide a seamless installation of your app from a Web page. The benefits of using the badge.swf file are as follows:

✓ The badge.swf installer checks to see whether the AIR runtime is installed. If the AIR runtime isn't detected, the runtime is automatically installed prior to installation of your app.

✓ The user has a choice of whether to install the AIR app without saving the .air file onto his or her computer.

✓ You can easily customize the graphic, badge color, and button color by setting parameters. You can even customize the badge.swf source code to give the badge a personalized look and feel.

✓ Using badge.swf provides a seamless, friendly installation experience for your users that will make them smile uncontrollably at their computer monitor.

To set up the badge.swf file for your AIR app, follow these steps:

1. **Locate three files in your samples/badge subdirectory of the AIR SDK:** badge.swf, AC_RunActiveContent.js, and default_badge.html.

   You'll copy these files up to your Web server in a moment.

2. **Open** default_badge.html **in your HTML editor.**

   The default_badge.html file contains boilerplate code for including the "install badge" (the Flash-based installer) on a Web page.

   You can customize the default_badge.html page to use it on your Web site. Or, more likely, you'll want to simply copy and paste the install badge code into your existing Web page.

3. **Locate the** AC_FL_RunContent() **function call in the JavaScript code.**

   It's the one with a bunch of parameters inside its parentheses.

4. **Customize the** `flashvars` **parameter (the string parameter that follows** `'flashvars'`**).**

   You have three required parameters to update:

   - `appname`: Enter the name of your application that you want to be displayed in a message under the Install button (shown only if the AIR runtime is not present).

     These parameters need to be escaped, so use a `%20` in place of a space in your app's name. For example, AIR Mate is

   ```
   AIR%20Mate
   ```

   - `appurl`: Enter the full (not relative) URL of the `.air` file.

   - `airversion`: If necessary, update the version of the AIR runtime required for your app.

   In addition, you may want to customize three optional parameters:

   - `imageurl`: Indicates the URL of the `.jpg` file to display in the badge interface.

   - `buttoncolor`: Specifies a hex color value for the button background.

   - `messagecolor`: Provides a hex color value for the color of the text message displayed under the Install button.

   Here's an example:

   ```
   'appname=AIR%20Mate&appurl=http://www.dummies.com/air/
        airmate.air&airversion=1.0&imageurl=test.jpg'
   ```

5. **If needed, adjust the** `width` **and** `height` **parameters of the** `AC_FL_RunContent()` **function call.**

   The `badge.swf` needs a minimum size of 217 x 180 pixels. If you need to make it bigger, then adjust.

6. **Save the HTML file or copy and paste the source code to another Web page.**

7. **Upload the** `badge.swf`**,** `AC_RunActiveContent.js`**, and** `default_badge.html` **files (or your own Web page) to your Web server.**

   Figure 14-1 shows the customized badge displayed for my AIR app.

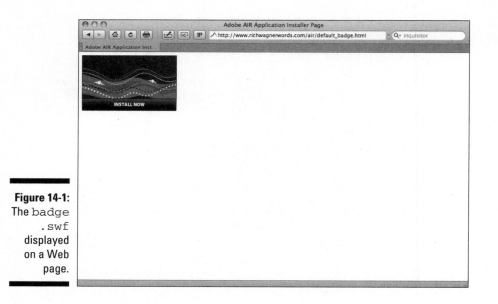

Figure 14-1:
The `badge`
`.swf`
displayed
on a Web
page.

When the badge is clicked by the user, helper text is displayed that indicates to the user what to do next to begin the installation. See Figure 14-2 for details.

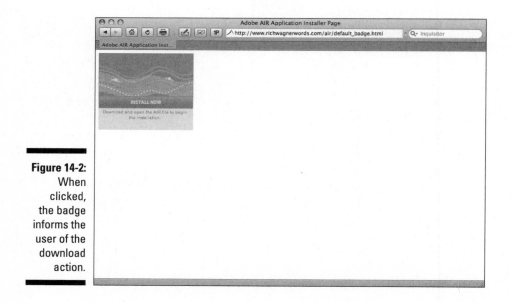

Figure 14-2:
When
clicked,
the badge
informs the
user of the
download
action.

If clicked again, the installation process begins (see Figures 14-3 and 14-4).

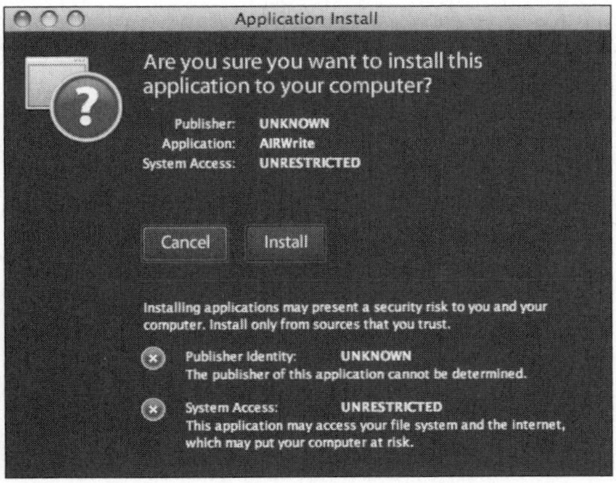

Figure 14-3:
Application
Setup dialog
box.

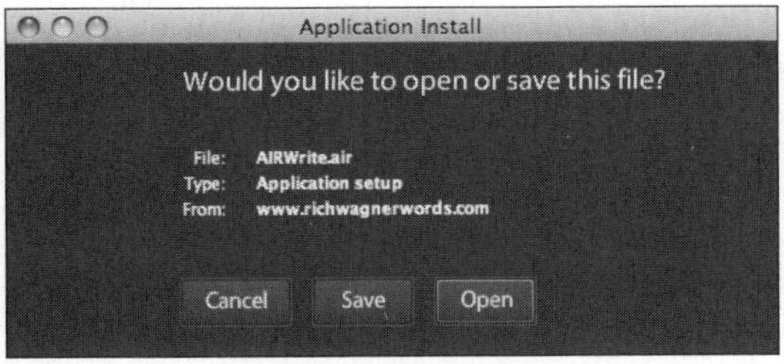

Figure 14-4:
User has
the option
of saving
or opening
without
saving.

The AIR SDK also includes the source files for the `badge.swf` file. These files are included in the `src` folder of the SDK. The `badge.fla` is the source Flash CS3 file, and `AIRBadge.as` is an ActionScript 3.0 class that defines the base class used in `badge.fla`.

Auto-Updating Your AIR Application

As I mention at the start of this chapter, one of the major benefits of a Web app is that it's easy to update. Because users access it remotely, all the application code is located on the server. Therefore, when a bug is fixed or a new feature is introduced, a developer can seamlessly update the application code base without any user intervention.

By contrast, because desktop apps run off a locally installed file, versioning and performing updates have always been much more complicated tasks for desktop applications. Fortunately, Adobe AIR comes with an auto-updating framework that makes the task of updating your app a snap. In fact, after you integrate the update framework into your app, you receive several features for free:

✔ Checking for updates periodically based on a specific interval or user request

✔ Displaying version info to user

✔ Downloading an updated version and displaying Install dialog box

✔ Informing the user the first time the new version is being run

To add these capabilities to your app, you need to do four tasks:

1. Add the update framework to your app.

2. Update the updater descriptor file for your app/version.

3. Upload the descriptor file and updated `.air` file to your Web server.

4. Add update framework code to your app.

I describe these tasks in the following sections.

Adding the AIR update framework

Before beginning the task of dealing with the specifics of your app, you need to add the AIR Update Framework to your application. To do so, follow these steps:

1. **Download the AIR Update Framework at** `http:// labs.adobe.com/ wiki/index.php/Adobe_AIR_Update_Framework.`

   At the time of writing, this framework was still in development and not considered part of the final SDK.

2. **After you download and decompress the framework, copy the folder to your AIR SDK directory so that you can have it on hand.**

3. **Add the appropriate framework file to your project.**

   For HTML apps, you'll want to reference either `ApplicationUpdater. swf` or `ApplicationUpdater_UI.swf`. (The UI version includes additional calls to display a UI for showing update and install options.) After copying the desired `.swf` file to your application directory, add the following script element:

```
<script src="applicationUpdater_UI.swf" type="application/
           x-shockwave-flash"/>
```

For Flex apps, you want to use either `ApplicationUpdate.swc` or `ApplicationUpdate_UI.swc`. (As with the `.swf` files mentioned previously, the UI equivalent includes additional calls to display a UI for showing update and install options.) To do so, copy the `.swc` to the `lib` directory of your app or add its existing directory to your library path. You can then import the updater UI and event packages with the following declarations:

```
import air.update.ApplicationUpdaterUI;

import air.update.events.UpdateEvent;
```

For most purposes, I recommend using the `_UI` versions of the framework files. You'll save yourself a lot of time. I'll focus on the UI versions in the remainder of this chapter.

Creating the updater descriptor file

The update framework uses an XML-based updater descriptor file to define the update versioning. An AIR app accesses this XML file from a Web server when it performs a version check, checking to see whether a new version has been uploaded.

Here's a sample file:

```
<?xml version="1.0" encoding="utf-8"?>
<update xmlns="http://ns.adobe.com/air/
            framework/update/description/1.0">
  <version>2.0</version>
  <url>http://richwagnerwords.com/air/AIRUpdates.air</url>
  <description><![CDATA[
AIRUpdates has an exciting new version for you. Version
            2.0 update includes:

  * Bug fixes
  * New UI

  ]]>
</description>
</update>
```

The `version` element specifies the new version of the app. This value is compared to the `version` element in the application descriptor file. The `url` element indicates the location of the new `.air` file to download. The `description` element is optionally used to provide release notes and other info you want the user to see prior to installation.

After you've updated this file, you want to upload it to the Web server.

Adding the updater to your source code

After you have the update framework added to your AIR app project and the updater descriptor file set, you're ready to add the updater to your application code.

Creating an instance of ApplicationUpdaterUI

You first want to create an instance of the `ApplicationUpdaterUI` object. In JavaScript, use

```
var appUpdater = new ApplicationUpdaterUI();
```

In ActionScript, use:

```
private var appUpdater:ApplicationUpdaterUI = new
        ApplicationUpdaterUI();
```

Customizing the updater from code

You can customize the settings of the updater by working with the properties of the `ApplicationUpdaterUI` instance. The properties are shown in Table 14-1.

Table 14-1	ApplicationUpdater and ApplicationUpdaterUI Settings		
Application UpdaterUI or Application Updater Property	*XML Configuration File Element/Attribute*	*Default*	*Description*
updateURL	`<url></url>`		Specifies the URL of the XML-based updater descriptor file that you create in the "Creating the updater descriptor file" section
delay	`<delay></delay>`	1	Specifies the interval (number of days) in which the app should check for an update

Application UpdaterUI or Application Updater Property	XML Configuration File Element/Attribute	Default	Description

isCheckFor UpdateVisible	`<defaultUI>`
	
	 `<dialog name= "check ForUpdate" visible="true |false" />`
	
	 `</defaultUI>`
		true	Indicates whether the Check for Update, No Update, and Update Error dialog boxes are visible

isDownload UpdateVisible	`<defaultUI>`
	
	 `<dialog name= "downloadUp date" visible= "true|false" />`
	
	 `</defaultUI>`
		True	Indicates whether the Download Update dialog box is visible

isInstall UpdateVisible	`<defaultUI>`
	
	 `<dialog name= "installUpdate" visible="true |false" />`
	
	 `</defaultUI>`
		true	Determines whether the Install Update dialog box is visible

isDownload Progress Visible	`<defaultUI>`
	
	 `<dialog name= "download Progress" visible="true |false" />`
	
	 `</defaultUI>`
		true	Specifies whether the Download Progress and Download Error dialog boxes are visible

isFile UpdateVisible	`<defaultUI>`
	
	 `<dialog name= "fileUpdate" visible="true |false" />`
	
	 `</defaultUI>`
		true	Determines whether the Install Update dialog box shows

(continued)

Table 14-1 *(continued)*

Application UpdaterUI or Application Updater Property	XML Configuration File Element/Attribute	Default	Description

isUnexpected ErrorVisible	`<defaultUI>`
	
	`<dialog name= "unexpected Error" visible= "true|false" />`
	
	`</defaultUI>`
		true	Indicates whether the Unexpected Error dialog box can be visible

The following code sets the URL, prompts the updater to check every half day, and hides the Check for Updates dialog box:

```
appUpdater.updateURL = "http://dummies.com/air/AIRUpdates_versions.xml";
airUpdater.delay = 0.5;
airUpdater.isCheckForUpdateVisible = false;
```

Customizing the updater from an XML configuration file

You can also configure the updater through an XML configuration file. Table 14-1 shows the elements and attributes you can use in the markup. The following file provides identical configuration as the earlier scripting code:

```
<?xml version="1.0" encoding="utf-8"?>
<configuration xmlns="http://ns.adobe.com/air/framework/
           update/configuration/1.0">
   <url>http://dummies.com/air/AIRUpdates_versions
           .xml</url>
   <delay>0.5</delay>
   <defaultUI>
      <dialog name="checkForUpdate" visible="false" />
   </defaultUI>
</configuration>
```

To load the configuration file, add the following line to your app code:

```
appUpdater.configurationFile = new [air.]File("update-
           config.xml");
```

Initializing the ApplicationUpdaterUI instance

The next step is to add event listeners to the updater and then initialize it. The code looks like this:

```
appUpdater.addEventListener([air.]UpdateEvent.INITIALIZED,
        onUpdate);
appUpdater.addEventListener([air.]ErrorEvent.ERROR,
        onError);

appUpdater.initialize();
```

You want to add this code to the `init()` function that is executed when the application loads.

Adding event handlers

Next, you need to add event handlers that will kick off when `appUpdater` is ready to check for an update or when an error occurs. Here's the JavaScript:

```
function onUpdate(event) {
   // Add code here
}

private function onError(event) {
   alert(event.toString());
}
```

In ActionScript:

```
private function onUpdate(event:UpdateEvent):void {
   // Add code here
}

private function onError(evt:ErrorEvent):void {
   Alert.show(evt.toString());
}
```

Checking for updates

Your final step is for the `appUpdater` instance to check for a new version using the `checkNow()` method. You want to add this code to the `onUpdate()` event handler:

```
appUpdater.checkNow();
```

Listings 14-1 and 14-2 provide full source code for an HTML and Flex app.

Listing 14-1:   AIRUpdates.html

```html
<html>
<head>
<title>AIRUpdates</title>
<script type="text/javascript" src="AIRAliases.js" />
<script src="applicationUpdater_UI.swf" type="application/x-shockwave-flash"/>
<script type="text/javascript">

var appVersion:String;
var file:File;
var airFileURL:String = "http://richwagnerwords.com/air/AIRUpdates.air";

var appUpdater = new air.ApplicationUpdaterUI();

    function init() {
        initAutoUpdate();
    }

    function initAutoUpdate() {
        appUpdater.updateURL = "http://richwagnerwords.com/air/AIRUpdates_
            versions.xml";
        appUpdater.addEventListener(air.UpdateEvent.INITIALIZED, onUpdate);
        appUpdater.addEventListener(air.ErrorEvent.ERROR, onError);
        appUpdater.initialize();
    }

    function onError(event) {
        alert(event.toString());
    }

    function onUpdate(event) {
        appUpdater.checkNow();
    }

</script>
</head>
<body onload="init()" bgcolor="#0080C0">
<p>AIRUpdates</p>
</body>
</html>
```

As you consider the Flex version, note that there is additional code that checks to see whether the app has been run before. If not, a welcome message is displayed. The updater process kicks in after this initial check.

Listing 14-2:   AIRUpdates.mxml

```
<?xml version="1.0" encoding="utf-8"?>
<mx:WindowedApplication xmlns:mx="http://www.adobe.com/2006/mxml"
               layout="vertical" title="AIRUpdates"
    applicationComplete="init()">
  <mx:Script>
  <![CDATA[
      import flash.filesystem.*;
      import mx.controls.Alert;
      import flash.events.ErrorEvent;
      import air.update.ApplicationUpdaterUI;
      import air.update.events.UpdateEvent;

      [Bindable] public var appVersion:String;
      public var file:File;
      private var airFileURL:String = "http://richwagnerwords.com/air/
           AIRUpdates.air";

      private var appUpdater:ApplicationUpdaterUI = new ApplicationUpdaterUI();

      public function init():void {
        var appDescriptor:XML = NativeApplication.nativeApplication.
             applicationDescriptor;
        var ns:Namespace = appDescriptor.namespace();
        appVersion = appDescriptor.ns::version;
        checkRunStatus();
        initAutoUpdate();
      }

      private function initAutoUpdate():void {
        appUpdater.updateURL = "http://richwagnerwords.com/air/AIRUpdates_
             versions.xml";
        appUpdater.addEventListener(UpdateEvent.INITIALIZED, onUpdate);
        appUpdater.addEventListener(ErrorEvent.ERROR, onError);
        appUpdater.initialize();
      }

      private function onError(evt:ErrorEvent):void {
        Alert.show(evt.toString());
      }

      private function onUpdate(event:UpdateEvent):void {
        appUpdater.checkNow();
```

(continued)

Listing 14-2 *(continued)*

```
    }

    private function checkRunStatus():void {
      file = File.applicationStorageDirectory;
      file = file.resolvePath(«Preferences/vercheck.txt»);
      if (file.exists) {
        checkAppVersion();
      } else {
        runFirstTime();
      }
    }

    private function checkAppVersion():void {
      var fs:FileStream = new FileStream();
      fs.open(file, FileMode.READ);
      var prevVersion:String = fs.readUTFBytes(fs.bytesAvailable);
      fs.close();
      var av:Number = Number(appVersion);
      var pv:Number = Number(prevVersion);
      if (av > pv) {
        Alert.show(«Welcome to the updated version of AIRUpdates, the coolest
              app in the biz.»);
        saveVersionToFile();
      }
    }

    private function runFirstTime():void {
      Alert.show(«Welcome to AIRUpdates, the coolest app in the biz.»);
      saveVersionToFile();
    }

    private function saveVersionToFile():void {
      var stream:FileStream = new FileStream();
      stream.open(file, FileMode.WRITE);
      stream.writeUTFBytes(appVersion);
      stream.close();
    }
  ]]>
  </mx:Script>

  <mx:VBox backgroundColor=»#6AA16A» x=»0» y=»0» width=»100%» height=»100%»
              horizontalAlign=»center» verticalAlign=»middle»>
    <mx:Label color=»white» text=»{appVersion}» fontSize=»134»/>
  </mx:VBox>

</mx:WindowedApplication>
```

When the app runs, the updater kicks in. Because the `isCheckForUpdate Visible` property defaults to `true`, the Check for Updates dialog box is displayed (see Figure 14-5).

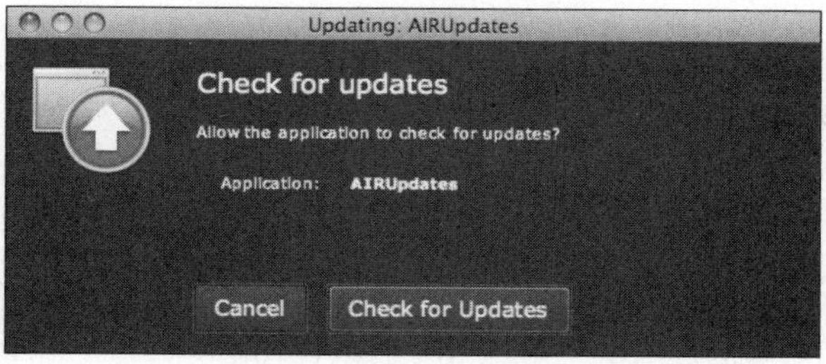

Figure 14-5:
Check for
Updates
dialog box.

When the Check for Updates button is clicked, the updater checks the server-based XML file. Because the remote file is for 2.0 and the current app is 1.0, the Update Available dialog box is displayed (see Figure 14-6). If the Release Notes text is clicked, the description content of the XML is displayed (see Figure 14-7).

Figure 14-6:
Update
Available
dialog box.

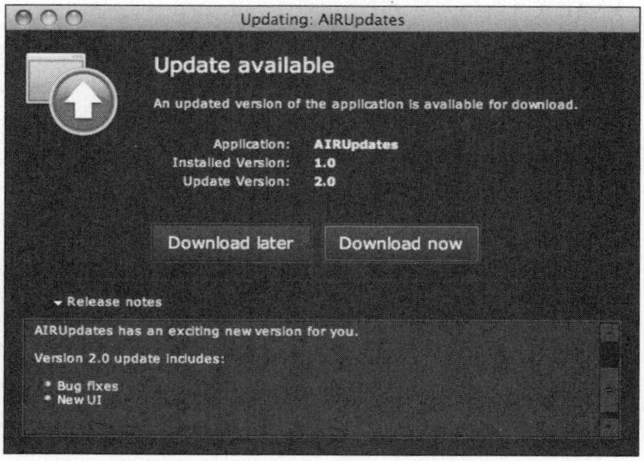

Figure 14-7:
Release
notes are
shown.

Figure 14-8 shows the Download Progress dialog box. When the download is complete, the Install Update dialog box is displayed (Figure 14-9).

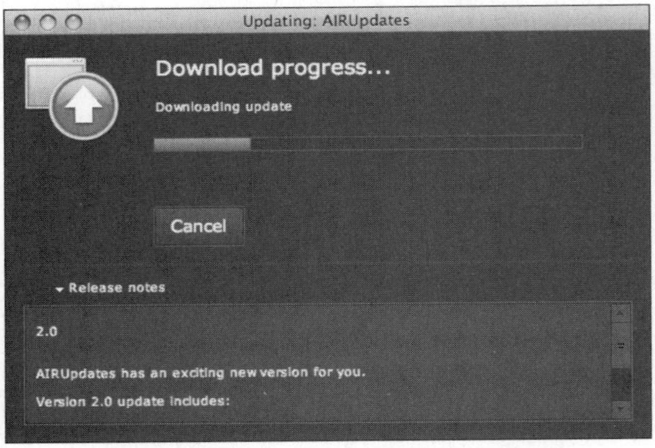

Figure 14-8: Down-loading the update.

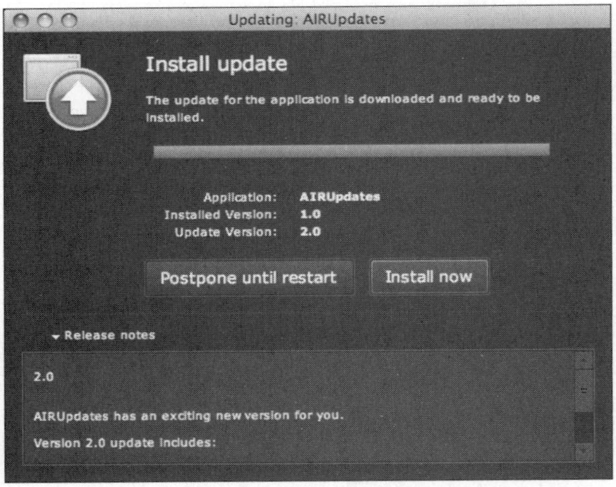

Figure 14-9: Installing the update.

Part IV
The Part of Tens

The 5th Wave   By Rich Tennant

"I couldn't get this 'job skills' program to work on my PC, so I replaced the motherboard, upgraded the BIOS, and wrote a program that links it to my personal database. It told me I wasn't technically inclined and should pursue a career in sales."

In this part . . .

If one is the loneliest number, ten is surely the "dumbest": the the Part of Tens section is a tradition in For Dummies books. This book therefore offers you a Part of Tens for "AIR-heads." In this part, you're privy to ten useful tips to help you with that oh-so-fun task of debugging your app. Also, if you're looking for AIR application examples, you've come to the right place; here I present my choices for the ten best ones.

Chapter 15

Ten Tips for Successful AIR Debugging

Debugging is one of those necessary evils of application development. It's never much fun but is essential to producing a quality, bug-free app. Adobe AIR provides various ways of debugging depending on the type of AIR application you're making. HTML-based apps can take advantage of the AIR HTML Introspector, which comes with the SDK. Flex Builder sports its own powerful debugger environment. Flash allows you to tap into the Adobe Flash Debugger.

In this chapter, I introduce you to these powerful tools as well as other tips and techniques that you'll want to be sure to incorporate into your debugging process.

Use ADL (AIR Debug Launcher) as the Starting Point

As I mention in Chapter 2, the AIR Debug Launcher (or ADL) is a command-line utility that comes with the Adobe AIR SDK. You can use ADL to test your apps without packing them up into an installable AIR app. Not only is it much quicker to test your app, but also any runtime errors that occur will be output to the ADL console window. Therefore, as you test your apps, consider ADL as your starting point for any debugging that you perform.

To use ADL from the command line, be sure it is in your path and then enter the following at a prompt, where `application.xml` is your AIR application descriptor file:

```
adl application.xml
```

Better yet, if you're using Flex Builder or Aptana Studio, you can launch ADL directly through the IDE. See related tips later in this chapter for more details.

ADL will run until your app closes. However, if your app freezes or you forgot to add a Close button to your app, simply close the command-line window.

Make Aptana Studio Your Home Base for HTML-Based Apps

To be effective in your development and debugging processes, you need to be equipped with the right tools. If you're creating HTML/Ajax-based AIR apps, you need to check Aptana Studio.

Aptana Studio is a full-featured integrated development environment (IDE) for Web developers. It offers an optional Adobe AIR plug-in that, when you install it, turns Aptana Studio into an IDE for Adobe AIR applications.

Using Aptana Studio, you can quickly create AIR apps with its AIR Project Creation Wizard (shown in Figure 15-1), use AIR API-supported auto completion in its source editor, and deploy final releases using its AIR package exporter (shown in Figure 15-2). However, what's most beneficial for debugging is that Aptana Studio frees you from the command line when working with ADL. It lets you run a test version of the app by clicking a toolbar button rather than typing everything at the command line (shown in Figure 15-3).

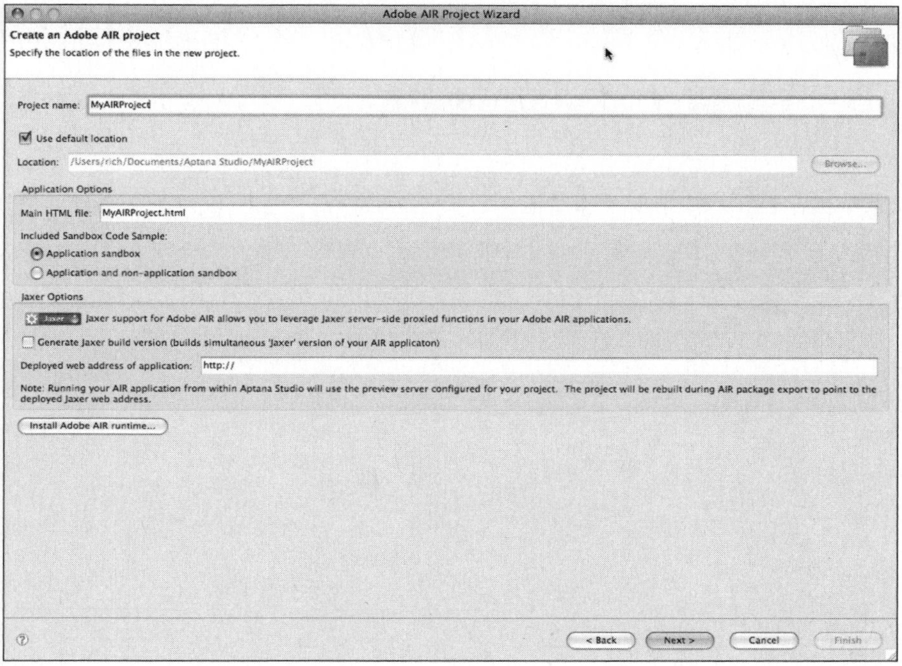

Figure 15-1:
Creating a
new AIR
project in
Aptana
Studio.

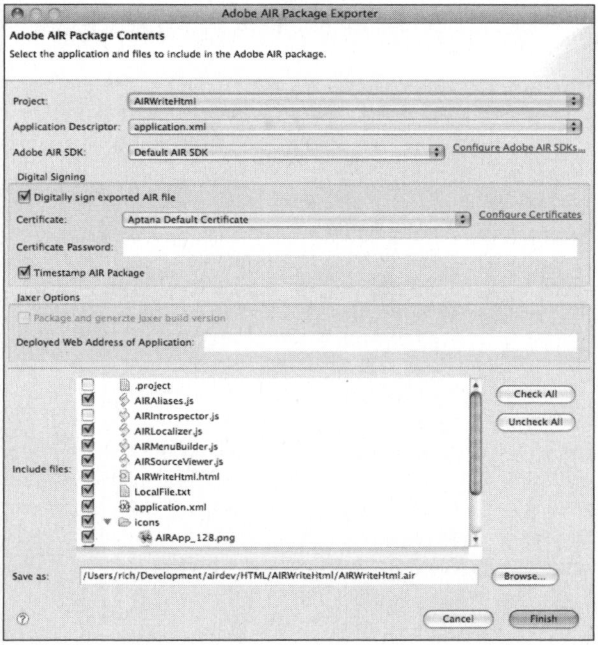

Figure 15-2:
Package
your app
inside the
Aptana
Studio IDE.

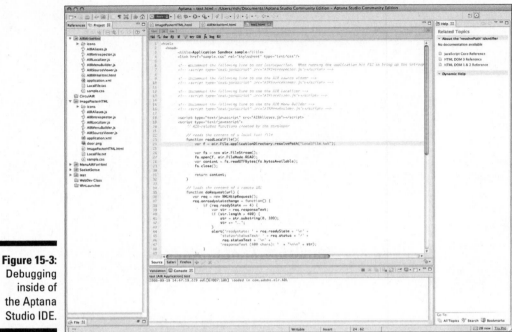

Figure 15-3:
Debugging
inside of
the Aptana
Studio IDE.

To download the free community edition or purchase the professional edition, visit www.aptana.com/air.

Quick and Easy Debugging: Use the alert Command

Sure, the alert command is usually considered the "poor man's debugger." Despite its clumsiness, it can be a handy quick and easy way to initially debug part of your application.

In JavaScript, you use the ubiquitous window.alert() method:

```
alert("Yikes, a problem occurred.");
```

In ActionScript, you call the Alert object's show() method:

```
import mx.contols.Alert;
Alert.show(("Yikes, a problem occurred.");
```

The `alert` command is particularly handy when you are doing initial testing on event handlers. In most cases, you will want to replace these alerts with more sophisticated techniques before final deployment. Here's a handler for a File IO error that lets you know whether something went awry when a file was being read:

```
function onIOReadError(evt) {
   alert("Something wacky happened. We are unable to open "
         + file.nativePath);
}
```

Although `alert()` can be useful, I recommend using it in your code during initial development phases and stripping out the `alert()` calls from your code as your app gets closer to being final.

Better Yet: Use the trace ( ) Method Instead of alert ( )

The `alert()` debugging method displays debug info in a message box, and the execution of the app is interrupted to show those details. Adobe AIR enables you to use an alternative method, the global method called `trace()`, which enables you to output debugging info to the ADL console window. Here's the syntax:

```
[air.]trace("This text will be output");
```

Any nonstring objects that you add to `trace()` will automatically be converted to a string (its `toString()` method is called for you) during the output.

Here's a JavaScript example of using `trace()` to output the error message that is generated during a `SQLErrorEvent.ERROR` event:

```
sql.addEventListener(air.SQLErrorEvent.ERROR, function
          error(event) {
   air.trace(event.error.message);
   sql.removeEventListener(air.SQLErrorEvent.ERROR, error);
});
```

The `trace()` method offers two key advantages over "alert box debugging." First, one of the problems when using alert boxes to display debugging info is that the dialog box itself can get in the way of normal flow of events in the execution of the app. However, because `trace()` doesn't require any user input, it never gets in the way of normal flow. Second, although debug alert boxes will need to be cleaned out of application code before the app is final, you can leave `trace()` commands in the code without the info ever being visible to users when run outside of ADL.

Create Your Own Debug Window

Although the `trace()` command is a great way to output debugging info, sometimes you may want to view debugging info outside the ADL console window.

If you're developing an HTML/JavaScript-based AIR app, you use a `div` element inside your app for this task and toggle its visibility, depending on whether you're in debug mode. Follow these steps:

1. **Add the following `div` to the bottom of your HTML document:**

   ```
   <div id="debugConsole">
   </div>
   ```

2. **Add the following CSS rule to your stylesheet:**

   ```
   div#debugConsole
   {
     display: none;
   }
   ```

   You can add any additional formatting properties you want.

3. **In your JavaScript code, add a global variable that indicates whether you're in debug mode:**

   ```
   var debugMode = false;
   ```

4. **Add a function that toggles visibility of the debug `div`:**

   ```
   enableDebugMode(state)
   {
     debugMode = state;
     d = document.getElementById("debugConsole");

     if (debugMode)
       d.style.display = "block";
     else
       d.style.display = "none";
   }
   ```

5. **Create a** `doDebug()` **function that outputs any debugging data you specify into the** `debugConsole div`:

```
function debug(output)
{
  if (debugMode)
  {
    d = document.getElementById("debugConsole");
    d.appendChild(document.createTextNode(output));
  }
}
```

To use the window, simply enable debug mode when your app loads. For example:

```
function init()
{
  enableDebugMode(true);
}
```

Then, add the following line of code to output to the debug console:

```
debug("debug text you want to display");
```

Outputting to a Log File with AIRLogger

AIRLogger is a handy utility available from the `ear-fung.us` developer blog that enables you to create a log file for debugging your HTML-based AIR app.

To enable this utility, all you need to do is add a downloadable script file called `AIRLogger.js` to your HTML document. You can then write to the log file by using the following command:

```
log.write("my debugging info");
```

The debugging info is output to a log file called `application.log` on your desktop.

To download AIRLogger.js, go to: `www.ear-fung.us/wp-content/uploads/2008/08/airlogger10.js`.

For more general AIRLogger info, go to `www.ear-fung.us/apps/airlogger`.

Debug HTML-Based Apps with the AIR HTML Introspector

The AIR HTML Introspector is an interactive debugging utility that you can use to test your HTML-based AIR applications. The AIR HTML Introspector goes beyond the basic debugging output that you get with alert boxes, `trace()`, your own homegrown debug console, or even AIRLogger. You can use the AIR HTML Introspector to navigate the UI and DOM, adjust JavaScript properties, and even access local files in the application root directory.

To enable the AIR HTML Introspector, you need to include the `AIRIntrospector.js` file in your HTML application source.

You can find the `AIRIntrospector.js` file in the `frameworks` subdirectory of the Adobe AIR SDK. You should copy the JavaScript file to your application directory and then add the following code to every HTML file in your app that will be visible:

```
<script type="text/javascript" src="AIRIntrospector.js"></
          script>
```

When the code is executed, a `Console` class is created and is accessible by calling `air.Introspector.Console`.

The `log()` method can be used to send objects to the Introspector:

```
new file = new air.File();
air.Introspector.Console.log(file);
```

When that line is encountered, the AIR HTML Introspector is displayed, as shown in Figure 15-4.

After the AIR HTML Introspector is shown, you may find yourself becoming like a kid in a candy store. You can access the current state of UI elements (see Figure 15-5) and DOM, view application assets, and view application source files. What's more, the XHR tab allows you to watch all `XMLHttpRequest` communications of the app.

The AIR HTML Introspector is designed to work primarily with sandboxed content (HTML files in your application directory). However, you can use the Introspector with nonsandboxed content that is inside an iframe or frame. To enable the AIR HTML Introspector, both the parent and frame HTML files need to include the `AIRIntrospector.js file`.

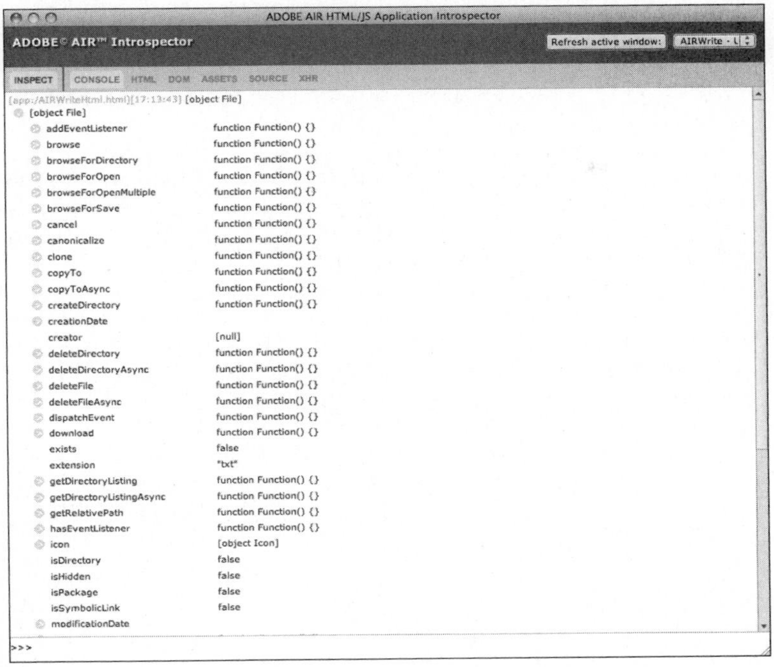

Figure 15-4:
Inspecting a
File object.

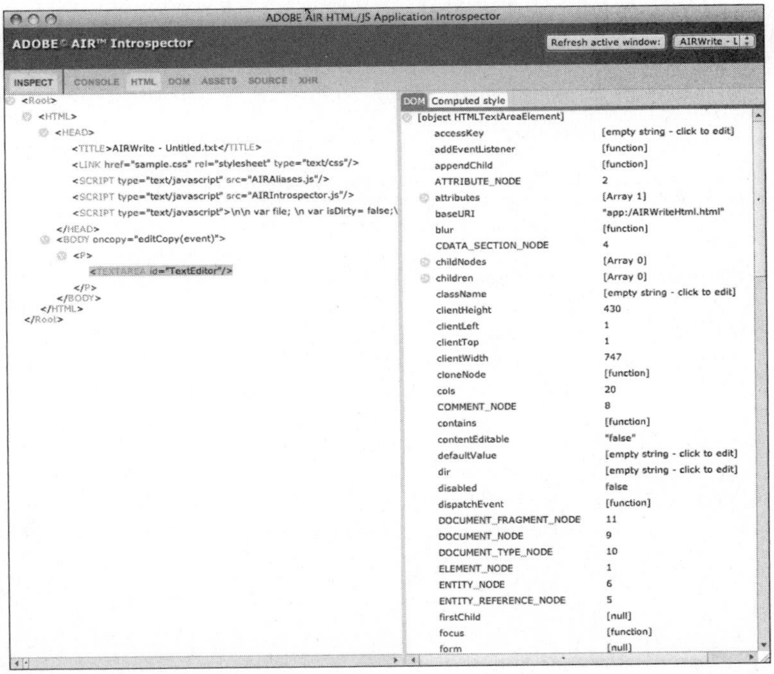

Figure 15-5:
Inspecting
elements of
the UI.

Debug with Flex Builder

If you're already using Flex Builder to develop Adobe AIR applications, this tip is a no-brainer. However, if you have not checked out Flex Builder's IDE, I recommend doing so. Flex Builder provides a full-featured debugging environment for your AIR apps, including breakpoints, the ability to step line-by-line through code, variable/object inspection, and so on. After you debug AIR apps inside Flex Builder (as shown in Figure 15-6), it becomes hard to want to ever leave its environment.

Figure 15-6: Flex Builder provides powerful debugging.

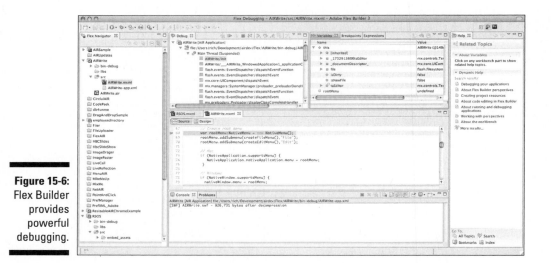

Test on Multiple Platforms

Because Adobe AIR apps work in Windows, Mac, and Linux, testing your application across multiple platforms is important. Although much of the functionality of your app will work as you designed, it could have some UI glitches or inconsistencies that you don't expect. Therefore, before your final release, at a minimum, do a sanity check on your app.

View Source Code

You can enable the source code of your app to be viewed by users of your application or by yourself in a deployed environment. For HTML apps, you want to add the following script element to your page header:

```
<script type="text/javascript" src="AIRSourceViewer.js"/>
```

By including that JavaScript file, you have access to the `air.SourceViewer` object. You can access a `SourceViewer` instance through the `getDefault()` method and then view the source by calling the `viewSource()` method. Here's the code:

```
function viewAppSource() {
  var sourceViewer = air.SourceViewer.getDefault();
  sourceViewer.viewSource();
}
```

You can exclude certain files or folders from the code that is displayed by specifying a `configObject` array as the parameter when calling `viewSource()`. For example:

```
function viewProtectedSource() {
  var sourceViewer = air.SourceViewer.getDefault();
  var configObj = {};
  configObj.exclude = ["supersensitive.html", "trade-
          secrets.html", "TopSecret"]
  sourceViewer.viewSource(configObj);
}
```

Figure 15-7 shows the viewer when called.

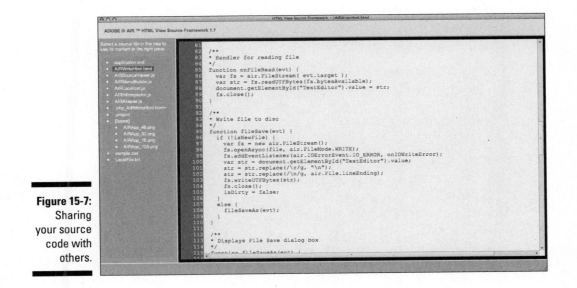

Figure 15-7:
Sharing
your source
code with
others.

Chapter 16

Ten Killer RIAs to Explore

Since the official release of the Adobe AIR SDK, hundreds of rich Internet applications (RIAs) have been developed and released on the Web. Some are new takes on desktop utilities and widgets. Some are parts of existing Web apps. A few are even full-scale commercial apps.

Rather than show you the ten most *useful* RIAs, I use this chapter to highlight ten killer examples that demonstrate the power and flexibility of the AIR platform. Consider these ten to be inspiration for the type of applications that you can develop using Adobe AIR.

One of the most beneficial aspects of surveying these RIAs is that they help you see how you can take a Web app that you've been working with online for years — such as eBay or Google Analytics — and seeing how AIR offers an entirely new take on how to tackle its respective problem domain.

Pure Usefulness: Google Analytics Reporting Suite

www.aboutnico.be

Google Analytics is one of the most popular Web site traffic analysis tools available. The Google Analytics Reporting Suite takes much of the functionality of what Google offers on its Web site and packages it into a well-designed, visually attractive, and very responsive AIR application (see Figure 16-1).

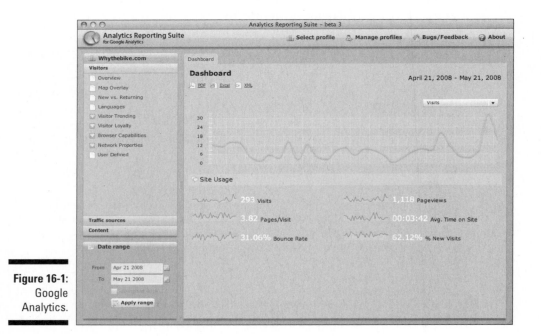

Figure 16-1:
Google
Analytics.

The Google Analytics Reporting Suite is an ideal desktop-based monitoring tool for Web site owners and administrators, eliminating the need to have a browser open to www.google.com/analytics. The application, written in Flex, makes effective use of charts, tabs, tabular lists, and a variety of other UI elements. You can also export data to PDF, Excel, or XML format.

One of the smart moves that its developer Nicholas Lierman made was to lay out and organize the UI in a format complementary to the Google Analytics Web site, thereby making the transition to the AIR app a no-brainer for existing Web app users. If you're porting an app from the Web to AIR, check out what Nicholas did.

You can read an article about the development of this app by its developer at the following URL: `www.adobe.com/devnet/air/flex/articles/analytics_reporting_suite_print.html`.

Pure Power: eBay Desktop

`http://desktop.ebay.com`

eBay Desktop may well be the poster child demonstrating the power of Adobe AIR. Inside of its desktop UI, it packs a huge amount of features for searching, bidding, watching, and buying items on eBay (see Figure 16-2).

Figure 16-2: eBay Desktop packs a true AIR punch.

If you've bid on an item before at the end of the auction, you've probably found yourself constantly hitting the browser Refresh button to see the latest bid. eBay Desktop eliminates that hassle because it offers live updating of bids in the main auction screen.

However, perhaps the most impressive part of eBay Desktop is how it transforms searching for items. Because the UI can be more sophisticated than the ordinary HTML version on the Web site, the AIR app delivers an intuitive and speedy way to search for items and drill down for products inside categories and subcategories.

The app was built using Adobe Flex. You can view a case study of the app at www.adobe.com/cfusion/showcase/index.cfm?event=casestudyde tail&casestudyid=383833.

Innovative Use of Media: AOL Music — Top 100 Videos

http://music.aol.com/help/syndication/desktop-widgets

AOL's entry into the AIR world is AOL Music — Top 100 Videos, a stylish media player for browsing (see Figure 16-3), playing (see Figure 16-4), sharing, bookmarking, and rating popular music videos. Top 100 Videos provides a great example of how you can combine the slickness and savvy of a Flash-based UI with the speedy performance of a desktop app.

Figure 16-3: Top 100 Videos makes browsing for videos easy.

Figure 16-4:
Integrated
video player
provided
for playing
videos.

Top 100 Videos also shows you how to toggle between normal, full-screen, and side Dock views with an AIR app.

Web App Upgrades: twhirl and Snitter

www.twhirl.org

http://snook.ca/snitter

Some Web apps are used so frequently throughout the day that you don't want to have a browser open to work with them. Twitter is one such example. For the uninitiated, Twitter is a social-networking app in which you can communicate quick messages to friends and colleagues. Rather than constantly refresh your Twitter page, you can use either of these two Twitter clients: twhirl (see Figure 16-5) and Snitter (see Figure 16-6).

Both encapsulate the functionality of Twitter for the desktop and do what a desktop client can do best — be instantly available when you need it.

The full-featured functionality of twhirl (which was built using Flex) goes beyond basic emulation. It allows you to connect to Twitter using multiple accounts, cross-post to Pownce and Jaiku, and post images to TwitPic. You can also follow other users and search tweets using the tweenScan and terraminds Web services.

Figure 16-5:
twhirl is a
full-featured
desktop
Twitter
client.

Figure 16-6:
Snitter
also brings
Twitter
functionality
to the
desktop.

Business Use: AgileAgenda

www.agileagenda.com

I include AgileAgenda in this chapter because it's a good example of a
real-world, business-oriented AIR application. AgileAgenda is a project

scheduling and management system (shown in Figure 16-7) that enables you to manage tasks, milestones, resources, and schedule. One of the advantages of AgileAgenda over a pure Web app is its ability to store project data either locally or remotely on AgileAgenda's Web service.

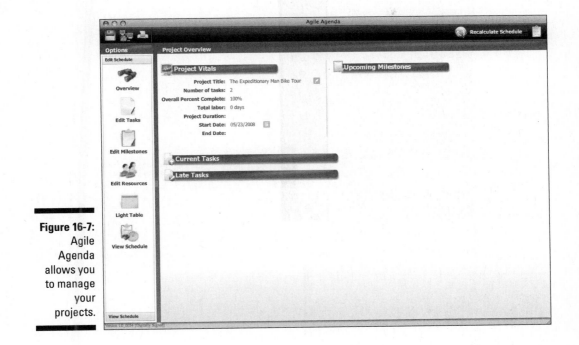

Figure 16-7: Agile Agenda allows you to manage your projects.

For the Niche Crowd: RichFLV

www.richapps.de/?p=48

RichFLV, shown in Figure 16-8, is one of those useful niche apps that, by the way, just so happens to be written in AIR. You can use it to edit Flash Video (FLV) files, such as modify metadata, edit cuepoints, and trim down videos. RichFLV also allows you to convert FLV files into different formats, including SWF, audio MP3, or a JPG image.

Yes, RichFLV could have been written as a native app, but the fact that it was written in AIR is a good testimonial to the power of AIR.

The Cool Factor: Snackr

`http:// snackr.net`

Snackr (see Figure 16-9) is an RSS aggregator that continuously displays newsfeed entries as a scrolling ticker on your desktop. If you see a story that looks interesting, you can click it and Snackr displays the full story in a pop-up window.

You can dock Snackr to one of the edges of your screen — top, left, right, bottom — and can tweak the speed of the scrolling. You can also import feeds from another reader using an OPML file or simply paste a new feed address into its dialog box.

Snackr's main selling point is its simple yet slick UI. It just looks cool docked to your desktop. However, in terms of overall RSS reading functionality, Snackr is bare bones. Clearly, Snackr is not meant as a replacement to a full-featured RSS reader, such as Google Reader or NetNewsWire.

Snackr is one of those apps that you'll probably either love or hate. When I first tried it docked to the top of the desktop, I found it completely distracting. However, when I slowed the scroll and moved it to the right side, it actually started to grow on me.

Figure 16-9:
Snackr displays RSS entries as a ticker.

If nothing else, Snackr provides a great example of a well-designed RIA that solves a problem in a way that a Web app alone can't do.

The developer, Narciso Jaramillo, wrote the app in Adobe Flex and has a write-up about his development approach at www.rictus.com/ muchado/2008/05/12/snackr-an-rss-ticker-built-using-air- and-flex.

For the Geek Crowd: Snippely

http://code.google.com/p/snippely

Snippely is a rather nifty utility you can use to organize source code and random text snippets. It uses a simple method of organizing snippets into distinct categories. Each snippet has a title, optional description, and one or more snippets. When you're working with source code, you can specify the language, which Snippely then uses to provide syntax highlighting.

Snippely is a handy way for me to get rid of countless .txt files all over my hard drive in which I store a script, CSS style, or serial number for my software.

Figure 16-10 shows the Snippely user interface.

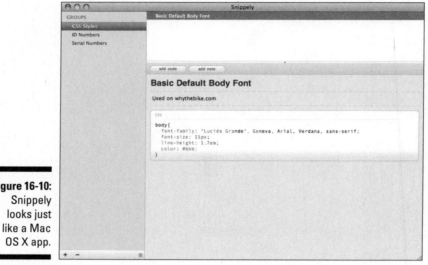

Figure 16-10:
Snippely
looks just
like a Mac
OS X app.

Snippely is written in HTML and JavaScript and stores data locally using AIR's SQLite database.

Groundbreaking Look and Feel: uvLayer

www.uvlayer.com/download

uvLayer, shown in Figure 16-11, is a social video application for discovering videos, sharing video media with friends, and organizing your own online video content. What is immediately striking about uvLayer is its innovative drag-and-drop desktop canvas, using tiles as a primary UI metaphor.

You can search for media across multiple sources and then add them to your desktop canvas. Search results are displayed as tiles. You can fan them out over your desktop or create stacks of videos.

You can share videos you collect with your friends through Facebook, Google Talk, or AIM, simply by dragging the video on top of the user's icon.

Figure 16-11: uvLayer sports an innovative futuristic UI metaphor.

Index

BUSINESS, CAREERS & PERSONAL FINANCE

Accounting For Dummies, 4th Edition*
978-0-470-24600-9

Bookkeeping Workbook For Dummies†
978-0-470-16983-4

Commodities For Dummies
978-0-470-04928-0

Doing Business in China For Dummies
978-0-470-04929-7

E-Mail Marketing For Dummies
978-0-470-19087-6

Job Interviews For Dummies, 3rd Edition*†
978-0-470-17748-8

Personal Finance Workbook For Dummies*†
978-0-470-09933-9

Real Estate License Exams For Dummies
978-0-7645-7623-2

Six Sigma For Dummies
978-0-7645-6798-8

Small Business Kit For Dummies, 2nd Edition*†
978-0-7645-5984-6

Telephone Sales For Dummies
978-0-470-16836-3

BUSINESS PRODUCTIVITY & MICROSOFT OFFICE

Access 2007 For Dummies
978-0-470-03649-5

Excel 2007 For Dummies
978-0-470-03737-9

Office 2007 For Dummies
978-0-470-00923-9

Outlook 2007 For Dummies
978-0-470-03830-7

PowerPoint 2007 For Dummies
978-0-470-04059-1

Project 2007 For Dummies
978-0-470-03651-8

QuickBooks 2008 For Dummies
978-0-470-18470-7

Quicken 2008 For Dummies
978-0-470-17473-9

Salesforce.com For Dummies, 2nd Edition
978-0-470-04893-1

Word 2007 For Dummies
978-0-470-03658-7

EDUCATION, HISTORY, REFERENCE & TEST PREPARATION

African American History For Dummies
978-0-7645-5469-8

Algebra For Dummies
978-0-7645-5325-7

Algebra Workbook For Dummies
978-0-7645-8467-1

Art History For Dummies
978-0-470-09910-0

ASVAB For Dummies, 2nd Edition
978-0-470-10671-6

British Military History For Dummies
978-0-470-03213-8

Calculus For Dummies
978-0-7645-2498-1

Canadian History For Dummies, 2nd Edition
978-0-470-83656-9

Geometry Workbook For Dummies
978-0-471-79940-5

The SAT I For Dummies, 6th Edition
978-0-7645-7193-0

Series 7 Exam For Dummies
978-0-470-09932-2

World History For Dummies
978-0-7645-5242-7

FOOD, GARDEN, HOBBIES & HOME

Bridge For Dummies, 2nd Edition
978-0-471-92426-5

Coin Collecting For Dummies, 2nd Edition
978-0-470-22275-1

Cooking Basics For Dummies, 3rd Edition
978-0-7645-7206-7

Drawing For Dummies
978-0-7645-5476-6

Etiquette For Dummies, 2nd Edition
978-0-470-10672-3

Gardening Basics For Dummies*†
978-0-470-03749-2

Knitting Patterns For Dummies
978-0-470-04556-5

Living Gluten-Free For Dummies†
978-0-471-77383-2

Painting Do-It-Yourself For Dummies
978-0-470-17533-0

HEALTH, SELF HELP, PARENTING & PETS

Anger Management For Dummies
978-0-470-03715-7

Anxiety & Depression Workbook For Dummies
978-0-7645-9793-0

Dieting For Dummies, 2nd Edition
978-0-7645-4149-0

Dog Training For Dummies, 2nd Edition
978-0-7645-8418-3

Horseback Riding For Dummies
978-0-470-09719-9

Infertility For Dummies†
978-0-470-11518-3

Meditation For Dummies with CD-ROM, 2nd Edition
978-0-471-77774-8

Post-Traumatic Stress Disorder For Dummies
978-0-470-04922-8

Puppies For Dummies, 2nd Edition
978-0-470-03717-1

Thyroid For Dummies, 2nd Edition†
978-0-471-78755-6

Type 1 Diabetes For Dummies*†
978-0-470-17811-9

* Separate Canadian edition also available

† Separate U.K. edition also available

Available wherever books are sold. For more information or to order direct: U.S. customers visit www.dummies.com or call 1-877-762-2974.
U.K. customers visit www.wileyeurope.com or call (0)1243 843291. Canadian customers visit www.wiley.ca or call 1-800-567-4797.

INTERNET & DIGITAL MEDIA

AdWords For Dummies
978-0-470-15252-2

Blogging For Dummies, 2nd Edition
978-0-470-23017-6

**Digital Photography All-in-One
Desk Reference For Dummies, 3rd Edition**
978-0-470-03743-0

Digital Photography For Dummies, 5th Edition
978-0-7645-9802-9

**Digital SLR Cameras & Photography
For Dummies, 2nd Edition**
978-0-470-14927-0

**eBay Business All-in-One Desk Reference
For Dummies**
978-0-7645-8438-1

eBay For Dummies, 5th Edition*
978-0-470-04529-9

eBay Listings That Sell For Dummies
978-0-471-78912-3

Facebook For Dummies
978-0-470-26273-3

The Internet For Dummies, 11th Edition
978-0-470-12174-0

Investing Online For Dummies, 5th Edition
978-0-7645-8456-5

iPod & iTunes For Dummies, 5th Edition
978-0-470-17474-6

MySpace For Dummies
978-0-470-09529-4

Podcasting For Dummies
978-0-471-74898-4

**Search Engine Optimization
For Dummies, 2nd Edition**
978-0-471-97998-2

Second Life For Dummies
978-0-470-18025-9

**Starting an eBay Business For Dummies
3rd Edition†**
978-0-470-14924-9

GRAPHICS, DESIGN & WEB DEVELOPMENT

**Adobe Creative Suite 3 Design Premium
All-in-One Desk Reference For Dummies**
978-0-470-11724-8

**Adobe Web Suite CS3 All-in-One Desk
Reference For Dummies**
978-0-470-12099-6

AutoCAD 2008 For Dummies
978-0-470-11650-0

**Building a Web Site For Dummies,
3rd Edition**
978-0-470-14928-7

**Creating Web Pages All-in-One Desk
Reference For Dummies, 3rd Edition**
978-0-470-09629-1

**Creating Web Pages For Dummies,
8th Edition**
978-0-470-08030-6

Dreamweaver CS3 For Dummies
978-0-470-11490-2

Flash CS3 For Dummies
978-0-470-12100-9

Google SketchUp For Dummies
978-0-470-13744-4

InDesign CS3 For Dummies
978-0-470-11865-8

**Photoshop CS3 All-in-One
Desk Reference For Dummies**
978-0-470-11195-6

Photoshop CS3 For Dummies
978-0-470-11193-2

Photoshop Elements 5 For Dummies
978-0-470-09810-3

SolidWorks For Dummies
978-0-7645-9555-4

Visio 2007 For Dummies
978-0-470-08983-5

Web Design For Dummies, 2nd Edition
978-0-471-78117-2

Web Sites Do-It-Yourself For Dummies
978-0-470-16903-2

Web Stores Do-It-Yourself For Dummies
978-0-470-17443-2

LANGUAGES, RELIGION & SPIRITUALITY

Arabic For Dummies
978-0-471-77270-5

Chinese For Dummies, Audio Set
978-0-470-12766-7

French For Dummies
978-0-7645-5193-2

German For Dummies
978-0-7645-5195-6

Hebrew For Dummies
978-0-7645-5489-6

Ingles Para Dummies
978-0-7645-5427-8

Italian For Dummies, Audio Set
978-0-470-09586-7

Italian Verbs For Dummies
978-0-471-77389-4

Japanese For Dummies
978-0-7645-5429-2

Latin For Dummies
978-0-7645-5431-5

Portuguese For Dummies
978-0-471-78738-9

Russian For Dummies
978-0-471-78001-4

Spanish Phrases For Dummies
978-0-7645-7204-3

Spanish For Dummies
978-0-7645-5194-9

Spanish For Dummies, Audio Set
978-0-470-09585-0

The Bible For Dummies
978-0-7645-5296-0

Catholicism For Dummies
978-0-7645-5391-2

The Historical Jesus For Dummies
978-0-470-16785-4

Islam For Dummies
978-0-7645-5503-9

**Spirituality For Dummies,
2nd Edition**
978-0-470-19142-2

NETWORKING AND PROGRAMMING

ASP.NET 3.5 For Dummies
978-0-470-19592-5

C# 2008 For Dummies
978-0-470-19109-5

Hacking For Dummies, 2nd Edition
978-0-470-05235-8

Home Networking For Dummies, 4th Edition
978-0-470-11806-1

Java For Dummies, 4th Edition
978-0-470-08716-9

**Microsoft® SQL Server™ 2008 All-in-One
Desk Reference For Dummies**
978-0-470-17954-3

**Networking All-in-One Desk Reference
For Dummies, 2nd Edition**
978-0-7645-9939-2

**Networking For Dummies,
8th Edition**
978-0-470-05620-2

SharePoint 2007 For Dummies
978-0-470-09941-4

**Wireless Home Networking
For Dummies, 2nd Edition**
978-0-471-74940-0